Who Is Mother Neff And Why Is She a Texas State Park?

The Story Behind the Names of the State Parks of Texas

Allan C. Kimball

EAKIN PRESS ⚏P Fort Worth, Texas
www.EakinPress.com

Contents

Caddoan Mounds State Historic Site
Daingerfield State Park
Huntsville State Park
Lake Bob Sandlin State Park
Lake Livingston State Park
Martin Creek Lake State Park
Martin Dies, Jr. State Park
Mission Tejas State Park
Starr Family State Historic Site
Texas State Railroad and Rusk and Palestine Parks
Tyler State Park
Village Creek State Park

Acton State Historic Site
Bastrop State Park
Bonham State Park
Buescher State Park
Cedar Hill State Park
Cleburne State Park
Confederate Reunion Grounds State Historic Site
Cooper Lake State Park
Dinosaur Valley State Park
Eisenhower State Park
Eisenhower Birthplace State Historic Site
Fairfield Lake State Park
Fanthorp Inn State Historic Site
Fort Boggy State Park
Fort Parker State Parker
Lake Mineral Wells State Park and Trailway
Lake Somerville State Park and Trailway
Lake Tawakoni State park
Lake Whitney State Park
Lockhart State Park
Meridian State Park
Monument Hill and Kreische Brewery
     State Historic Site
Mother Neff State Park
Palmetto State Park
Purtis Creek State Park
Ray Roberts Lake State Park

Introduction

It all began with Mother Neff.

One day I was driving north on Interstate 35 from Austin to Dallas and noticed a highway sign I'd never paid attention to before. It read, "Mother Neff State Park." A question immediately leaped to my mind: "Just who in hell is Mother Neff and why is she a state park?"

I'm certain that many people can enjoy a park and not wonder for even a moment who the park was named after. But I can't. I guess I've always been a curious person. That ingrained nosiness naturally led to my career as a journalist.

So this Mother Neff thing left me a little obsessed. First chance I had, I found some information on the park. I discovered the entire state park system all began with Mother Neff. She was not only the mother of a Texas governor but she donated the land that most sources credit as the very first state park. And her son, Governor Pat Neff, was one of the most instrumental forces in creating the Texas parks system. To me, that was a clear invitation to write this book.

I checked around. No single source existed to explain who the people were who had state parks named after them. Some I already knew. I knew who the Leaton was in Fort Leaton State Historic Site, for example, because of the research I did for my book *The Legend of Fort Leaton*. But most others were named for folks I didn't have a clue about. Unless you happen to be a native in a certain park area, or maybe a descendant of someone who has had a park named after him or her, you probably don't know who most of these people were either.

Sure, you may know who Austin, Eisenhower, Fannin, and perhaps even Garner were. But who were Acton, Cleburne, Griffin, Inks, Maxey, Navarro, Richardson, or Umphrey, and many, many others?

Some parks—Enchanted Rock, Fairfield Lake, or Possum Kingdom, for example—aren't named for people and while I could make an educated guess why some had their names, I didn't know for sure. Sometimes, as with Fairfield, I got surprised.

One question led to one source, to another source, and so on until I found I had compiled a significant amount of information that no one else had, including the Texas Parks and Wildlife Department (TPWD) itself.

For some parks' namesakes the biographical information was easy to come by and more copious than I have used. For some, the information was far more interesting than I could have imagined. For others, that information is obscure and remains hidden. Thankfully, only one park—Purtis Creek—completely eluded my research. So if you have any documented information about who Purtis was, or other information on the few other parks for which I have scant details, please let me know and I'll include it in the next edition of this book.

Although some park sites were preserved by the state as early as the 1850s, funding was sparse and unreliable with no controlling authority. The Texas state park system as we know it today began in 1923, and the Civilian Conservation Corps built many of the earlier parks during the 1930s—beginning with Mother Neff.

Today, more than 500,000 acres are preserved within Texas' state parks. When we think of a state park, we usually think of a beautiful place outdoors, a place where we can find a little rest, relaxation or recreation. That's what most parks are, but this book also includes state natural areas, state historic sites and buildings. Because of Texas' huge size and geological diversity, you can find just about anything you could hope for in our state parks from marshes to deserts, mountains to sand dunes, coastal lands to forests, lakes to prairies. And you'll find historic homes, a battleship, a hotel, a railroad, battlegrounds, western outposts, an aerial tramway, and ancient rock art. Our parks are nothing less than living museums of Texas' natural and cultural legacies.

Little public money goes into our parks. According to the Texas Coalition for Conservation, Texas ranks 49th in per capita state government spending on parks and recreation, averaging $3 per person while the national average is $13. Because of this, parks must charge an entry fee and other fees for camping. Some parks provide shelters, cabins, lodging or group facilities for additional fees. An annual Texas State Parks Pass costs $60 and allows members and others in their vehicle free entry to all parks, and discounts on camping, lodging and park store merchandise. Pass holders also receive a discount on the cost of a subscription to the monthly *Texas Parks & Wildlife* magazine. A discounted pass is offered to senior citizens over the age of 65 and those who are disabled.

TPWD lists about 120 parks in the state. I say "about" because the number varies from one year to the next, especially as the state accepts land for a new park, like Chinati Mountains State Natural Area, or considers decommissioning an older park, like Lake Rita Blanca. Also, I've included many state historic sites that were transferred from TPWD to the Texas Historic Commission in 2008.

You'll find general information on Texas state parks by calling 800-792-1112 or visiting the web site at www.tpwd. state.tx.us. For camping reservations, call 512-389-8900 or visit the web site.

After reading this book, you'll be able to enjoy the park you're visiting just a little bit more because you'll know just a little bit more about the park than the person at the picnic table next to yours. And you'll know it all began with Mother Neff. Happy trails.

Big Bend and West Texas

Balmorhea State Park

Balmorhea State Park is a welcome oasis at the edge of the vast Chihuahuan Desert with the world's largest spring-fed swimming pool.

Crystal clear San Solomon Springs Pool, formed by damming Toyah Creek, covers 1.75 acres and maintains a 72-to-76-degree temperature year-round. More than a million gallons of water flow through the spring each hour. Canals lead to a restored wetland where windows built below ground provide visitors with a turtle-eye view of the underwater world. The state acquired the property in 1934 and it opened as a park in 1968. In the late 1930s, the Civilian Conservation Corps built the pool and San Solomon Courts, 18 southwestern style cabins.

At an elevation of 3,200 feet, Balmorhea enjoys warm days and cool nights from May through September with August usually being the wettest month.

San Solomon Springs has provided water for travelers for thousands of years. The springs were first named Mescalero Springs for the Mescalero Apaches who controlled the area for centuries. The name *mescalero* is a Spanish word meaning "mescal eaters" since this particular Indian tribe baked the heart of the mescal plant as a cabbage-like staple food.

The name *San Solomon*—Holy Solomon, the wise son of the biblical King David—came from the first settlers, Mexican farmers who hand-dug the first irrigation canals here to use spring water for their crops.

Toyah is a Comanche word meaning "a lot of water."

Balmorhea is the oddest of all park names. It's neither a word from a foreign language nor someone's name; it's a combination of several names. In 1907, E. D. Balcom, H. R. Morrow, and brothers J. E. and J. W. Rhea formed a partnership and bought the area around Toyah Creek to provide water for irrigation and parcels of land were subdivided into home sites.

The town that grew up around the land was called Balmorhea, combining the names of the four investors.

His father told Luke Bradley, a great-grandson of Balcom, that a conductor of the train they were riding on suggested the name during a dispute between Balcom, Morrow and the Rhea brothers. Another version claims Ira M. Cole, the men's agent, came up with the name as a way to be fair to all the investors.

E. D. Balcom was born in Marlborough, Massachusetts, educated in Nova Scotia, Canada, and moved to a Nebraska farm when he was fourteen and later to Colorado. In 1889, he moved to New Mexico and in 1906 came to the Toyah Valley as a real estate developer, founding both the Toyah Valley Live Stock Company and the Toyah Valley Irrigation Company. His goal was to put 20,000 acres under cultivation and, with the coming of a railroad, attract thousands to the Toyah Valley. Balcom was also part owner of the Pecos Valley Southern Railway Company. In 1918, he joined the U.S. Army and served as a first lieutenant in the Quartermaster Department. He later went into a real estate business in Dallas because his wife didn't care for the desolation of West Texas.

Hugh R. Morrow was from Amarillo in the Texas panhandle and was instrumental in organizing Potter County there. He also served as an officer in the Amarillo Chamber of Commerce.

Morrow was a railroad agent and founder of Morrow-Thomas Hardware in Amarillo and Roswell, New Mexico, and acquired other hardware stores in Plainview and Hereford. He died in California in 1912.

Joseph E. Rhea was born in Collin County, Texas, in 1858. He married Florence Bass of Denton County in 1883. John W. Rhea was also born in Collin County, in 1861. He never married. Their family came to Texas from Tennessee and their father, John R. Rhea, was killed at Corinth, Mississippi, while fighting for the Confederacy during the Civil War. Because of the similarity of their initials, the brothers are often confused in historical records with their father.

The brothers worked on the family farm until Joseph accumulated a little money then, borrowing more, they bought cattle and headed west. By the 1880s, they were prominent in the cattle business in West Texas and New Mexico and renowned for their fair dealings with others.

Location: The park is in Reeves County on Texas Highway 17, four miles south of Interstate 10, about forty miles from Pecos. Busy season is Spring Break through Labor Day.

Amenities: Camping, dump station, lodging, nature trail, park store, playground, picnicking, SCUBA and skin diving, showers, swimming, wheelchair accessible, wireless Internet access.

Contact: Balmorhea State Park, P.O. Box 15, Toyahvale, TX 79786, 432-375-2370, www.tpwd.state.tx.us.

Pool at Balmorhea State Park
—Texas Department of Transportation Photo

Big Bend Ranch State Park

The majority of Big Bend Ranch State Park's 300,000 acres remains inaccessible to the public and most of what is accessible is so far off the beaten path that wandering its dirt roads and hiking trails is a truly primitive experience.

The easily reached portion of park lies along Farm Road 170, also called the River Road that follows the Rio Grande between Lajitas and Presidio. Before this remote, scenic route was paved in 1961, locals called it *Muerto del Burro*, or "donkey's death." Today, the road's Big Hill with its steep westward incline has caused similar problems for large RVs. *National Geographic* magazine called this stretch of road one of the prettiest drives in all America. In this area, visitors will find the Barton Warnock Environmental Education Center at Lajitas, a couple of trailheads, scenic Closed Canyon, and the fake adobe buildings at the Contrabando Creek Movie Set where films such as *Streets of Laredo* were made. Fort Leaton State Historic Site, near Presidio, is part of the Big Bend Ranch State Park complex but is treated in a separate entry.

Contrabando means "smuggling" in Spanish. Items of all sorts have been smuggled across this remote international border since Texas won its independence from Mexico onward. In the earliest days it was mostly just to avoid paying custom fees when entering at official border crossings, then it became various forms of alcoholic beverages during the Prohibition era in the U.S. Other goods over the years have included illicit drugs and candelilla plants into the United States and firearms into Mexico.

If you're new to the Big Bend, the Barton Warnock Center is the perfect starting point where you can roam its botanical garden and amble through its museum to get a comprehensive feel for the area's 570 million years of natural and cultural history. Originally the Lajitas Museum and Desert Garden, it was built in 1982 by Lajitas on the Rio Grande resort owner and Houston financier Walter M. Mischer after suggestions and guidance from Big Bend botanist Barton H. Warnock. The state purchased the museum in 1990, named it after Warnock, and included it in Big Bend Ranch State Park.

Warnock was the leading authority on plant life in the Big Bend, and one of the most respected botanists in the United States. He taught at Sul Ross University in Alpine for thirty-three years and authored *Wildflowers of the Big Bend Country, Texas*, the botanist's bible on the subject. He also wrote *Wildflowers of the Guadalupe Mountains and the Sand Dune Country, Texas* and *Wildflowers of the Davis Mountains and the Marathon Basin, Texas*.

Over his career, Warnock discovered many plant species and had more than a dozen others named after him. He hand-picked most of the specimens for the center that was eventually named after him in Lajitas, and cataloged all the plants in what would become Big Bend National Park.

Born in Christoval in 1911, Warnock grew up on the family farm near Fort Stockton and was a star running back on the Fort Stockton High School football team. In 1998, he suffered a heart attack while driving north of Alpine. The state trooper who discovered his body said Doc, as he was known throughout the Trans Pecos area, seemed to be serenely gazing at the Davis Mountains he loved. He was eighty-six.

Big Bend Ranch State Park is so large—more than 300,000 acres today—that when it was acquired by the state in 1988 it effectively doubled the size of the entire state park system. The bulk of the park is exceptionally remote, lying north of FM 170, and is only recently being developed with hiking, biking, and equestrian trails. The park also hosts a longhorn herd. The visitor center is in the heart of the park at the old ranch headquarters, twenty-eight miles on gravel roads from Presidio. This road is remote and rough and you will not make good time on it—count on about an hour and half to travel those twenty-eight miles.

Brothers James M. "Manny" Fowlkes and Edwin H.

Cinco Tinajas Trail at Big Bend Ranch State Park
—Allan C. Kimball

Who Is Mother Neff
and Why Is She a
Texas State Park?

Fowlkes, Jr., founded the Big Bend Ranch in 1932 by buying up and consolidating many smaller ranches in the area. The name of the ranch headquarters area is *La Sauceda*, Spanish for "the willow grove." This was the name given to the core ranch area by the Bogel brothers—Gus, Gallie, Graves, and Edward—in 1908 when they owned this portion. Three rooms in the main Big House are now available for guests. A nearby bunkhouse accommodates visitors in separate men's and women's facilities.

The original 216,000 acres of Big Bend Ranch were acquired by the state from partners Robert O. Anderson and Walter Mischer, developer of the original Lajitas resort in the 1970s. Subsequent land purchases enlarged the park to its current, unprecedented size.

The term "big bend" comes from a geological feature that gives Texas its distinctive shape. The Rio Grande flows southeast from El Paso until it reaches the Chisos Mountains where it makes a rather sudden turn—a big bend—to the northeast before it begins another southeasterly flow to the Gulf of Mexico.

No one is certain where the word *chisos* comes from. One version says it's a corruption of *chivos*, a Spanish slang word for goats. One theory says it derives from the word *chishi*, a Jumara Indian word that means "people of the forest" and was used to refer to the Apache who once roamed the mountains in Big Bend. Another version says it is derived from the word *hechizos*, an Apachean word meaning "enchantment." Anyone who has ever seen the early morning mists rise over the high Chisos will know which version is more poetic.

Rio Grande is Spanish for "big river," an appropriate name for a 1,885-mile long stream that flows from southern Colorado to the Gulf of Mexico. In Mexico, the river is known as the Rio Bravo del Norte, or "Wild Northern River." In recent years the rio has become a little less grande and not very bravo thanks to the vast amount of water used by the sprawling metropolis of El Paso, Texas/Juárez, Mexico. In fact, much of the water in the Rio Grande, which flows through Big Bend to the Gulf, is actually Mexican water from the Rio Conchos that joins the Rio Grande near Ojinaga, Mexico (across from Presidio). *Rio Conchos* means "shell river." It's uncertain where the name came from, but early Spanish explorers called it a river of pearls since many of the mussel shells found in it contain freshwater pearls, but it could also be named after the thousands of fossils found in the riverbed and banks.

Although the Rio Grande is narrow and so shallow in many places in the Big Bend area that you would barely get your shins wet crossing into Mexico, at present no legal crossings exist between Presidio and Amistad Dam near Del Rio, a distance of about 250 river miles.

Location: The park lies in a generally triangular-shaped area in southern Presidio County with the villages of Lajitas to the east, Presidio to the west, and Marfa to the north. Turn north off Farm Road 170 about six miles east of Presidio onto Casa Piedra Road, a gravel road. Follow that road about seven miles to the small sign for the park and turn east on another dirt and gravel road. The Sauceda Visitor Center and lodging are found along this road about twenty-one miles from Casa Piedra Road. The Barton Warnock Center is located on 99 acres in Brewster County, one mile east of Lajitas on FM 170. The center is open from 8 A.M. to 4:30 P.M. daily.

Amenities: Backpacking, bicycling, camping, canoeing and kayaking, dump station, equestrian trails and facilities, fishing, 4x4 roads, hiking, lodging, nature trails, park store, restrooms, showers, tours, wheelchair accessible, wireless Internet.

Contact: Big Bend Ranch State Park, P.O. Box 2319, Presidio, TX 79845, 432-229-3416. Barton Warnock Environmental Education Center, HC 70 Box 375, Terlingua, TX 79852, 432-424-3327, www.tpwd.state.tx.us.

Visitors descend into Closed Canyon at Big Bend Ranch State Park.
—Allan C. Kimball

Chinati Mountains State Natural Area

Chinati Mountains State Natural Area is a wild place, 40,000 acres of stark contrasts just west of Big Bend Ranch State Park.

Formerly known as the Mesquite Ranch, it was owned by Heiner and Philippa Friedrich until the family sold it to the R. K. Mellon Foundation as part of the foundation's American Land Conservation Program and The Conservation Fund. When the land was donated in 1996, it became the largest gift ever to TPWD.

The site features spectacular scenery and a variety of wildlife, including sixteen species of bats, one of the most diverse congregations of bats in the U.S. Terrain includes granite bluffs, spring-filled woodland canyons, and grass and woodland plateaus. Standing at more than 7,700 feet, the Chinatis are the fourth highest mountain range in Texas. Unfortunately for visitors, all of this is closed to the public until TPWD decides how much will be accessible. That may not be soon—it took nearly twenty years for the heart of Big Bend Ranch State Park to be opened to the public on anything other than guided tours.

A number of stone cabins and shelters were built at strategic points around the ranch before state acquisition.

Chinati is a corruption of *chanate*, the Spanish word for "blackbird" and a wide diversity of birds are found in the higher elevations of the mountains here. Some sources believe the mountains are named for an Indian leader, Chief Chinati who was prominent in the area around 1840 to 1850. It's quite possible both explanations are correct since many Native Americans in the area took their name from animals. Yet another version of the name claims it came from a Spaniard named Jose Rodriquez, who called himself "Chanata" and named these mountains the Sierra Chanate when he explored the area in 1650.

Location: The park is east of Farm Road 2810 near Ruidosa, about thirty-eight miles west of Presidio. Access to the park is currently closed as TPWD determines a management plan for future use.

Amenities: Closed at this writing.

Contact: Chinati Mountains State Natural Area has no separate headquarters or visitors facilities as of this writing, but information may be obtained through Big Bend Ranch State Park, P.O. Box 2319, Presidio, TX 79845, 432-229-3416, www.tpwd.state.tx.us.

Davis Mountains State Park

Davis Mountains State Park is one cool place. At more than a mile high, the park is one of the best places to escape the sometimes overbearing heat of the Big Bend. You may even be dusted with snow in the winter. The park has several hiking trails, including one that meets a trail from Fort Davis National Historic Site.

The park was established in 1933 after Jesse W. and Richard K. Merrill and other ranchers donated the land.

Since the 2,708-acre park is at such a high elevation and yet sits at the edge of the Chihuahuan Desert it is home to a wide variety of plant and animal life. The area of the park south of Texas Highway 118 is more developed while the area north of the highway is designated the Limpia Canyon Primitive Area with ten miles of backcountry trails and primitive campsites for visitors and for horses.

The Limpia Canyon is named for Limpia Creek that flows through it, a major source of water when Fort Davis was built. The name *limpia* means "clear" in Spanish referring to the water in that creek.

Its location near Fort Davis and McDonald Observatory, about halfway between Big Bend National Park and Guadalupe Mountains National Park and Carlsbad Caverns, makes the park a favorite resting place for travelers. Accordingly, the park accommodates everyone regardless of whether they prefer staying in primitive campsites, in RVs, or comfortable rooms.

Part of the park is the historic Indian Lodge, a Southwestern style inn built by the Civilian Conservation Corps in 1933. The Lodge has thirty-nine rooms, a restaurant, and a swimming pool. The furniture in many of the rooms was hand carved by CCC workers.

Jefferson Davis
—National Archives

The park is named for the volcanic mountains that were named for Jefferson Davis. When Davis was U.S. Secretary of War before the Civil War, he ordered the construction of the fort that now bears his name and the surrounding mountains were also named in his honor. He also served in the U.S. House of Representatives and U.S. Senate.

Davis is best known, though, as the only president of the Confederate States of America.

He was born in Fairview, Kentucky, in 1808, the tenth child of Samuel Emory Davis, a Georgia-born planter of Welsh ancestry who was an American Revolutionary War veteran. When Davis was three, his family moved to a plantation called Rosemont near Woodville, Mississippi.

Davis graduated from the U.S. Military Academy in 1828, and served in the Black Hawk War under future president, Colonel Zachary Taylor. He married Sarah, Taylor's daughter, in 1835 but she died several months later of malaria.

In 1845, Davis married Varina Howell and was elected to Congress. He resigned that seat to fight in the Mexican War and gained fame for winning the Battle of Buena Vista. Wounded in the war, he was later elected to the Senate where he spoke widely in the North and South urging harmony in the increasingly strife-torn years before the Civil War. In 1853 he was appointed Secretary of War by President Franklin Pierce and expanded the army, strengthened coastal defenses, and directed three surveys for railroads to the Pacific.

Until 1861 both northerners and southerners admired Davis as a "virtuous and resolute man." When Mississippi officially seceded, Davis resigned from the Senate and the Confederate convention quickly chose him provisional president.

Indian Lodge at Davis Mountains State Park
—Allan C. Kimball

He was sworn in on February 18, 1861, and his first act was to send a peace commission to Washington to prevent an armed conflict. President Abraham Lincoln refused to meet with the commission, the overture failed, and Davis presided over the Confederacy until its last day in 1865.

After the war he was imprisoned for two years on charges of treason, then given bail. He went to Canada and made several trips to Europe seeking employment. He retuned to the United States after the treason charges were dropped on Christmas Day, 1868. He wrote a memoir, *The Rise and Fall of the Confederate Government*, and turned down requests to enter the U.S. Senate again.

He died of a bronchial ailment in New Orleans in 1889, at the age of eighty-one.

Location: The park is in Jeff Davis County, four miles northwest of the city of Fort Davis on Texas Highway 118.

Amenities: Biking, camping, dump station, hiking, lodging, park store, picnicking, playground, restaurant, restrooms, showers, swimming pool, water and electric camp sites, water/electric/sewer sites.

Contact: Davis Mountains State Park, P.O. Box 1707, Fort Davis, Texas 79734, 432-426-3337, www.tpwd.state.tx.us. Indian Lodge, 432-426-3254.

Devil's River State Natural Area

Devil's River State Natural Area in Val Verde County offers visitors a glimpse at an untamed Texas, a harsh experience whether across the brush country, through canyons, or along the river because the park is at the crossroads of three major ecological areas: desert, brushlands, and the Hill Country.

This now seldom-visited area was once heavily traveled by Apache, Comanche, Kickapoo, Kiowa, and earlier Native American tribes. Their presence kept white settlement at a minimum until the 1880s.

The river flows 95 miles from Crockett County to the Rio Grande at the Amistad Reservoir. Many springs rejuvenate the river through the park, some of which actually gush out of cliff walls on the riverbank. Even when droughts dried up the river north of the park area, the springs always flowed and this fact is what attracted so many Indian groups. The river can be volatile as rains upriver alter its nature from placid to rabid. The river changes from wide, shallow areas to long, deep pools to turbulent rapids rushing through high-walled canyons of bleached limestone. Whitewater boaters will discover Class III rapids and twelve-foot waterfalls. Being free flowing and so inaccessible, the river is primitive and unpolluted, making it a favorite of wilderness paddlers in Texas. However, visitors cannot access the river by vehicle within the park and although the park has a put-in point for paddlers, it has no take-out access. That's another ten miles downriver. Lake Amistad is thirty-two miles downriver, near the city of Del Rio. *Amistad* means "friendship," and the name is applied to the dam impounding the Rio Grande that has one end in the U.S. and the other in Mexico and to the lake formed by that dam.

The park also has limited bunkhouse accommodations with a kitchen, restroom and a cold-water shower. Visitors must bring in their own water and carry out all trash.

When Texas Ranger Jack Hays was on his journey of exploration through South and West Texas in the 1840s, he came to a formidable gorge, at the bottom of which he could see water. He asked what the name of the river was. Told it was the Rio San Pedro, Hays replied, "Saint Peter's, hell! It looks like the devil's river to me." And it was from then on.

Those who love the area are fond of quoting a poem, *Hell in Texas*, by some anonymous author. The key portion goes:

The Devil put thorns and brambles all over the trees
and mixed up the sand with chiggers and fleas;
he scattered tarantulas along the roads;
put thorns on the cactus and horns on the toads;
he lengthened the horns of the Texas steers
and added a few inches to the jackrabbits' ears.
He put a little devil in the bronco steed
and poisoned the feet of the centipede.
The rattlesnake bites you, the scorpion stings,
the mosquito delights you with his buzzing wings;
sand burrs cause you to jig and dance;
and when you sit down, you'll get ants in your pants.
The heat in the summer is a hundred and ten,
too hot for the devil, too hot for the men.
Go see for yourself and you can tell,
it's a hell of a place he has for a hell.

The park's 20,000 acres were acquired in 1988 from the Fawcett, Finegan, and Whitehead families. In 1883, eighteen-year-old Erasmus K. Fawcett lived in a cave and tended a flock of sheep near Dolan Falls for several years. He eventually built a house, acquired more property, and established a huge goat and sheep ranch. The Finegans, who established Dolan Creek Ranch, are also his descendants along with the Fawcetts who still live in the area. The falls and Fawcett's cave are part of the adjacent Dolan Falls Preserve, owned by The Nature Conservancy, and has severely limited access.

Location: The park is on Dolan Creek Road in Val Verde County, about sixty-five miles north of Del Rio. Visitors should travel only in proper high-clearance vehicles with adequate tires and a full tank of gas since no facilities exist in the park or anywhere near it. Advance reservations must be made, even for day use.

Amenities: Biking, camping, canoeing and kayaking, hiking, picnicking, tours to pictograph sites.

Contact: Devil's River State Natural Area, HCR 1, Box 513, Del Rio, Texas 78840, 830-395-2133, www.tpwd.state. tx.us.

Fort Lancaster State Historic Site

Fort Lancaster State Historic Site is so desolate that it conjures a forlorn feeling when you try to imagine the soldiers who were stationed at this wasteland so far from civilization before the Civil War.

The fort was established on August 20, 1855, to guard the San Antonio-El Paso Road and to attempt to stop raiding by Comanches along one fork of their War Trail that led into Mexico. It was abandoned by federal troops on March 19, 1861, at the start of the Civil War and was never recommissioned. At its peak, seventy-two soldiers were posted here.

Unlike many other old military forts in Texas, Fort Lancaster has not been restored and remains a lonely sentinel shaped by nature and time. The fort was a dull and dreary place and its soldiers saw little action in the short time it was active. The soldiers are long gone; the dreariness remains. Although it was in such a remote location that cavalry would have been more effective in patrolling the vast areas under the fort's authority, Congress opted for lower costs and ordered it manned by infantry troops.

Captain Stephen Carpenter established the post and named it for a West Point classmate of his, Job Roberts Hamilton Lancaster of Ohio. Lancaster was seventh in the class.

Lancaster and Carpenter were commissioned as second lieutenants in the First Infantry in 1840, but Lancaster was killed by lightning on July 5, 1841, while fighting in the Seminole War in Florida.

Private owners donated the site to Crockett County in 1965. The fort was transferred from Texas Parks and Wildlife Department to the Texas Historical Commission in 2008.

Location: The park is eight miles east of Sheffield. Open daily from 9 A.M. to 5 P.M.

Amenities: Historic ruins, interpretive trail, museum, picnicking, restrooms. Day use only.

Contact: Fort Lancaster State Historic Site, P.O. Box 306, Sheffield, Texas 79781, 432-836-4391, www.thc.state.tx.us.

Fort Leaton State Historic Site

Not a military structure, Fort Leaton was a trading post and home to the toughest of pioneer families on the frontier of Texas.

Today, the twenty-three-acre site has been significantly restored. The fort is made of two-foot thick adobe bricks and covers an entire acre. At one time, a cannon was mounted on a wall to protect the fort's inhabitants and workers from hostile Indians. The F. O. Skidmore family donated the property to TPWD in 1967, and it was opened to the public in 1978.

The fort was named after Ben Leaton, one of the first Anglo settlers in the area along the Rio Grande known as *La Junta de los Rios*—the meeting of the rivers—where the Rio Conchos flows into the Rio Grande near Ojinaga, Mexico, and Presidio, Texas.

Not much is known about Leaton. Some say he came from Kentucky, others that he hailed from Virginia. What is known is that in the 1830s he was in Mexico making a living as a scalphunter, tracking down Indians for the bounty on their heads. He got caught up in the Mexican War and while in Chihuahua City met Juana Pedraza, who he eventually married.

Leaton and several other American soldiers of fortune traveled north to settle around what is now Presidio. Leaton chose land that was claimed by his wife, but whether she actually owned it remains unknown. On that property were the ruins of an old Spanish fort, the presidio of the current city's name.

Leaton, some friends, and Juana's relatives built a new fort of thick adobe, covering an entire acre, with hopes of turning it into a major trading post and shipping enterprise between Chihuahua and San Antonio. They also traded with Native Americans in the area.

Nearly all contemporary accounts agree on one thing about

Corral area at Fort Leaton, part of the Big Bend Ranch State Park complex
—Allan C. Kimball

Leaton: he was *un mal hombre*—a bad man—yet he was also renowned for his hospitality to travelers. The fort provided respite for both Texas Ranger Jack Coffee Hays' survey of the west and the U.S. Army's experiment to replace mules with camels.

Leaton ran the trading post; partner John D. Burgess ran the shipping. They hauled goods on huge ox carts, a replica of which is in the park's courtyard. They prospered for several years. Leaton died in 1851 but details about his death are uncertain. One version says an unknown man assassinated him at the fort, but most sources agree he died of an illness, either in San Antonio or New Orleans.

Juana Pedraza soon married Edward Hall, one of Leaton's friends and the local customs official, and they tried to continue running the trading post, but when the Civil War broke out trade dropped and Hall had to borrow money from Burgess. When Hall was unable to repay the loan, unknown assailants murdered him in 1864 and Burgess took possession of the fort. Ben's son, William Leaton, avenged his stepfather's death by shooting Burgess to death in Fort Davis in 1875. Unknown assailants later killed William Leaton in Ojinaga, Mexico, in 1880.

The Burgess family continued to run the fort until 1926.

It is now part of the Big Bend Ranch State Park complex and permits and maps for the park may be obtained at Fort Leaton.

Location: The park is four miles east of Presidio on Farm Road 170. Open from 8 A.M. to 4:30 P.M. daily. Busy season is September through April.

Amenities: Guided tours, historic site, interpretive trails, museum, park store, picnicking, restrooms.

Contact: Fort Leaton State Historic Site, P.O. Box 2439, Presidio, Texas 79845, 432-229-3613, www.tpwd.state.tx.us.

Franklin Mountains State Park

Franklin Mountains State Park is a remote, natural wonderland located smack in the middle of one of the largest cities in Texas.

The park exists because the Texas Legislature was troubled about growing development in the city, development that was encroaching on the mountains that tower over the West Texas town of El Paso. The Legislature acted in 1979, directing TPWD to acquire the property in order to preserve its ecological, historic, and scenic wonders. That was accomplished in 1981 and the park opened in 1987.

Covering thirty-seven square miles, the park is the largest urban park in the nation. The highest point in the mountains is 7,192 feet and the Trans-Mountain Highway, one of the highest roads in Texas, crosses the park at 5,120 feet.

Overlooking the Rio Grande, the Franklin Mountains are the northern ramparts of what the city was named for: El Paso del Norte (Pass of the North). Native Americans, soldiers, priests, traders, adventurers, gold-seekers, entrepreneurs, and pioneers have passed through the gap in both directions for thousands of years. Evidence of Indian use of plant and animal resources here dates back at least 12,000 years.

Although located completely within the city limits of El Paso, the park is home to reptiles; birds such as eagles, falcons and owls, and a wide variety of animals—from squirrels to mule deer, bats to mountain lions. Plant life is what you would expect to find in the Chihuahuan Desert with cactus, lechuguilla, ocotillo, sotol, and yucca. The Franklins are the only known location in Texas for a number of plant species, including the Southwest barrel cactus.

The mountains are named for Benjamin Franklin Coons, an early pioneer. After the Mexican War, Coons bought property along the north bank of the Rio Grande from an earlier pioneer, Juan Maria Ponce de León, who was the first settler north of the river in 1827. A small town grew in the area and was called variously Coons' Rancho or Franklin. The city didn't have an official name until it was incorporated in 1860 as El Paso, reflecting the historical importance of the Pass of the North.

Born in St. Louis, Missouri, Coons led wagon trains to Santa Fe in 1846, 1847, and 1848. He moved to the El Paso area from Santa Fe in 1849, establishing a ranch and other businesses on both sides of the Rio Grande. He also leased a portion of his sprawling ranch to the U.S. Army. Those enterprises repeatedly failed and he traveled back to Santa Fe, to California, returned to El Paso, then went to St. Louis where he died in 1892.

A tale persists that the mountains were so named because the profile of patriot Benjamin Franklin is said to be visible along a portion of the mountain ridge. A visitor should have a good imagination in order to see this profile.

An unusual feature of the park is the Wyler Aerial Tramway, a cable car that gives visitors a bird's eye of the rugged Franklin Mountains. From the high end of the ride at 5,632-foot high Ranger Peak is a view of Texas, New Mexico, and Mexico across 7,000 square miles. It's the highest cable car facility in the U.S.

The tramway is named for Karl O. Wyler, Sr., a local radio and television broadcast pioneer and philanthropist. Wyler, who was born in the city in 1906, helped found KTSM Radio in 1929 and performed as Karl the Kowhand, telling funny stories while strumming a ukulele. In the 1940s, he also taught radio broadcasting at the Texas College of Mines (now the University of Texas at El Paso) and helped create the college's major in radio. Wyler was one of the first to take the path into television, simply by putting a camera in his radio studio in 1953, founding KTSM-TV. He died in 1990.

Location: The park is on the northern edge of El Paso off the Trans-Mountain Road. Open for day use only from 8 A.M. to 5 P.M. daily. Busy Season is Spring (especially Easter) and Fall. The Wyler Aerial Tramway is located at the end of McKinley Street in the park. The tramway operates from noon to 6 P.M. weekdays, to 9 P.M. weekends and holidays, closed Tuesdays and Wednesdays.

Amenities: Bicycling, camping, hiking, horseback riding, park store, picnicking, restrooms, rock climbing, tram. Ranger-led tours are available with advance reservations.

Contact: Franklin Mountains State Park, 1331 McKelligon Canyon Road, El Paso, TX 79930, 915-556-6441, www.tpwd.state.tx.us.

Hueco Tanks State Historic Site

Hueco Tanks State Historic Site has the largest gallery of prehistoric pictographs in the nation, a gallery of jumbled granite tucked away in the desert, a gallery crawling with rock climbers.

The rock here dates back about thirty-five million years. Rainwater-catching hollow spots in the granite have made the place a natural rest stop for more than ten thousand years.

The tanks have a stunning and unmatched collection of rock paintings. Not only are the pictographs here abundant and ancient, this conglomeration of rock art here has been said to be second in the world only to that in Lascaux, France. From prehistoric times, Native Americans have been drawn to this site with its life-giving collection of water and drawn more than two thousand intriguing designs and figures on the rocks to commemorate their presence here and to pay tribute to their cultures. The art includes more than two hundred thirty kachina masks left by the oldest of those cultures.

Mescalero, Kiowas, and other Indian groups camped here and left behind their own pictographs telling of their adventures. And these tanks served as watering places for the Butterfield Overland Mail Route and other travelers who left

Hueco Tanks State Historic Site

—Allan C. Kimball

Who Is Mother Neff and Why Is She a Texas State Park?

behind their own nineteenth century graffiti painted in wagon-axle grease or scratched in the rock. Hueco Tanks was also the site of the last Indian battle in the county.

Hueco Tanks is also a sacred place to the Tigua Indians of El Paso and the tribe held meetings here as far back as the 1600s. Still does. Evidence also suggests that the vast Puebloan culture of the Southwest may have had its beginnings right here. The site also includes the historic Escontrías ranch house that serves as the park's interpretive center, and the ruins of a stagecoach station.

Another item of unusual interest in the rock basins are seasonal explosions of fairy shrimp—tiny, translucent freshwater shrimps—that attract foxes, bobcats, prairie falcons, golden eagles, lizards, and other predators.

Hueco Tanks is also popular for bouldering—difficult climbing that is low enough to attempt without ropes for protection. The climbing season from October through March attracts climbers from all over the world to the park.

In 1898, Silverio Escontrías acquired Hueco Tanks for a ranch. The Escontrías family held the property until 1956, charging a small fee for visitors who came to enjoy the scenic area. Facing developments of golf courses, housing, lakes, movie sets, and resorts, El Paso County acquired Hueco Tanks in 1965 as a county park. In 1969, the county transferred Hueco Tanks to the Texas Parks and Wildlife Department. TPWD bought an additional 121 acres from Barney Wieland, the man who had sold Hueco Tanks to the county, and in 1970 the park was opened to the public. The site is listed on the National Register of Historic Places.

In order to preserve the unusual natural and cultural resources of Hueco Tanks, visitation now is severely limited.

The 860-acre park is named for its *huecos*, Spanish for the large natural rock basins or tanks that have furnished a supply of trapped rain water to dwellers and travelers in this arid region of West Texas for millennia. Because *hueco* means "tank," calling the park Hueco Tanks is a little like calling the nearby international boundary the Rio Grande River.

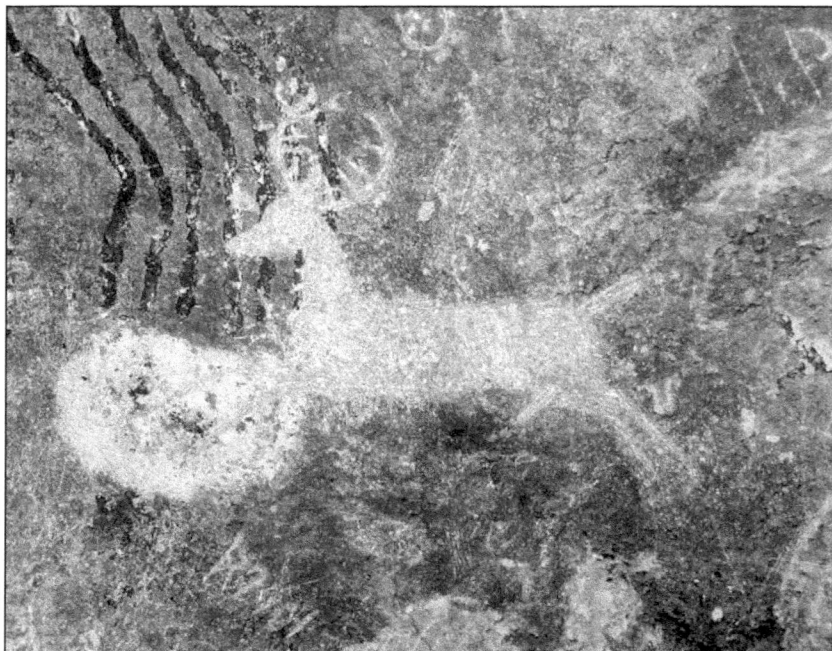

Pictographs at Hueco Tanks State Historic Site
—Allan C. Kimball

Location: The park is thirty-two miles northeast of El Paso off U.S. Highway 62, then Ranch Road 2775. Open daily 8 A.M. to 6 P.M. in winter, extended hours of 7 A.M. to 7 P.M. Friday through Sunday in summer.

Amenities: Camping, dump station, hiking, park store, picnicking, restrooms, rock climbing, showers, wireless Internet access. Bouldering, birding, pictograph and hiking tours are available. Reservations for all uses must be made at least two days prior to a visit, and the number of people admitted is restricted.

Contact: Hueco Tanks State Park, 6900 Hueco Tanks Road No. 1, El Paso, TX 79938, 915-857-1135, www.tpwd. state.tx.us.

Who Is Mother Neff and Why Is She a Texas State Park?

Magoffin Home State Historic Site

See what life was like in the nineteenth century for one of the founding families of El Paso at the Magoffin Home State Historic Site, one of the oldest buildings in the city.

Located in downtown El Paso, the nineteen-room adobe house is a prime example of Territorial-style architecture, popular throughout the Southwest. It combines both Victorian wood trim and locally made adobe bricks—the wood was cut in the Sacramento Mountains of New Mexico and the adobe walls are more than two feet thick, keeping the house cool in the El Paso summers. The house has three wings, each built at different times. In addition to the prized antiques on display, one of the treasures in the home is a ninth edition set of the *Encyclopedia Brittanica* printed in 1878.

The Magoffin Home was named for its builder and first occupant, pioneer Joseph Magoffin. He was born in 1837 in Chihuahua, Mexico, where his father, James, was a merchant. The family moved to Missouri in 1845 just before the start of the Mexican War. While his family was safely away from the conflict, James fought in the war, was captured, and spent many months as a prisoner. On his release at the end of the conflict, James bought property in the El Paso area and moved his family there in the 1850s. Joseph, who was away at college, joined the family in 1856 in the portion of the village that had become known as Magoffinville.

Joseph served in the Confederate Army during the Civil War and married Octavia MacGreal in 1864 while he was stationed in Victoria. The couple moved to Houston after the war and had two children. In 1868 he returned to Magoffinville, built the family home in 1875, and saw El Paso grow from the untamed frontier villages of Magoffinville and Franklin to the bustling city of El Paso.

Magoffin served as county judge, justice of the peace, customs inspector, and as mayor for four terms. During his tenure as mayor, all the city's utilities were established, the first schools and hospitals were built, and the city fire department was set up. He was also president of the first street car company to operate in El Paso and was founder and vice president of El Paso's first bank.

He also worked closely with the Mexican state of Chihuahua to complete flood control projects on the Rio Grande. Joseph Magoffin died in 1823 in Washington, D.C., at the home of his daughter.

The family occupied the home for one hundred ten years until the city of El Paso and the state of Texas jointly purchased the home in 1976. TPWD operated the site until 2008 when supervision was transferred to the Texas Historic Commission. Persistent legends say some ghostly family members still roam the home.

Location: The site is located just east of the intersection of Octavia Avenue and Magoffin Avenue. Open Tuesday through Sunday 9 A.M. to 5 P.M.

Amenities: Historic site, park store, restrooms.

Contact: Magoffin Home State Historic Site, 1120 Magoffin Avenue, El Paso, TX 79901, 915-533-5147, www.thc.state.tx.us

Joseph Magoffin
Texas Historical Commission

Monahans Sandhills State Park

You can surf the sand at Monahans Sandhills State Park.

Sandriding is popular with just about everyone, from the smallest children to senior citizens, and has become quite trendy among young adults who surf under the full moon that makes the sands glisten as if they were diamonds. Bring your own boards or rent sliding discs at the park headquarters.

The 3,840 acres of dunes, some as high as seventy feet, are part of a two-hundred-square-mile dune field that stretches into New Mexico.

Humans have visited the area date for the past 12,000 years because of abundant game—including wooly mammoths—attracted to the plentiful fresh water beneath the dunes. The water occurs at shallow depths, sometimes just a foot below the surface of the sand, and sometimes stands in shallow ponds between dunes.

These dunes are active; they constantly change with the rains or the winds, altering views or even burying picnic tables, requiring park personnel to scrape the roads clear of sand on a regular basis.

Midland native J. Conrad Dunagan visited the area with a hiking party of Cub Scouts in 1934 and fell in love with it. Dunagan founded and served on the boards of several banks in the Monahans area and had a long career with the Coca-Cola Bottling Company, eventually serving as chairman of the board. He was also active in many West Texas historical societies. Conrad and wife Kathlyn, along with famed Texas naturalist Roy Bedichek, led the effort to acquire the dunes for a state park in the 1950s. Bedichek called the dunes as unique as Yellowstone or the Painted Desert. The land was leased for ninety-nine years from the Sealy-Smith Foundation in 1956 and the park was opened to the public in 1957. The visitor center is named in the Dunagans' honor.

The park lies just six miles from the oil boom town of Monahans. Thomas John (Pat) Monahan, a Texas and Pacific

Railway surveyor, dug the area's first well to supply water for the railroad which reached the dunes in 1881. The town that grew up in the area was called Monahan's Wells and was incorporated as Monahans.

Location: The park is located six miles northeast of the city of Monahans on Park Road 41, off Interstate 20. Open daily; busy season March through August.

Amenities: Camping, dump station, horseback riding, nature trails, park store, picnicking, restrooms, sand surfing, showers, wheelchair accessible.

Contact: Monahans Sandhills State Park, P.O. Box 1738, Monahans, TX 79756, 432-943-2092, www.tpwd.state. tx.us.

Monahans Sandhills State Park
—Texas Department of Transportation

Seminole Canyon State Park and Historic Site

Seminole Canyon is a beautiful mystery. The steep, rugged canyon walls drop through the Chihuahuan Desert hiding prehistoric rock shelters full of ancient graffiti. If only these colorful pictographs could tell us their stories, but their meanings are lost in the mists of time.

For at least 12,000 years, prehistoric people have been visiting this area where the Pecos River flows into the Rio Grande. Some of these visitors painted arcane pictographs in the various rock shelters found along the lower Pecos River. One of the best known of these shelters is found in Seminole Canyon where well-preserved pictographs date back 8,000 years. Among the most intriguing of the pictographs is one that looks like a 1950s-era television set complete with rabbit ears. Many of the recognizable pictographs are of tribal shamans, and an imposing sculpture by Bill Worrell commemorates them at the top of the strenuous trail to the Fate Bell Shelter. The shelter was named for Fate Bell, the woman who owned the land the shelter is on. Other sites include an annex to Fate Bell, Presa Canyon, and Panther Cave.

While access to the shelters in the park is restricted to guided tours, other trails across the brushlands, one leading to a Rio Grande overlook, are open to bikers and hikers.

The 2,173 acres just above the Rio Grande was bought from private owners in 1973-1977 and opened as a park in 1980.

The park is named for the U.S. Army's Seminole Negro Indian Scouts garrisoned at Fort Clark in Brackettville. The scouts helped protect this area from Apaches and Comanches between 1872 and 1912 and never lost a man. Four of them won the Medal of Honor—you may visit their final resting place at the Seminole Negro Indian Scout Cemetery near Brackettville.

Black Seminoles are descended from runaway slaves who sought asylum in the Florida swamps. After the Seminole Wars in the mid-1800s, many Seminoles, including the former slaves, were rounded up and marched to a reservation in the Indian Territory (present-day Oklahoma). Along the trek, many of the black Seminoles escaped into Mexico and others who found life on the reservation unbearable soon joined them. Most settled in Nacimiento, across the Rio Grande in Mexico.

Desperate for scouts who knew West Texas, the U.S. Army made a deal in 1870 with many of the black Seminoles, promising them land in return for serving in the military.

They became known as the Seminole Negro Indian Scouts and served all over Texas but were stationed primarily at Fort Clark and Fort Duncan. Their commander for many years was Lieutenant (later Brigadier General) John L. Bullis. Camp Bullis, near San Antonio, is named in his honor. Bullis and the scouts operated extensively in the Seminole Canyon area, and they blasted a wagon road into the Pecos Canyon near the Rio Grande to provide the military with a shorter route between Fort Clark and Fort Davis.

The scouts' knowledge of English, Spanish, and various Indian dialects, along with their knowledge of lands unknown to the soldiers, made them indispensable to the Army. They were critical to the success of Colonel Ranald S. Mackenzie's famous raid on an Indian camp near Remolino, Mexico.

Despite the Seminoles' heroic service to the Army, the government ultimately reneged on its promise of land to those who served, saying the officer who initiated the negotiations did not have authority to make the offer. Some returned to the Nacimiento area, some sought refuge on the Seminole reservation in Oklahoma, but many stayed near Fort Clark where their descendants live today.

Location: The park is located nine miles west of Comstock off U.S. Highway 90, just east of the Pecos River Bridge. Open daily; busy season March through May. Tours to the Fate

Bell Shelter rock art site are held Wednesdays through Sundays at 10 A.M. and 3 P.M., summers at 10 A.M. only.

Amenities: Biking, camping, dump station, hiking, interpretive center, park store, picnicking, restrooms, showers, wireless Internet, wheelchair accessible.

Contact: Seminole Canyon State Park and Historic Site, P.O. Box 820, Comstock, TX 78837, www.tpwd.state.tx.us.

Visitors inspect pictographs at Seminole Canyon State Park
—Allan C. Kimball

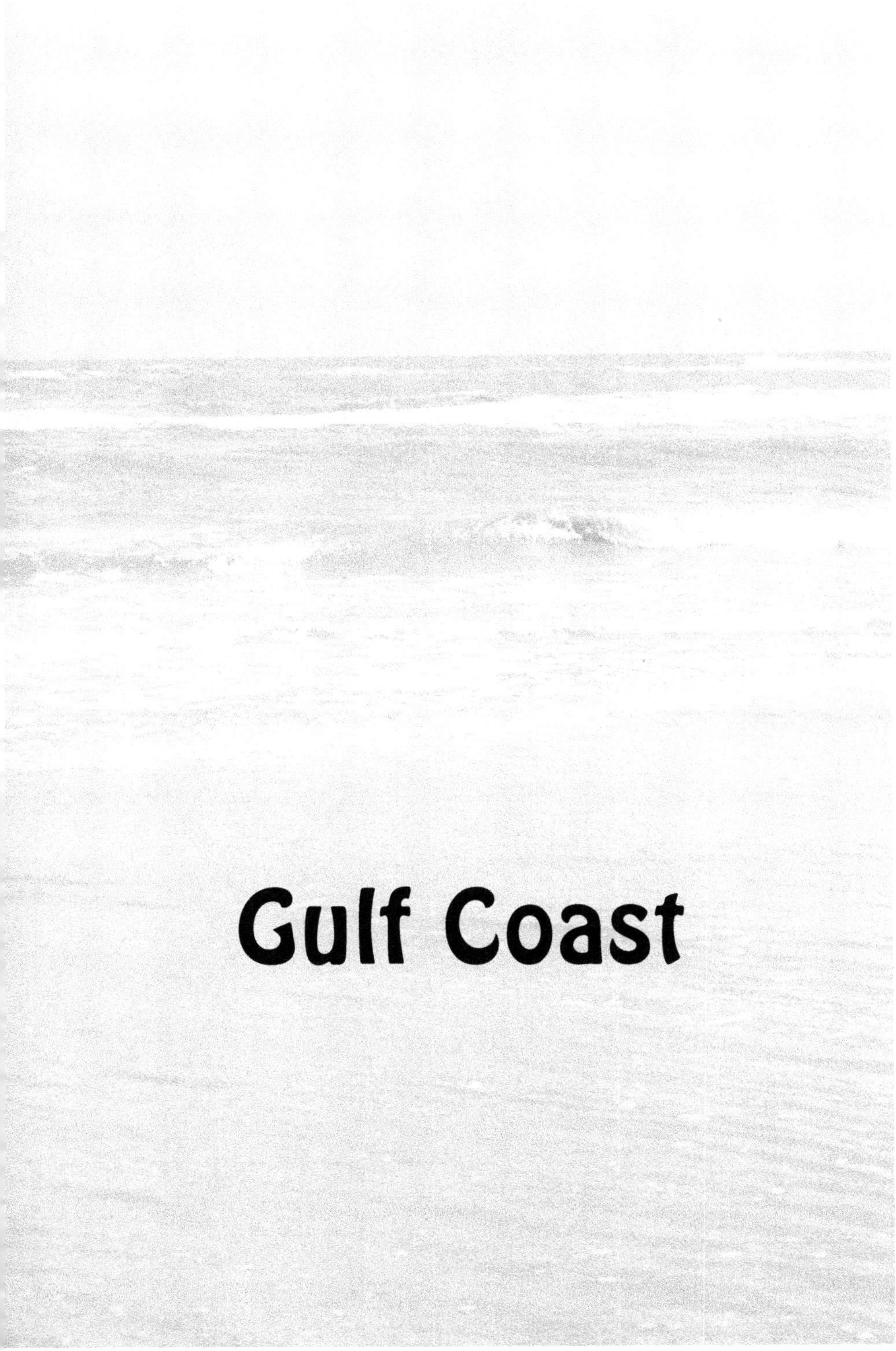

Gulf Coast

Battleship Texas State Historic Site

The Battleship Texas is a floating museum where you can tread on decks that saw service in two World Wars and that at one time was the most powerful military weapon on the face of the earth. It is the first ever state memorial battleship.

The USS *Texas* is the oldest Dreadnaught class battleship in the world, and the only surviving battleship to have served in World War I and World War II. When it was commissioned in 1914 it carried the first 14-inch naval guns in the world.

Over the years, the battleship became a platform for cutting-edge naval warfare technology. It was the first to launch an aircraft from its decks, the first to mount anti-aircraft weapons, and the first to use radar. And in 1977 was designated a National Historic Landmark.

The keel of the USS *Texas* was laid at the Newport News Shipbuilding Company in Virginia on April 17, 1911. The ship was christened on May 18, 1912, and commissioned on March 12, 1914.

The *Texas* was 573 feet long with a beam of 95 feet, and it displaced 27,000 tons. It had two four-cylinder steam engines developing 28,100 horsepower, driving two three-blade propellers with diameters of nearly nineteen feet. The ship had fourteen coal-burning boilers and was designed for a speed of twenty-one knots.

The USS *Texas* served in the Atlantic Fleet during World War I, and was present at the surrender of the German Fleet in 1918.

In 1925 the ship was modernized with new oil-fired boilers and an updated superstructure. Two years later, the *Texas* was the flagship for the commander-in-chief of the United States Fleet.

After the outbreak of World War II, the *Texas* served in the North Atlantic, and in 1942 it supported the Allied landings in North Africa. On D-Day, June 6, 1944, the USS *Texas* was the flagship for the bombardment group supporting the Allied landings on Omaha Beach.

By February 1945, the battleship was in the Pacific and supported the landings at Iwo Jima and Okinawa.

In 1946—after more than thirty-four years of service—the venerable ship was slated for retirement. Texas Governor Coke R. Stevenson accepted the USS *Texas* from the United States Navy to be used as a state shrine, the first battleship ever to become a state memorial.

In 1948 the ship was permanently moored at the San Jacinto Battleground on the Houston Ship Channel.

The ship was acquired through efforts of the Battleship Texas Commission that led efforts to raise money to bring the ship to Texas. The ship was officially decommissioned in 1946 and presented to the state of Texas. The Commission administered the floating museum until 1983 when the *Texas* was transferred to TPWD. Restorations of the ship began in 1988 at a Galveston shipyard and were completed in 1990.

Several groups are currently pushing to move the *Texas* to its own site in Galveston.

The battleship is named for Texas, the twenty-eighth state in the Union and one of only two states that were independent republics before becoming part of the U.S. Vermont is the other (1777-1791); Hawaii was a monarchy before being acquired by the U.S. Texas is the second largest state in both area (after Alaska) and population (after California).

The flags of six different countries have flown over Texas: Spain (1519-1685, 1690-1821), France (1685-1690), Mexico (1821-1836), the Republic of Texas (1836-1845), the United States (1845-1861, 1865-present), and the Confederate States (1861-1865).

The name Texas comes from *Tejas*, the Spanish pronunciation of a Caddoan Indian word, *tayshas*, that means "friend."

Location: The park is located at the San Jacinto Battleground, twenty-five miles west of Houston. Open daily 10 A.M. to 5 P.M.

Amenities: Historic site, park store, picnicking, tours, wheelchair accessible.

Contact: Battleship Texas State Park, 3523 Battleground Road, La Porte, TX 77571, 281-479-2431, www.uss texasbb35.com, www.battleshiptexas.org, www.tpwd. state.tx.us.

Brazos Bend State Park

Named one of America's top ten state parks by *National Geographic* magazine, Brazos Bend has 5,000 acres of lakes, prairies, and forests. Large oak trees—some more than two hundred years old—draped in Spanish moss provide shade and offer a comfortable and scenic location to relax or have a picnic.

Those low roars you often hear are alligators.

Visitors can wander over thirty-four miles of trails by foot, on a bicycle, or on horseback. On the way they'll see abundant wildlife that can include alligators, more than two-hundred-ninety species of birds (including the elegant white ibis and rare masked duck), fifty species of butterflies, and thirty-nine species of dragonflies. And by the way, all those dragonflies keep the mosquito population at bay.

The Nature Center has an aquarium, live snakes, and an unusual hands-on alligator exhibit. One of the trails has interpretive signs and touchable bronze statues of wetland wildlife. So many alligators call the park home that visitors need to read—and heed—Alligator Etiquette directions on signs and in pamphlets.

As if all that weren't enough, the park also hosts the George Observatory for evening stargazing and simulated space missions. The observatory was established in 1987 in the wake of the visit of Halley's Comet in 1986 when Brazos Bend was virtually the only place dark enough in the Houston area to see the legendary comet. The observatory expanded in 1993.

The state purchased the property in 1976 and it was opened to the public as a park in 1984.

The park is named for the many bends in the Brazos River that forms its eastern boundary.

The Brazos River flows for 840 miles from Stonewall County in the Panhandle to the Gulf of Mexico, near Freeport. It is the longest river wholly within Texas.

The full name of the river used by Spanish explorers is *Los Brazos de Dios*, "the arms of God." Many legends have grown up explaining the name.

One tale says that Francisco Vázquez de Coronado and his men wandering around the Llano Estacado were suffering from lack of water when local Indians guided them to a small stream that the men named *Brazos de Dios*.

Another story tells of a Spanish ship caught in a storm in the Gulf of Mexico that lost its supply of drinking water. The sailors were parched with thirst, lost, and unable to determine which direction they should go to find land, when one of the crew noticed a muddy streak in the waters. The ship followed the streak's current to the mouth of a wide river. The ship sailed up the river, and the sailors drank fresh water and were saved. In gratitude they christened the river *Brazos de Dios*.

The final legend says the river was named in the 1760s when a drought made it impossible for the Spanish miners on the San Saba River to work. They headed toward an Indian village where they found a stream full of water. Many of the men and beasts had died en route, but the few who survived named the river *Brazos de Dios*.

The George Observatory is one of many Fort Bend County projects funded by the George Foundation. Albert P. George

(1873-1955) and Mamie E. George (1877-1971) established the foundation in 1945 as a private charitable trust.

Location: The park is located twenty-eight miles southwest of Houston. Open 7 A.M. to 10 P.M. Friday through Sunday, 8 A.M. to 10 P.M. Monday through Thursday. Observatory open 3 P.M. to 10 P.M. Saturday.

Amenities: Biking, camping, dump station, hiking, horseback riding, park store, picnicking, playground, restrooms, screened shelters, showers.

Contact: Brazos Bend State Park, 21901 Farm Road 762, Needville, TX 77461, 979-553-5101, www.brazosbend .org, www.georgeobservatory.org, www.tpwd.state.tx.us.

Fulton Mansion State Historic Site

The Fulton Mansion seems a little out of place. It's a true mansion, ornate and elegant, but it's located in a small town on the Gulf of Mexico where humble homes and weathered boats are much more common.

The three-story house is one of few remaining examples of a high-style Victorian home exemplifying classic French Second Empire architecture. George and Harriet Fulton built this extravagant home on Aransas Bay in 1877. The house was not only architecturally impressive for its time and place, but made full use of the latest technology such as modern plumbing, central heating, and a gas lighting system.

The mansion was listed on the National Register of Historic Places in 1975. It was restored in 1983. The state purchased the property in 1976, and the Texas Parks and

Wildlife Department operated the site until it was transferred to Texas Historical Commission in 2008.

George Ware Fulton was born in Philadelphia in 1810 and became a schoolteacher and watchmaker. He later made mathematical instruments in different towns in Indiana. He traveled to Texas to help in the fight for independence in 1837 but arrived after the battle of San Jacinto established the new republic. He did serve in the Texas Army, however, earning a land grant in San Patricio County.

He later met Henry Smith, a former provisional governor of Texas and Secretary of the Treasury under President Sam Houston. Fulton married Henry's daughter Harriet in 1840 and they moved to the northeast in 1846. After Harriet's father died, the couple returned to Texas and George became involved in several business enterprises, including cattle, railroading, and land development in the town that would bear his name.

George Fulton died in 1893 at the mansion and was buried in Rockport.

Fulton Mansion State Historic Site

—Allan C. Kimball

Location: The park is located off Texas Highway 35, five miles north of Rockport on the Texas Gulf Coast. Open Monday 10 A.M. to 1 P.M., Wednesday 10 A.M. to 4 P.M., Saturday 10 A.M. to 3 P.M., Sunday 1 P.M. to 3 P.M.

Amenities: Guided tours.

Contact: Fulton Mansion State Historic Site, 317 Fulton Beach Road, Fulton, TX 78358, 361-729-0386, www.thc.state. tx.us.

Galveston Island State Park

Enjoy all sorts of tropical fun on Galveston Island's sandy beaches or in the warm, gently rolling surf of its gulf waters. Here's a romantic location adjacent to a quaint city full of museums, galleries, unusual shopping opportunities, and one of the largest and best-preserved concentrations of Victorian architecture in the country. And it's all just forty minutes from Houston, the fourth largest city in America.

The island is believed to be about 5,000 years old. The state purchased this 2,000-acre site between the Gulf of Mexico and Galveston Bay from private owners in 1969 and opened it as a park in 1975.

Cabeza de Vaca and his crew were shipwrecked here in 1520 and eventually made their way from the island to colonies in Mexico. The LaFitte brothers, fleeing the prosecution of pirates in the U.S., established a government here in 1817, and legends say Jean LaFitte buried a treasure somewhere on the island.

The city of Galveston thrived for a while—it was considered the financial capital of the Southwest in the days after the United States annexed Texas—but its progress suffered in the wake of major storms in 1867, 1871, 1875, and 1886. Then the Great Storm of 1900 devastated the island, a disaster from which the city never fully recovered. The storm killed 5,000 to 10,000 people, and prompted the construction of the seawall that now protects the northern half of the island.

Galveston is named for Bernardo de Gálvez who was born in Malaga, Spain, in 1746. He fought Apaches in New Spain and rose to the rank of colonel. In 1777 he was named governor of Louisiana and served in that capacity until 1783.

During his governorship of Louisiana, he ordered the survey of the Texas coast. Surveyor and mapmaker José de Evia named the largest bay on the Texas coast Bahía de Galvezton for the governor.

Gálvez helped patriots during the American Revolution by capturing Florida, Jamaica, and the Bahamas from the British. He also secured the port of New Orleans so that only

Bernardo de Galvez

American, French, and Spanish ships could move arms, ammunition, and other supplies up and down the Mississippi River. He was so influential that he helped draft the Treaty of Paris that ended the war, and was later commended by the American Congress.

The king of Spain named him captain general of Florida, Louisiana, and Cuba, and governor of Cuba.

He was named viceroy to Mexico in 1785. When Mexico City suffered from disease and famine that winter, Gálvez opened government warehouses and used his personal fortune to help the population. During his tenure, he began reconstruction of the Castle of Chapultepec, installed street lights in Mexico City, and started construction of the Cathedral of Mexico, the largest cathedral in the Western hemisphere.

Gálvez died of an illness in Mexico City in 1786. He was buried in the San Fernando cemetery there, but his heart was removed and placed in an urn in the Cathedral of Mexico.

Location: The park is located on the west end of Galveston Island. Open daily.

Amenities: Biking, camping, dump station, fishing, hiking, kayaking, park store, picnicking, restrooms, screened shelters, swimming, wireless Internet access.

Contact: Galveston Island State Park, 14901 Farm Road 3005, Galveston, TX 77554, 409-737-1222, www.tpwd.state. tx.us.

Beachgoers at Galveston Island State Park
—Richard Reynolds/Texas Department of Transportation

Goose Island State Park

Goose Island is a park where brown pelicans, herons, and rare whooping cranes soar overhead and where an ancient giant spreads its branches.

Fishing and photography are two of the main draws to this 320-acre coastal park that has documented more than 300 species of birds and is home to the largest oak tree in Texas, one of the largest in the world.

Appropriately named Big Tree, the State Champion Coastal Live Oak is 35 feet around and 44 feet tall with a crown spread of 90 feet. By some estimates, it's about 2,000 years old. Over the years, the tree has served as a hanging tree, a pirate's rendezvous, and a ceremonial site for cannibalistic Karankawa Indians.

Although located on Aransas Bay, the park does not allow swimming because the shoreline is made up of concrete bulkheads, oyster shells, mud flats, and marsh grass. Guided nature tours are offered year round and guided birding tours are held from January through April.

The 320-acre property was acquired in 1931-35. The Civilian Conservation Corps constructed many of the park's early facilities.

Goose Island is one of the Gulf Coast's prime spots for viewing water birds, including herons, bitterns, rails, turnstones, spoonbills, egrets, sandpipers, skimmers, plovers, avocets, ducks, frigatebirds, cormorants, cranes, ibises, willets, and, of course, geese. Lots of geese.

A goose is a medium to large size water bird with a long neck that usually migrates over great distances. Powerful and high fliers, they fly in a distinctive V formation. They are in the Anatide family, sized between ducks and swans.

Location: The park is located at the southern tip of Lamar

Peninsula, ten miles northeast of Rockport off Texas Highway 35. Open daily.

Amenities: Boating, camping, dump station, fishing, kayaking, park store, picnicking, restrooms, showers, tours.

Contact: Goose Island State Park, 202 S. Palmetto Street, Rockport, TX 78382, 361-729-2858, www.tpwd.state .tx.us.

Lake Corpus Christi State Park

While away some time boating, swimming, waterskiing, or sailboarding. Or just drop a line in the waters and pull in some bass, catfish, and crappie.

Lake Corpus Christi is a 14,112-acre park opened in 1934 with many of its facilities built by the Civilian Conservation Corps. This is a manmade lake, created by damming the Nueces River.

The open waters of the lake and the surround riparian woodlands give the park a diverse ecology that provides habitat to a wide variety of wildlife.

The city and lake of Corpus Christi take their name from Corpus Christi Bay, which was discovered by Spanish explorer Alonzo Alvarez de Pineda in 1519 on the Roman Catholic Feast Day of Corpus Christi. However, the first reference to the area using the name Corpus Christi was made in 1766 by Colonel Diego Ortiz Parilla. The feast celebrates the Eucharist that Jesus instituted at the Last Supper when he told his disciples to eat bread blessed in his memory saying, "This is my body." *Corpus Christi* means "Body of Christ" in Latin.

The Nueces River rises in Edwards County and flows southeasterly 315 miles to its mouth on Nueces Bay at the

Gulf of Mexico. In 1689, explorer Alonso De León named it Rio de las Nueces, or River of Nuts, for the plentiful pecan trees growing along its banks.

The Nueces was once the disputed boundary of Texas. After gaining independence, Texas insisted the boundaries of the Republic would be the Rio Grande while Mexico insisted it was the Nueces River. The conflict was one of the prime factors leading to the Mexican War, the result of which brought Texas and land that became several western states into the Union.

Location: The park is located on Park Road 25, four miles southwest of Mathis and thirty-five miles northwest of Corpus Christi. Open daily.

Amenities: Boating, camping, dump station, fishing, picnicking, restrooms, screened shelters, showers, swimming, water/electric/sewer sites, water skiing.

Contact: Lake Corpus Christi State Park, Box 1167, Mathis, TX 78368, 361-547-2635, www.tpwd.state.tx.us.

Lake Texana State Park

Woodlands, water, and wildlife all converge at Lake Texana to make this pristine park a great family recreation locale. Here are scenic landscapes and plenty of opportunities for boating, birding, fishing, picnicking, watching wildlife, or strolling through the woods thick with oak and pecan trees.

Whitetail deer are so common in the park visitors might find them competing for food at campsites. Visitors are also certain to hear the howl of a coyote and growl of an alligator and perhaps catch sight of armadillos and a bobcat.

The park also rents kayaks and hydrobikes.

The park's 575 acres were acquired in 1977 and opened as a park in 1981. It's located on Lake Texana—a reservoir on the Navidad River—with 125 miles of shoreline.

The lake is named for the nearby town of Texana, founded in 1832. The town was originally named Santa Anna in honor of General Antonio López de Santa Anna, the president of Mexico, but it was changed after Texas won its independence by defeating that general. The town disappeared after the railroad passed it by in 1883.

The name Texana honors Texas.

The Navidad River rises near Schulenberg and flows southeasterly seventy-four miles to the Lavaca River below Lake Texana. The river's name means "Christmas" in Spanish and honors the birth of Christ.

Location: The park is located about halfway between Corpus Christi and Houston on Texas Highway 111 about seven miles east of Edna. Open daily.

Amenities: Biking, boating, camping, dump station, fishing, hiking, kayaking, park store, picnicking, playground, restrooms, showers, swimming, waterskiing, wheelchair accessible.

Contact: Lake Texana State Park, 46 Park Road 1, Edna, TX 77957, 361-782-5718, www.tpwd.state.tx.us.

Lipantitlan State Historic Site

Lipantitlan is a very small park—only five acres—and it is mostly undeveloped, with no facilities other than picnic tables.

Two forts have occupied this wilderness area near Corpus Christi. The first was built in 1734 and was soon abandoned. A second fort of earth and wood pickets was built here in 1831 by Mexican forces anticipating trouble with Anglo settlers. In 1835 the small guard force manning the fort surrendered it to Texan forces without firing a shot.

The state acquired the property in 1937 and opened it as a park in 1949.

Lipantitlan is an Aztec word meaning "Lipan land" and although its origin is uncertain, it is believed to refer to a band of Lipan Apaches that camped near the fort.

Lipan Apaches are an Athabascan people who have lived in Texas since the seventeenth century. They were known as excellent buffalo hunters, living in bison-hide tipis, and relied on large pack dogs for transport. Over the years, the Lipans had conflicts with Mescalero Apaches, Comanches, the Spanish, and Anglo settlers. The Apachean word *lipan* is an apparent corruption of the word *ipa-n'de* meaning "light gray people." Today some Lipans live on the Mescalero Reservation in New Mexico and others in and around Corpus Christi, Texas.

Location: The park is located nine miles east of Orange Grove, near Lake Corpus Christi. Open daily.

Amenities: Historic site, picnicking.

Contact: Lipantitlan State Historic Site, Box 1167, Mathis, TX 78368, 361-547-2635, www.tpwd.state.tx.us.

Mustang Island State Park

Mustang Island is one of the popular areas in Texas thanks to its unspoiled beauty. It has five miles of shoreline, abundant wildlife, great fishing, opportunities for basking in the surf, and vistas that seem to stretch out into the Gulf of Mexico forever.

The park is full of sand dunes, grasslands, freshwater marshes, salt marshes, tidal flats, and beaches that support a wide variety of plant and animal life within the park's 3,950 acres.

Some of the dunes reach heights of thirty-five feet, anchored by vegetation with deep roots. The vegetation, in turn, helps support a population of gophers, squirrels, mice, rats, rabbits, opossums, skunks, armadillos, snakes, lizards, and coastal water birds, and the rare Kemp's Ridley sea turtle. It's

Visitors enjoy the surf at Mustang Island State Park
—Jack Lewis/Texas Department of Transportation

also prime wintering grounds for many water fowl and shore-birds.

The park is on the southern end of Mustang Island, one of several coastal barrier islands that lie between the mainland of Texas and the open waters of the Gulf of Mexico. Mustang Island, like the others, was created from sandy beach deposits brought in by ocean currents and waves, then built into dunes by the wind. They provide a narrow buffer protecting bays and the mainland from the sometimes violent Gulf waters. These barrier islands cover about half of Texas' 367-mile coastline.

Despite growth in the Corpus Christi area, Mustang Island remained in a primitive state because until the 1950s it could be accessed only by boat.

Port Aransas, at the northern tip of the island, has always been, and remains, one of the most popular tourist spots in Texas.

The Texas Parks and Wildlife Department bought the park site from private owners in 1972 and was opened to the public in 1979.

The island was named for the herds of wild horses that once roamed the area. The horses were brought in by Spanish explorers, primarily a priest, Padre Nicholas Balli, in about 1800. The Balli family operated ranches on the barrier islands and this ranching tradition continued for at least another one hundred years with other owners. Nearby Padre Island was named for Padre Nicholas. "Mustang" is a corruption of the Spanish word *mesteño* that refers to livestock belonging to ranchers.

Location: The park is located about twenty-five miles southeast of Corpus Christi on Texas Highway 361. Open daily.

Amenities: Camping, dump station, hiking, fishing, kayaking, park store, restrooms, shade shelters, showers, surfing, swimming.

Contact: Mustang Island State Park, P.O. Box 326, Port

Aransas, TX 78373, 361-749-5246, www.tpwd.state
.tx.us.

Port Isabel Lighthouse State Historic Site

Port Isbael Lighthouse has been a dominant feature at the southern tip of the Texas Gulf Coast for more than a century. Visiting here is a rare treat because it's the only lighthouse in the state open to the public.

With a viewing platform 50 feet in the air that looks out over the coast and the Gulf of Mexico, the lighthouse is a favorite with photographers. A number of couples have climbed the 75 winding stairs and three short ladders to get married on top of the tower.

As shipping increased in Texas during the 1800s, the low-lying coast made charting a seagoing course extremely difficult and sixteen lighthouses were built along the coast from the Louisiana border to the Mexican border to ease the woes of ship captains.

The 72-foot tall Port Isabel Lighthouse was built in 1852. As railroads became more prevalent, shipping declined. Money to operate the lighthouse became scarce. Technology changed. Accurate charts became more available. As a result of all of this, the Port Isabel light was extinguished in 1905.

The lighthouse was neglected for decades until the state bought it in 1950. Renovation followed and it was opened to the public in 1952. The site's Visitor Center was completed in 1996, a replica of the original lighthouse keeper's cottage. Another major renovation was completed in 2000.

Although ownership of the historic site remains with the Texas Parks and Wildlife Department, the city of Port Isabel currently operates it.

Port Isabel State Historic Site
—Richard Reynolds/Texas Department of Transportation

The lighthouse was named for the city it is located in. The original name of Port Isabel was *El Fronton de Santa Isabella*. It was named for the Spanish land grant given to Don Rafael Garcia in the early 1800s. *Fronton* means "bluff" or "wall" and refers to the steep face of a lightly colored hill that faced the bay. Over the years it was also known as *Potrero de Santa Isabella*, *portrero* meaning "pasture," and as *Punta de Santa Isabella*, *punta* meaning "point." The town became known as Point Isabel and, in 1928, incorporated as Port Isabel.

Santa Isabel refers to Queen Isabella of Spain who reigned with her husband King Ferdinand II in Spain and helped finance Christopher Columbus' voyages that led to the discovery of the New World of the Americas.

Isabella was born in 1451 at Madrigal into the royal family of Castile. When she married Ferdinand of Aragon in 1469, it united the two kingdoms and Spain emerged as one country once the pair conquered the Muslim stronghold in Granada. The result of their support of Columbus was that Spain annexed the majority of land in the Americas.

One of the queen's primary interests was in education, becoming proficient in Latin herself, a rare accomplishment for a woman in those times.

Queen Isabella of Spain

She was a patron of the arts. Isabella was also concerned with the future of the Indians in the lands discovered by Columbus and wanted their rights to be officially recognized. She was involved in this struggle when she died in 1504.

Location: The park is located on the Lower Laguna Madre in Port Isabel, sixteen miles northeast of Brownsville. Open daily for day use only.

Amenities: Historic site, museum, restrooms, tours.

Contact: Port Isabel Lighthouse State Historic Site, 421 East Queen Isabella Boulevard, Port Isabel, TX 78578, 956-943-2262, 800-527-6102, www.portisabelmuseums.com, www.portisabellighthouse.com, www.tpwd.state.tx.us.

Sabine Pass Battleground State Historic Site

Relive a piece of the Civil War at the site of one of the few important battles of that war in Texas.

In 1863, the Union Navy tried to invade Confederate Texas through the Sabine Pass and eventually to Houston, the rail center of the state. On September 8, Lieutenant Dick Dowling and forty-six of his men in Company F of the First Texas Heavy Artillery used six cannons behind a mud fort to defeat four gunboats and halt the invasion. The majority of the Confederates were Irish dockhands from the Houston and Galveston area and not professional soldiers.

Dowling's men captured two of the gunboats, killed nineteen enemy troops, wounded nine, thirty-seven were reported missing, and took 315 men prisoner. The remainder of the Union force retreated. Dowling's command did not lose a man. The victory allowed the Confederates to maintain control of Texas for the remainder of the war. Because Texas survived the war with its farms and industries intact—unlike most other Confederate states which were invaded—the state recovered much quicker than other Southern states.

In 1936 a bronze statue of a bare-chested and clean-shaven Dowling was erected by the state to honor the Confederate defenders. The names of Dowling's men are inscribed on the pedestal of the statue. A monument dedicated in 2007 lists the names of the Union troops who died in the battle.

An interpretive pavilion tells the story of the battle and a walking trail features historical markers.

Richard William Dowling was born in Ireland in 1838. His family moved to New Orleans in 1846 and in the early 1850s, after the death of his parents, he made his way to Texas and settled in Houston.

The red-headed Irishman made a name for himself as a businessman, opening saloons in the area and buying a bank. When the Civil War began, Dowling joined the Jefferson Davis Volunteer Guards guarding the Texas coast. Because the Union gave up on its invasion plans for Texas, the Battle of Sabine Pass became the highpoint of Dowling's military career. He spent the remainder of the war as a recruiting officer, reaching the rank of major by war's end.

After the war, he returned to Houston and got back into business, acquiring real estate, oil and gas leases, and a steamboat. He died of yellow fever in 1867. He is buried in St. Vincent's Cemetery in Houston.

The battleground is named for Sabine Pass, a narrow opening between Sabine Lake and the Gulf of Mexico at the Texas-Louisiana border at the Sabine River. Sabine comes from *sabina*, a slang Spanish word meaning "cypress," and refers to the large growth of cypress trees along the lower course of the river.

The state acquired the fifty-seven-acre site in 1972 and it was opened to the public in 1974. The site was transferred to the Texas Historical Commission in 2008.

Location: The park is located fifteen miles south of Port Arthur on Dick Dowling Road. Open daily.

Amenities: Boating, fishing, historic site.

Contact: Sabine Pass Battleground State Historic Site, 512-463-6323, www.thc.state.tx.us.

San Jacinto Battleground and Monument State Historic Site

San Jacinto Battleground is, in fact, the place that the West was first won. And April 21, 1836, is the most important date in Texas history and one of the most important for several Western states.

On that day, even though outnumbered two-to-one, a rag-tag, undisciplined army led by a cantankerous general called "Big Drunk" by the Indians, defeated a regular army led by a general who called himself the "Napoleon of the West." But General Sam Houston's men caught General Antonio López de Santa Anna's men literally napping and killed more than six hundred Mexicans, captured all the survivors including Santa Anna, and lost just nine men of their own.

That victory won Texas its independence from Mexico. Other territories included within the new republic's boundaries would become all or part of several Western states— Arizona, Colorado, Kansas, Nevada, New Mexico, Oklahoma, Utah, and Wyoming. Considering the battle lasted only eighteen minutes, and the land won, it has been called by historians one of the most decisive battles ever fought.

Visitors can explore San Jacinto Battleground today, take in a bird's-eye view from atop a huge monument, and relive the history of Texas in a first-class museum.

Commemorating the men who fought in the important battle here, the San Jacinto Monument is a 570-foot column topped by a thirty-four-foot star. It appears similar to the Washington Monument in the District of Columbia, but San Jacinto's is fifteen feet taller. The San Jacinto Monument is the tallest stone column memorial structure in the world.

The column is 125 feet square at its base, tapering to 30 feet square at the top. It is faced with blocks of fossilized shell stone that are more than 100 million years old. Its bronze doors are 15½ feet tall and weigh 3,000 pounds each. The

San Jacinto Monument

—Allan C. Kimball

monument was a Public Works Administration project started on April 21, 1936, and dedicated on April 21, 1939.

Visitors can ride an elevator to the observation floor of the monument at 489 feet above the battleground.

At the base of the monument is the San Jacinto Museum of History with a collection that spans more than four hundred years of Texas history.

The battle was fought along the banks of the San Jacinto River, hence its name. The river now flows southeast for twenty-eight miles from Lake Houston to Galveston Bay. The Spanish word *jacinto* means "hyacinth."

One version of the origin of the river's name says it was so named because it was choked with the aquatic plants when Spanish explorers first encountered it. The water hyacinth is an aggressive invader and can form thick mats covering the entire surface of the body of water they are growing in.

Another version claims the river was discovered on August 17, the feast day of Saint Hyacinth. Given the fact that the river bears the Spanish word for saint, *san*, the second version appears more plausible.

Saint Hyacinth was a Dominican priest born in Poland in 1185 who spent his life on missionary work in Denmark, Lithuania, Norway, Pomerania, Prussia, Russia, and Sweden. During an attack on a monastery, he is said to have rescued a statue of the Virgin Mary that weighed far more than he could have carried. He died in 1257 and was canonized in 1594.

Location: The park is located twenty-five miles west of Houston. Monument and museum open 9 A.M. to 6 P.M. daily.

Amenities: Fishing, historic site, museum, park store, picnicking, restrooms, wheelchair accessible.

Contact: San Jacinto Battleground, 3523 Battleground Road, La Porte, TX 77571, 281-479-2431, www.sanjacinto-museum.org, www.tpwd.state.tx.us.

Sea Rim State Park

Come face-to-face with alligators, skim across marsh grasses on an airboat, splash in the surf, comb the beaches for shells and sand dollars, and if you don't catch a fish here then you don't have a hook on your line. It's all at the 4,100-acre Sea Rim State Park with five miles of Gulf of Mexico shoreline.

The park is divided into two units: D. Roy Harrington Beach Unit and Marshlands Unit. The Beach Unit is where most of improvements are located, including exhibits, observation decks, nature trails, and miles of open beach. Marshlands is accessible only by boat and remains primitive. Fishing is allowed there but no swimming because of the prevalence of alligators.

Located along the Greater Texas Coastal Birding Trail, Sea Rim serves as a rest area for many species of migratory birds like buntings, flycatchers, grosbeaks, swallows, and vireos. Critters such as minks, opossums, river otters, and muskrats are seen frequently and coyotes are often heard at night. The catch of the day might include red drum, speckled trout or flounder.

The state acquired the land from an oil company in 1973. It opened as a park in 1977.

The park is named for that portion of the Gulf shoreline where marsh grasses extend into the surf in a zone termed Sea Rim Marsh.

D. Roy Harrington was a native of Port Arthur. He was elected to the Texas House in 1956, then to the Texas Senate in 1962 where he served until 1977. During his tenure in the Senate, he also served as its president pro tempore. He died in 2001.

Sea Rim State Park suffered significant damage from Hurricane Rita and repairs and renovation are ongoing. Visitors would be wise to call ahead to determine what portions, if any, are open.

Catamarans at Sea Rim State Park
—Greg White/Texas Department of Transportation

Who Is Mother Neff
and Why Is She a
Texas State Park?

Location: The park is located twenty miles south of Port Arthur. Open daily.

Amenities: Airboat tours, biking, boating, cabins, camping, dump station hiking, fishing, park store, picnicking, restrooms, showers, swimming, wheelchair accessible.

Contact: Sea Rim State Park, P.O. Box 356, Sabine Pass, TX 77655, 409-971-2559, www.tpwd.state.tx.us.

Sheldon Lake State Park and Environment Learning Center

Sheldon Lake is two parks in one. First you have the Lake Unit where you can fish and observe wildlife to your heart's content. Keep an eye out for the osprey and bald eagles in the winter. The Learning Center Unit is where you can study nature and birding through exhibits, a self-guided nature trail, and ponds full of alligators and other wildlife. And you can do all this while still in the Houston metropolitan area.

The Learning Center also demonstrates alternative energy technologies and green building techniques. A wildscape garden area shows how to use native plants and wildflowers that attract birds, butterflies, and other wildlife to your backyard. A composting area shows how to recycle household leaves and grass.

Sheldon Reservoir was created in 1942 by the federal government to provide water for war industries along the Houston Ship Channel. The state acquired it in 1952 and it was opened in 1955 as a wildlife management area. In 1984, Sheldon Lake was designated a state park.

The lake is named for the nearby town of Sheldon. Sheldon was established in the early 1860s along a railroad line and was named for Henry K. Sheldon of New York, a stockholder in the Texas and New Orleans Railroad Company.

Sheldon, a well-known patron of the arts and music, was born in 1826 in Windsor, Connecticut. He moved to Brooklyn when he was a child, studied abroad, and went into the hardware business with his father. He amassed a fortune through many business ventures and was president of the Brooklyn Savings Bank, and a board member or trustee of several other financial institutions in New York.

Sheldon also served for many years as president of the Brooklyn Academy of Music, president of the Brooklyn Philharmonic Society, and was a trustee of the Brooklyn Art Association and the Brooklyn Institute of Arts and Sciences. He died in 1902.

Location: The park is located two miles east of Beltway 8 on Business U.S. Highway 90, sixteen miles east of downtown Houston. Open daily for day use only. The Environmental Learning Center is open Monday through Friday from 8 A.M. to 5 P.M., Saturday and Sunday 8 A.M. to 7 P.M.

Amenities: Boating, hiking, fishing, tours.

Contact: Sheldon Lake State Park, 15315 Beaumont Highway, Houston, TX 77049, 281-456-2800, www.tpwd.state.tx.us.

Varner-Hogg Plantation State Historic Site

See what plantation life was like in antebellum Texas at the Varner-Hogg Plantation. This was a highly successful sugar plantation, whose elegant mansion was built by slave labor.

The property was originally owned by Martin Varner who in 1824 moved his family into a cabin here along the creek that would later be named for him. They raised livestock and farmed corn and some sugar cane.

Varner was a member of Stephen F. Austin's "Old 300," the original Anglo settlers of Texas. He was born in 1787 in Page County, Virginia, and lived in Missouri and Arkansas before coming to Texas in 1816. Varner worked as a fur trader on the Red River and married Betsy Inglish, sister of Baily Inglish who founded the city of Bonham.

Varner joined Austin's Colony in 1822 and in 1829 he built the first rum distillery in Texas.

Varner sold the property to Columbus R. Patton in 1834 for $13,000 and moved to the land in Wood County that he was granted for service during the Battle of San Jacinto. He was murdered there in 1844.

Varner, his eighteen-year-old son Stephen, and a black slave named Joe were building a fence on their property when

Varner-Hogg State Historic Site
—Jack Lewis/Texas Department of Transportation

a man named Simon Gonzales rode up. Varner and Gonzales argued over a debt. As Varner turned his back to return to the work, Gonzales mounted his horse, turned and shot Varner in the back with his rifle. When Stephen tried to grab Gonzales' horse, Gonzales shot Stephen through the heart with a derringer, killing him. Joe grabbed Gonzales from his horse, getting knifed in the process. Severely wounded, the slave dragged Gonzales over to Varner who stabbed Gonzales to death. Betsy sewed up Joe's stomach and he survived but Varner died several days later.

The Patton family came to Texas in the early 1830s from Kent, England. Columbus Patton fought in the Texas Army during the war for independence and his brother William was aide-de-camp to Sam Houston and guarded General Santa Anna after his capture at San Jacinto.

Patton was the owner who built the mansion and established the sugar plantation in 1840. He also ran a racetrack on the property.

In 1854, Patton was declared insane and died in 1856 of typhoid dysentery. After much litigation among Patton's heirs, the estate was bought by the New York and Texas Land Company. The Great Hurricane of 1900 devastated much of the plantation, destroying the sugarhouse and other buildings. The mansion survived.

James Hogg bought the property in 1902 as an investment but soon began to think of it as a second home. Hogg also believed the area held large quantities of oil, and drilled several wells trying to find some but he died before anyone did. However, in 1920 the West Columbia oil field was discovered and became very productive, becoming the cornerstone of the Hogg family fortune.

Hogg preferred to refer to the property as the Varner Plantation instead of the Patton Plantation because he had lived and worked for a while with Varner's daughter and her husband when Hogg was a young man in Wood County.

James Stephen Hogg was born in 1851 near Rusk. His father, Joseph Hogg, was a brigadier general during the Civil

War. His father died at the head of his command in 1862 and his mother, Lucanda, died a year later.

Hogg worked in newspapers after the war, running his own in Longview and Quitman. He also served as justice of the peace in Quitman. He married Sallie Stinson, and served as county attorney in Wood County and as district attorney for the Seventh District of Texas. He was elected Texas attorney general in 1886. He was elected governor in 1890, the first native-born governor of Texas.

He served as governor from 1890 to 1895. His wife died in 1895 and he went into private law practice but kept active in politics. He died in 1906 in Houston and was buried in Austin.

James S. Hogg
—Texas State Archives

The governor's daughter, Miss Ima Hogg—a well-known art collector and philanthropist—donated the property to the state in 1957. It was opened to the public in 1958. The historic site was transferred to the Texas Historical Commission in 2008.

Location: The park is located two miles north of West Columbia on Farm Road 2852. Open Tuesday through Saturday from 8 A.M. to 5 P.M.

Amenities: Historic site, tours.

Contact: Varner-Hogg Plantation State Historic Site, 1702 North 13th Street, West Columbia, TX 77486, 979-345-4656, www.thc.state.tx.us.

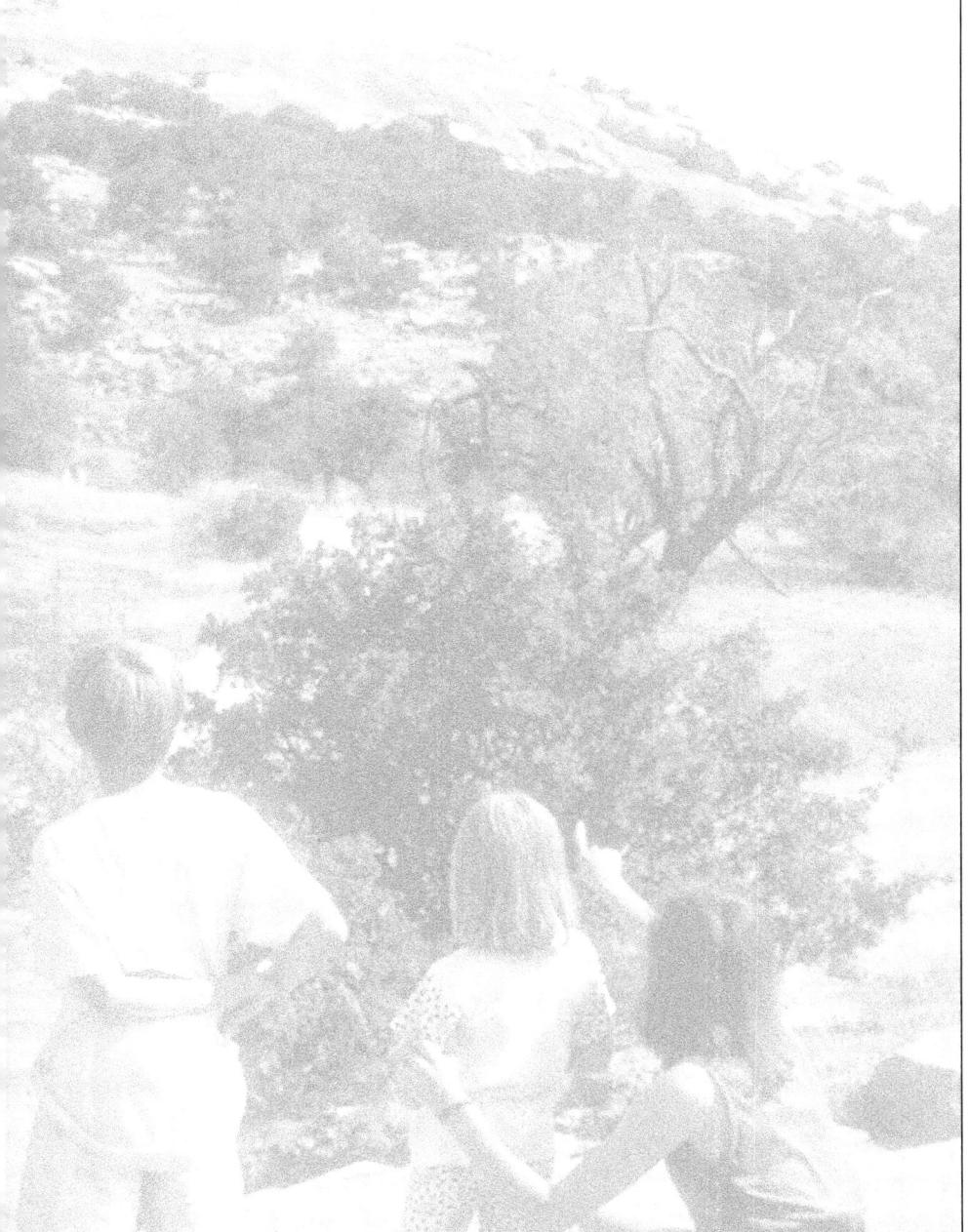

Hill Country

Admiral Nimitz State Historic Site
and Museum of the Pacific War

The Admiral Nimitz Museum is the most distinctive build-ing in Fredericksburg with one portion jutting out nearly into traffic on Main Street like the prow of a riverboat. In fact, the building is the former Nimitz Steamboat Hotel.

The museum is the only institution outside of Hawaii that is dedicated exclusively to the Pacific Theater of World War II. The nine-acre site includes the National Museum of the Pacific War, the George Bush Gallery, the Admiral Nimitz Museum, the Japanese Garden of Peace, and areas honoring the nation's presidents and war veterans.

The facility boasts an impressive display of Allied and Japanese aircraft, tanks, guns, and other artifacts from the war. The museum was recently transferred from Texas Parks and Wildlife to the Texas Historical Commission.

Fleet Admiral Chester W. Nimitz, the five-star admiral who commanded all Allied forces in the Pacific during World War II was born here in 1885 and grew up in the hotel. He gradu-ated seventh in his class of one hundred fourteen at the U.S. Naval Academy in 1905. but his naval career did not begin auspiciously. Serving onboard the USS *Decatur*, he ran the de-stroyer aground and was court-martialed, reprimanded, and assigned to submarine duty. After four undersea commands, he became a submarine expert which served him well in both world wars.

During World War I, he served as chief of staff to Ad-miral Samuel Robison, commander of the Atlantic Submarine Fleet, then as executive officer on the battleship USS *South Carolina*. He later supervised the building of the submarine base at Pearl Harbor and eventually commanded the Sub-marine Division.

Between the wars, Nimitz attended the Navy War College and served again as chief of staff to Admiral Robison who was then commander-in-chief of the U.S. Fleet. Promotions took him through several commands until he became chief of the Bureau of Navigation in 1939. In the aftermath of the Japanese attack on Pearl Harbor, Nimitz became commander-in-chief of the Pacific Fleet on Christmas Day, 1941.

Thanks to Nimitz's expertise in naval combat tactics, he eventually rose to the rank of fleet admiral and command over all Allied forces in the Pacific. Nimitz coordinated the offensive that brought the Japanese to unconditional surrender which he accepted onboard the battleship USS *Missouri* in Tokyo Bay on September 2, 1845.

He was then named commander-in-chief of the U.S. Fleet and served for the next two years. Nimitz never officially retired, being assigned to "duty as directed by the Secretary of the Navy," and later served as a roving ambassador for the United Nations, was a regent of the University of California, and became chairman of the Presidential Commission of Internal Security and Individual Rights.

Fleet Admiral Chester W. Nimitz
—Nimitiz Foundation/National Museum of the Pacific War

Nimitz died in 1966 after suffering a stroke in San Francisco and is buried in Golden Gate National Cemetery.

The George Bush Gallery is named after President George H. W. Bush. Before serving as the forty-first president from 1989-1993, he was vice president for eight years under President Ronald Reagan, served as director of the Central Intelligence Agency, ambassador to the United Nations, ambassador to China, and served in Congress from the Seventh District of Texas. He is the father of George W. Bush, the forty-third president of the U.S. and a former Texas governor, and Jeb Bush, former governor of Florida.

Born in 1924 in Massachusetts, Bush flew fifty-eight combats missions as a naval aviator in the Pacific during World War II. After graduating from Yale University he moved to Texas in 1948. He currently lives in Houston.

Location: The museum is located at the corner of Main Street and U.S. Highway 87 in downtown Fredericksburg. Open daily 9 A.M. to 5 P.M.

Amenities: Museum exhibits, restrooms, store.

Contact: National Museum of the Pacific War, 328 E. Main Street, Fredericksburg, TX 78624, 830-997-4379, www.nimitz-museum.org, www.thc.state.tx.us.

Blanco State Park

Although not very large, Blanco State Park is one of the most popular in Texas thanks to its shaded location on the spring-fed Blanco River. The one-hundred-four-acre family-friendly park borders one mile of the Blanco and attracts visitors who come to fish, picnic, swim, or just relax.

A group of local residents donated the land to TPWD in 1933, and the Civilian Conservation Corps built the original developments in the park. The park opened in 1934.

The area on the spring-fed river was used as a campsite by early explorers and settlers.

The park draws its name from the city and river also named Blanco, which means "white" in Spanish. By the way, locals don't use the proper Spanish pronunciation of the word;

they call it "Blank-oh." The river got its name in 1721 by Spanish explorer José de Azlor y Virto de Vera, the Marqués de San Miguel de Aguayo, who was impressed by the white limestone cliffs containing the river and covering its bed.

The marqués, a wealthy nobleman who was governor of New Spain's provinces of Coahuila and Tejas, led a force of nearly six hundred soldiers, colonists and priests along the King's Highway between San Antonio de Bexar and Natchitoches, Louisiana. His goal was to block any French expansion into New Spain by re-establishing a mission near Natchitoches that had been taken over by the French. He retook Mission San Miguel de los Adaes without firing a shot, built a presidio nearby, and it served as the Spanish capital of the province of Tejas for fifty years. At the beginning of his governorship, the entire European population of Tejas was only sixty soldiers in San Antonio de Bexar but Aguayo eventually established four presidios and ten missions in Tejas, recruiting four hundred families that would begin colonization in the province. He died in 1734.

Location: The park is located four blocks from the historic Blanco square on Park Road 23, off U.S. Highway 281. Open daily.

Amenities: Camping, dump station, fishing, hiking, park store, picnicking, playground, restrooms, screened shelters, showers, swimming, water/electric/sewer sites, wireless Internet.

Contact: Blanco State Park, P.O. Box 493, Blanco, TX 78606, 830-833-4333, www.tpwd.state.tx.us.

Colorado Bend State Park

Colorado Bend State Park is a true wilderness area with one of the most picturesque waterfalls in the Hill Country, an undeveloped cave where you can get dirty and get down, and all sorts of recreation along the Colorado River.

The area is so pristine that access to Gorman Falls and the caves is limited to guided tours.

The river here is in its natural state because the park is located upstream from the many dams that now line the Colorado River from Lake Buchanan to Austin. The river here cuts a deep gorge through the limestone. Indian artifacts have been discovered in the area and the park is also home to the rare golden-cheeked warbler and black-capped vireo, and a pure strain of Guadalupe black bass. Bald eagles nest near here during the cooler months.

The park is named for a horseshoe-shaped bend in the Colorado River in the area. The nearby community of Bend is also named for that twist in the river.

The Colorado River is the eighteenth longest river in the United States and the longest with its source and mouth in Texas, flowing for about six hundred miles from the eastern edge of Dawson County, near the New Mexico border, to the Gulf of Mexico at Matagorda Bay. The river's name means "red" in Spanish but it may not be the name it was supposed to have. "Colorado" was the name given by Alfonso de León in 1690 to what is now the Brazos River and many experts believe the two names were switched somehow during the Spanish exploration of Texas.

Property for the park was initially purchased in 1984, with more property acquired in 1987. The 5,328-acre park opened to the public in 1987.

Two legends give name to Gorman Falls, Gorman Creek, and Gorman Cave. One story says the park's premier landmarks are named for Sidney Alsup who killed a man in

Gorman Falls at Colorado Bend State Park
—Gay Shackelford/Texas Department of Transportation

Who Is Mother Neff
and Why Is She a
Texas State Park?

Tennessee in the 1840s. Alsup did what many with such problems did in that era: he was quickly "gone to Texas." Once in the Republic, he changed his name to J. P. Gorman and settled near the waterfall. Gorman died in 1886 and is buried in the Chappel Cemetery near Bend. The other story says the name comes from William Gorman who killed two men near Bend and fled downriver. He escaped by hiding in what is now Gorman Cave.

Location: The park is located in San Saba County, off Farm Road 580, ten miles on a gravel road. Open daily. Busy season is when the white bass make their run upriver in February through early April.

Amenities: Biking, boating, boat rentals, camping, fishing, hiking, park store, restrooms, swimming.

Contact: Colorado Bend State Park, P.O. Box 118, Bend, TX 76824, 325-628-3240, www.tpwd.state.tx.us.

Devil's Sinkhole State Natural Area

Devil's Sinkhole is simply breathtaking at sunset. As you peer into the depths of the earth, more than four million Mexican free-tailed bats emerge from the largest single-room cavern in Texas.

The cloud of bats swirls from the sinkhole just before sunset and the number of them seems to go on forever. Remarkably, cliff swallows dart into the cave to spend the night as the bats leave to forage throughout the darkness. The process then reverses as the sun rises.

The entrance hole is about 60 feet across and drops 140

feet into a room that measures 240 feet by 360 feet. The cave descends to a depth of nearly 400 feet and an underground river passes through it.

Access to the 1,860-acre natural area is limited to guided tours and reservations are required. Evening bat flight tours are offered Wednesday through Sunday from May through mid-October; daily day tours throughout the year allow visitors to look into the depths of the cavern from a viewing platform.

Travelers discovered the cave in 1867. The cave was acquired by the state in 1985 and opened to the public in 1992. It is a registered National Natural Landmark.

The Devil's Sinkhole was named in 1876 by pioneer Ammon Billings, who came to Edwards County from Kerr County. His family settled five miles above Hackberry and unlike others who brought cattle to the area, Billings brought 333 hogs.

Billings was ranging the hogs in the hills near his ranch when he came upon Indians while scouting along the old government road that came from Camp Wood. He fired at the Indians and they disappeared. Worried that the disappearance of the Indians might be a trick, Billings and his party fled. They returned the next day, found blood on the ground, and while following that trail came upon the opening to the cavern.

Billings returned home and told his wife, Coney, "I just came from the outlet to Hell, the Devil's own sinkhole."

Billings died in Sabinal in 1907.

Location: The park is located six miles north of Rocksprings off U.S. Highway 377. The Devil's Sinkhole Visitor Center is located at 101 N Sweeten Street in Rocksprings. All tours meet at the Visitor Center.

Amenities: Nature trail, tours, viewing platform.

Contact: For tour reservations, call 830-683-2287. Devil's Sinkhole State Natural Area, P.O. Box 678, Rocksprings, TX 78880, 830-683-3762, www.tpwd.state.tx.us.

Enchanted Rock State Natural Area

You won't have much doubt how Enchanted Rock got its name once you see it or, better yet, look out from the top of it.

First-time visitors get their breath taken away before they ever get to the park, as they round a bend in the road and see the huge, exposed dome rising in the distance. This is the second largest exposed batholith in the United States after Stone Mountain, Georgia, and its pink granite dome rises 425 feet above the surrounding countryside to an elevation of 1,825 feet above sea level.

The park has two main trails. One, short but very steep, ascends the face of the rock. Another wanders for four miles around and behind the rock, gradually approaching the peak from its back side. Many interesting rock formations and views are found along this secondary trail, but most visitors go up the face of the rock.

Once on top, Enchanted Rock offers astounding 360-

Unusual rocks found on the peak at Enchanted Rock State Natural Area
—Allan C. Kimball

degree views of the surrounding Hill Country. The view is made even more beautiful in the spring when the wildflowers are blooming.

The 1,643-acre park is so popular that it gets very crowded on weekends, especially weekends in late spring through early fall. When the parking lot fills up, rangers close the park, so call before you head out.

Enchanted Rock was designated a National Natural Landmark in 1971. The Nature Conservancy acquired it from private owners in 1979. The state assumed ownership in 1984. It opened as a park the same year.

Various Indian tribes that lived in the area called the granite dome Spirit Rock or Enchanted Rock, ascribing magical powers to it. The name comes not only from its natural beauty, but from eerie properties that an observant visitor may still see and hear today at the right times: the rock moans and sighs and sometimes sparkles.

The scientific explanations are that the glittering is caused either by water trapped in indentations in the rock's surface or by the moon reflecting off wet feldspar, and the moaning noises by the contraction of the rock's outer surface as it cools.

Many Indian legends speak of the rock being haunted. One tradition holds that a band of warriors, the last of their tribe, sought refuge on the rock from the attacks of other Indians, but the warriors were killed. Enchanted Rock has been haunted by their ghosts ever since. Another legend tells of an Indian princess who threw herself off the rock when she saw her people slaughtered by enemies. Her spirit now haunts the rock. Yet another tale tells of the spirit of an Indian chief who was doomed to walk the summit forever as punishment for sacrificing his daughter. The indentations on the rock's summit are his footprints. Another story describes a white woman who was kidnapped by Indians but escaped and lived on Enchanted Rock. Her moans can be heard at night.

One story is true. Texas Ranger Captain Jack Hays was surveying alone in the area in 1841 when he was trapped at Enchanted Rock by a band of Comanche. He was able to singlehandedly hold off the raiders thanks to his new pistol, a Colt Paterson, the first mass-produced revolver allowing Hays to fire several shots without having to reload. That was something the Comanche had never seen before and they attributed their adversary's firepower to the magic of Enchanted Rock and fled.

Hays' fight is commemorated with a plaque at the covered rest area at the base of the rock.

The park has more than one hundred Native American archeological sites, some dating back 10,000 years.

Location: The park is located on Ranch Road 965, eighteen miles north of Fredericksburg. Open daily.

Amenities: Camping, rock climbing, hiking, park store, picnicking, restrooms, showers.

Contact: Enchanted Rock State Natural Area, 16710 Ranch Road 965, Fredericksburg, TX 78624, 830-685-3636 (325-247-3903?), www.tpwd.state.tx.us.

Visitors impressed by the size of the single rock peak at Enchanted Rock State Natural Area

—Allan C. Kimball

Fort McKavett State Historic Site

Fort McKavett is an interesting blend of weathered ruins and restored historic buildings, showcasing what General William T. Sherman called "the prettiest post in Texas."

The eighty-acre historic site was established in 1852 at the headwaters of the San Saba River. Surgeons who served here called it an "exceedingly healthy" locale because of the breezes blowing over the hills and a good supply of fresh water from a nearby spring.

Among the many restored buildings are enlisted barracks, officers' quarters, the post headquarters, and hospital.

The first soldiers posted at Fort McKavett were five companies of the 8th Infantry who arrived in March 1852 to protect settlers and travelers along the Upper El Paso-San Antonio Road.

The fort was abandoned in March 1859 and reoccupied in April 1868. By 1880, the fort was no longer needed and it was decommissioned in 1883. Among the units stationed at the post were black regiments of the 24th Infantry and the 9th and 10th Cavalry. One of the commanders of the 24th was Colonel Abner Doubleday. Although Doubleday was erroneously credited in the 1930s with inventing the game of baseball and the sport's Hall of Fame was established in his hometown of Cooperstown, N.Y., he was certainly enamored of the game. Post records show that on June 12, 1872, Doubleday asked Washington for baseball equipment for his men. In support of his request, the colonel said that playing baseball would "add to the happiness of the men."

The post was originally named Camp San Saba because of its location.

In 1755, Spanish explorer Juan Antonio Bustillo y Zevallos led an expeditionary force looking for a site for a mission and presidio. On the day before Easter, Holy Saturday (*Santo Sabado* in Spanish), the small band came upon a clear, spring-fed stream and they selected that as the site for the mission.

The church was established there in 1757, and was named the Mission San Saba in memory of the day on which the site was discovered. The river took its name from the mission and, much later, the U.S. military post took its name from the river.

Soon after its establishment, Camp San Saba was renamed for Captain Henry M. McKavett of the 8th Infantry who was killed during the Mexican War at the battle of Monterey on September 21, 1846.

McKavett, a native of Truxton, N.Y., graduated from the U.S. Military Academy on July 1, 1834. Family tradition holds that McKavett was an orphan when he achieved his appointment to West Point. He was ranked twenty-fourth in his class. He was commissioned a second lieutenant and assigned to the 7th Infantry. He was promoted to first lieutenant on December 25, 1837.

From 1838 to 1840, McKavett served on the northern frontier during the Canadian boundary dispute. On October 1, 1840, he was transferred to the 8th Infantry and promoted to the rank of captain.

He served in the Florida War from 1840 to 1845, and aided in transferring a mixed band of Seminoles and Seminole Negroes to Arkansas. McKavett was credited with taking good care of his charges, ensuring they had generous rations of beef, corn, salt, pork, and flour.

During the Mexican War, McKavett fought in the battles of Palo Alto and Resaca de la Palma. He was killed at Monterrey by an enemy cannonball, but need not have died. Before the battle, General William Jenkins Worth told McKavett that in recognition for his meritorious service on May 9 during the battle of Resaca de la Palma he could avoid the upcoming battle if he wished.

McKavett replied "I have too much fighting Irish blood in me to withdraw."

His company held off a charge by Mexican lancers then came under withering cannon fire and eventually withdrew beyond the range of the cannon but not before McKavett was killed. In a September 24, 1846, letter to his wife, Lt.

Napoleon Jackson Tecumseh Dana wrote about witnessing McKavett's death: "The shot came out under his breast, and carried all his vitals with it."

The state acquired the fort from private owners over several years and opened it as a park in 1968. It was transferred from the Texas Parks and Wildlife Department to the Texas Historical Commission in 2008.

Location: The park is located twenty-two miles southwest of Menard near the intersections of Farm Roads 864 and 1674. Open daily 8 A.M. to 5 P.M.

Amenities: Interpretive center, nature trail, store, restrooms.

Contact: Fort McKavett State Historic Site, Farm Road 864, Fort McKavett, TX 76841, 325-396-2358, www.thc. state.tx.us, www.fortmckavett.org.

Garner State Park

Garner State Park is not only gorgeous, situated along the heavily wooded banks of the scenic Frio River, but it is the only state park ever to have a hit song written about it back in the 1960s.

In the western part of Texas
90 miles from San Antone,
There's a place I go each summer
When I get the urge to roam.
I stand out on the highway,
If I couldn't catch a ride I'd walk,

To Garner State Park.
Let's go to Garner State Park.

—Written by Mark Charron,
performed by B. J. Thomas
and the Triumphs

Here are canyons, crystal-clear streams, an abundance of birds, axis and white tail deer, limestone cliffs, dinosaur footprints, and nightly dances in its pavilion during the summer. The park is remote and parts are quite primitive, but so many people gather here that visiting Garner is often more a social event than a getaway. Visitors love to swim, ride inner tubes or kayak along the mild river rapids, hike, camp, play miniature golf, and observe the wildlife that seems to outnumber people. A few rustic cabins are also available for rent. The park is so popular that many families have turned visits here into a ritual, returning for yearly vacations through several generations.

Uvalde County acquired 640 acres for the park in 1934 through 1936, and the Civilian Conservation Corps constructed many of the park's original improvements. The state accepted the property from the county in 1936 and the park was dedicated in 1941. In 1976, an additional 790 acres along the Frio were added to the park.

The park is named for John Nance Garner, a Uvalde resident who served as vice president of the U.S. under President Franklin D. Roosevelt from 1933 to 1941.

Garner was born in a log

U.S. Congress Portrait by Howard Chandler

cabin on November 22, 1868, in Blossom Prairie, Texas. He first gained fame as a star shortstop for the combined Blossom Prairie-Coon Soup Hollow baseball team. He became a lawyer and moved to Uvalde in 1893.

His law practice served nine rural counties and Garner often accepted cattle or mohair goats for his services. He married a rancher's daughter and her inheritance helped the couple build their own fortune as ranchers, pecan growers, and bankers. One of his friends was Pat Garrett, the lawman who killed Billy the Kid. Garrett lived in Uvalde in the 1890s where he raised horses. Garner and Garrett were so close, the former sheriff named a racehorse for Garner.

Garner was elected to the Texas Legislature in 1898 and in 1903 was elected to the U.S. Congress. He worked with the Surgeon General to improve sanitation along the Rio Grande in an effort to curb yellow fever. The one piece of legislation Garner introduced that affects all Americans to this day was the establishment of the graduated income tax in 1913.

He rose to the post of Speaker of the House in 1931. Roosevelt placed him on the ticket during the 1932 election because he needed to carry Texas.

Garner wasn't too enamored of the job, however, and made only one campaign speech. He is reported to have said the vice presidency wasn't "worth a pitcher of warm spit." Actually, Garner compared the high office to a different bodily fluid, but a reporter cleaned up the quote for use in a newspaper. Garner then called the newsman a "panty-waist."

His prickly demeanor, cigar perpetually rammed into a corner of his mouth, and short, stocky body probably helped earn him the nickname of "Cactus Jack." He once had also unsuccessfully promoted the prickly pear cactus bloom as the official Texas state flower. The cactus flower lost out to the bluebonnet.

He was the first vice president in history to participate in Cabinet meetings and became a vital part of the Roosevelt administration even though he didn't agree with all the steps

FDR wanted to take to get the country out of the Depression. Their biggest disagreement came in their second term when Garner wanted the president to curtail the deficit. Garner was opposed to deficit spending, pointing out that his wife, Mariette, never had a charge account and he could see no reason why the country should have one either.

When Roosevelt chose to run for an unprecedented third term, Garner decided against continuing and returned to Uvalde, vowing, "I'll never cross the Potomac again."

Garner died in 1967, two weeks shy of his 99th birthday.

The John Nance Garner Museum is located in the Garner homestead in Uvalde, 31 miles south of the park.

Location: The park is located on Park Road 29, off Ranch Road 1050, eight miles north of Concan along the Frio River, and thirty-one miles north of Uvalde off U.S. Highway 83. Open daily. Busy season is from Memorial Day through Labor Day. The park closes when it reaches capacity, so call ahead.

Amenities: Biking, cabins, camping, dance hall, dump station, fishing, hiking, miniature golf, park store, picnicking, restrooms, showers, swimming, wheelchair accessible.

Contact: Garner State Park, 234 Ranch Road 1050, Concan, TX 78838, 830-232-6132, www.tpwd.state.tx.us.

Government Canyon State Natural Area

When you're in the midst of Government Canyon—strolling the trails shaded by thick stands of oaks and mountain laurels, enjoying the views of limestone bluffs, caves, and creeks, and listening to the song of the rare golden-cheeked warbler—you'll be hard pressed to remember you're just sixteen miles from the bustle of downtown San Antonio.

The 8,622-acre natural area lies astride the Balcones Fault Line at the edge of the oak and cedar-covered hills of the Edwards Plateau. Below is the Edwards Aquifer, the underground lake from which the second largest city in Texas gets all of its drinking water, and that valuable water is one of the main reasons the area was preserved since it is one of the prime recharge zones for the aquifer.

Government Canyon is surrounded by housing developments around San Antonio, one of the fastest growing metropolitan areas in the country. At one point in time, it was targeted for a similar development. Land speculators bought the canyon area from private ranchers in 1967 but the proposed development of 44,000 homes did not materialize because of the economic depression in the 1980s. The development went bankrupt, so the land was foreclosed on and ended up with the Resolution Trust Corporation in 1991. In 1993, the state acquired the property and Government Canyon State Natural Area was opened to the public in 2005.

Because the park is so new, much of it continues to be under development and some facilities and trails are still under construction.

In the 1850s, the U.S. Army from Fort Sam Houston in San Antonio blazed a government road from San Antonio to Bandera, going through the steep canyon and along a clear stream. Government wagons regularly used the road to supply military posts to the west. Government Creek and Government Canyon took their names from the road builders.

Location: The park is located about four miles west from Loop 1604, northwest of San Antonio. Open Friday through Monday, 8 A.M. to 6 P.M. with access to backcountry trails closed at 4 P.M.

Amenities: Biking, hiking, park store, picnicking, restrooms, wheelchair accessible, wireless Internet access.

Contact: Government Canyon State Natural Area, 12861 Galm Road, San Antonio, TX 78264, 210-688-9055, www.friendsofgc.org, www.tpwd.state.tx.us.

Guadalupe River State Park

Another pristine park not far from San Antonio is Guadalupe River State Park. The Guadalupe River—the state's most popular for river recreation—is the main draw here. The river's banks are lined with huge cypress trees and typical Hill Country limestone ledges frame the river as it courses over four rapids.

The 1,940-acre park has four miles of river frontage along nine miles of the river within the park. In addition to the cool waters of the Guadalupe, the shade of abundant trees, and several miles of wilderness trails, the park is home to a wide variety of birds and other wildlife. Anglers enjoying fishing for the feisty Guadalupe bass, Texas' state fish, that lives only in Central Texas streams.

What makes Guadalupe River State Park so special is that it is rarely crowded, unlike other portions of the river near the city of New Braunfels that, in the summer, can be as congested as a city freeway during rush hour.

The park takes its name from the Guadalupe River, a spring-fed stream that rises in Kerr County and flows for 250 miles to the Gulf of Mexico.

The name Guadalupe, or *Nuestra Señora de Guadalupe*, has been applied to the present river since 1689, when the stream was so named by Alonso De León. León was a renowned Spanish explorer who was born in Mexico in 1639,

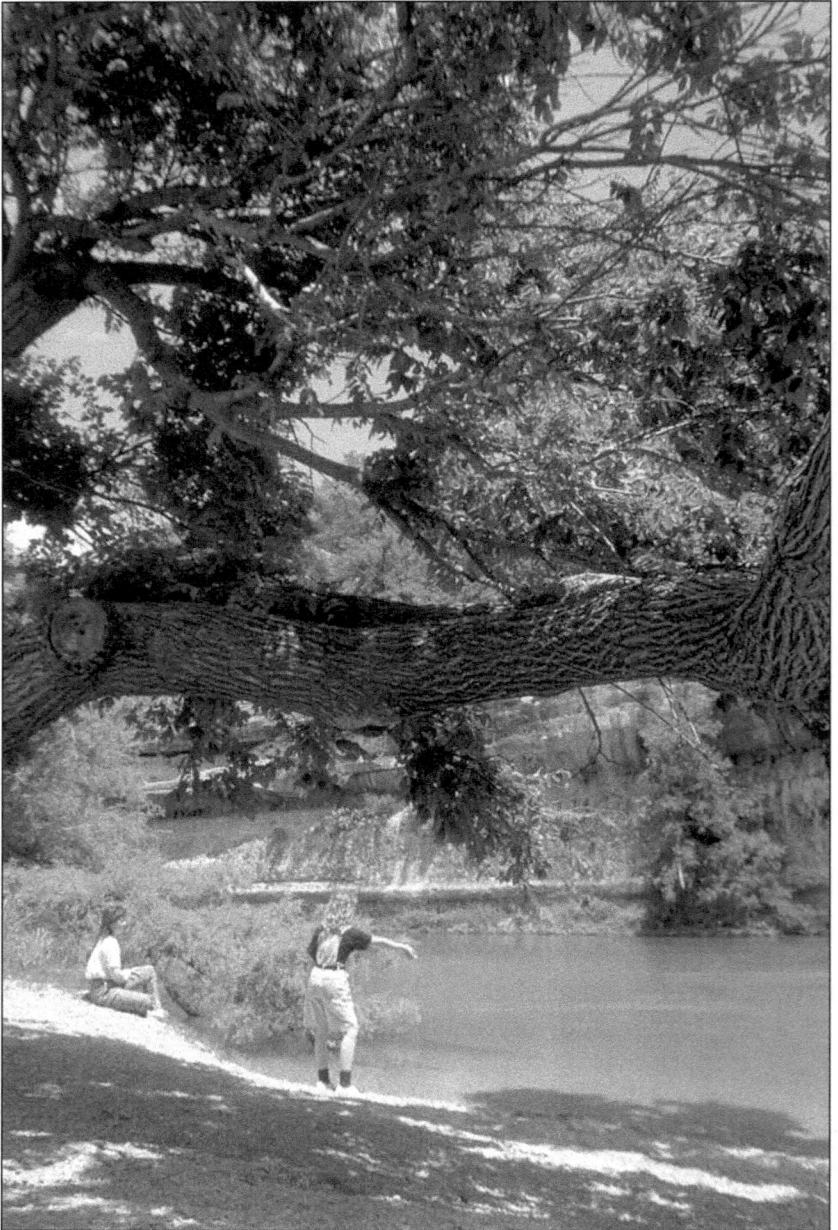

Visitors enjoy Guadalupe River State Park

—Allan C. Kimball

educated in Spain, and became governor of the province of Coahuila in 1867. He died in 1691.

The story of Our Lady of Guadalupe dates back to 1531 when an Aztec Indian Mexican peasant Juan Diego said the Virgin Mary appeared to him four times. She told Diego she wanted a shrine built on the sacred hill of Tepeyac, to the east of Mexico City. Almost everyone doubted Diego's visions but on his fourth visit, Mary had him place flowers inside his peasant cloak, made of crude maguey fiber, and take them to the local bishop. When Diego unwrapped the cloak, an imprint of the Virgin was found inside the cloak making believers of everyone.

Today, the cloak hangs in the Basilica of Guadalupe in Mexico City and its pigments have defied scientific analysis. The iconic portrait is perhaps the best known of any in Mexico.

The origin of the name *Guadalupe* is uncertain. Most scholars believe it derives from a Nahuatal word used by Mary during her apparitions. She is said to have used the word *coatl-axopeuh*. The word is pronounced *quatlasupe*. The word means "the one who crushes the serpent," and the Virgin's portrait often includes a writhing serpent under her feet. One of the primary Aztec gods was Quetzalcoatl, represented by a serpent, and Mary's appearance was seen as a symbol of Christianity replacing the old religion of the natives. Millions were converted in the following years.

The state acquired the property from private owners in 1974 and opened the park to the public in 1983.

Location: The park is located thirty miles north of San Antonio off Texas Highway 46. Open daily.

Amenities: Biking, camping, dump station, fishing, hiking, horseback riding, park store, picnicking, restrooms, river recreation, showers, swimming.

Contact: Guadalupe State Park, 3350 Park Road 31, Spring Branch, TX 78070, 830-438-2656, www.tpwd.state.tx.us.

Hill Country State Natural Area

Hill Country State Natural Area is a seldom-visited scenic and undeveloped collection of grasslands, rocky hills, springs, and steep canyons. Within its 5,370 acres are forty miles of multi-use trails.

The park is popular with horse riders and you can either bring your own or rent them from nearby ranches. (Call the park headquarters for contact information on who is renting horses at the time.) Mountain biking over the same trails is also becoming more popular. Several spring-fed streams provide fishing and swimming.

In 1976, Bar-O Ranch owner Louise Lindsey Merrick began donating portions of land on an annual basis to the Texas Parks and Wildlife Department. By 1982, the state owned 4,753 acres of former ranch land, and in 1984 opened it to the public. In 1987 an additional 617 acres were purchased from landowner Pat Boyle.

When Merrick donated the property, she asked that it "be kept far removed and untouched by modern civilization, where everything is preserved intact, yet put to a useful purpose." Hill Country State Natural Area is operated as closely to her request as possible. It remains a primitive area with few amenities.

The park is named for the Central Texas Hill Country it is in the midst of.

"Hill Country" is the common term applied to a region including all or part of twenty-five counties near the geographical center of Texas. The entire Hill Country region is much like a park with many scenic rivers and open forests dominated by several types of oak, with cedar brakes and prairies thick with mesquite and oak shrubs.

The Hill Country was so inhospitable to farming and settlement that most of it was left to roving Apache and Comanche bands until the mid-1800s. At that time, pioneers from mountainous areas like Arkansas, Missouri, and

Tennessee began to settle in, along with large groups of German immigrants. That German culture continues to dominate much of the region.

The Hill Country is located primarily on the Balcones Escarpment and the Edwards Plateau, creating an abundance of hills and, on the western edge, small mountains.

Balcones means "balconies" in Spanish and is the word Spanish explorers used to describe the jutting hills that impeded their expeditions.

The Edwards Plateau is named for Haden Edwards, an early Texas pioneer and land speculator who was a bitter rival of fellow land empresario Stephen F. Austin. Edwards was born in 1771 in Virginia. In 1823, he was in Mexico City trying to convince the government to authorize him to oversee Anglo colonization in Texas. Although Edwards often financed the father and son team of Moses and Stephen Austin, he believed they were able to get better lands than he could from the Mexican government and they had a falling out. A series of events led to the government canceling Edwards' land grants, leading to Edwards and his brother Benjamin heading up the Fredonian Rebellion in 1826. Before military action took place, Edwards fled to Louisiana but returned during the Texas Revolution, got back into the land business, and settled in Nacogdoches where he died in 1849. Edwards County, in southwest Texas, is also named for him.

Location: The park is located about sixty miles northwest of San Antonio, off Texas Highway 1077 (Dixie Dude Road) south of Bandera. Open daily February through November; December through January open Friday through Sunday.

Amenities: Biking, camping, fishing, hiking, horseback riding, swimming.

Contact: Hill Country State Natural Area, 10600 Bandera Creek Road, Bandera, TX 78003, 830-796-4413, www.tpwd.state.tx.us.

Honey Creek State Natural Area

Honey Creek State Natural Area is full of towering sycamores, bald cypress trees laced with Spanish moss, along with Texas persimmon, pecan, and walnut trees. It is so pristine and delicate, it is rarely open to the public.

The park's 2,294 acres were acquired in 1985 and opened for limited access the same year.

The park was named for Honey Creek Ranch that took its name from spring-fed Honey Creek that flows through the preserve. The creek rises in a limestone cave and Honey Creek Cave is the longest ever discovered in Texas—twenty miles so far and exploration is not complete.

Honey Creek was named for the large numbers of honeybees found along the creek and for the unusual "honeycomb rock" formations seen in much of the limestone bluffs in the area.

Honeybees are a flying insect, a type of bee renowned for its production and storage of honey and the construction of its nests out of wax. They apparently originated in Southeast Asia, but evidence of the bees has been found in Europe as far back as thirty-five million years ago. Humans have raided their nests for honey and wax for thousands of years, and within recorded history have raised and kept bees for the same purpose. Bees also pollinate a large number of crops as they fly from plant to plant. Honey is the sweet fluid produced by bees from the nectar of flowers.

Limestone, which is abundant throughout the Hill Country, is soluble and when rainwater seeps into cracks in the rock and mixes with sulfurous gases often present, it dissolves portions of the limestone resulting in a honeycomb of chambers of all sizes in the rock.

Location: The park is located adjacent to Guadalupe River

State park, off Texas Highway 46. Guided tours at 9 A.M. Saturdays only.

Amenities: Guided hikes.

Contact: Honey Creek State Natural Area, 3350 Park Road 31, Spring Branch, TX 78070, 830-438-2656, www.hon eycreekfriends.com, www.tpwd.state.tx.us.

Honey Creek State Natural Area

—Allan C. Kimball

Inks Lake State Park

Inks lake State Park is one of the most popular parks in Texas and for good reason: It has something for just about everyone to enjoy, from paddling on the lake to hiking in the red hills to getting up-close-and-personal with roaming deer to jumping off a cliff into the lake to playing a round of golf.

The park store rents canoes and paddle boats. The park features seven and a half miles of trails, a nine-hole golf course, and in addition to abundant camping and picnicking areas around the lake, limited-use cabins with air conditioning recently opened.

The state acquired the park's 1,201 acres in 1940. Prior to that, the area was a part of various ranches.

One of the things that makes Inks Lake State Park so popular is that the lake itself remains at a constant level so it is not affected by the frequent droughts that can plague the Hill Country.

The lake is also unusual because it's surrounded by red granite hills, the same rock that is extracted at nearby Marble Falls, home to the largest surface granite quarry in the U.S. Inks Lake was created in 1938 as one of seven of the Highland Lakes, all impounded by dams along the Colorado River. The lake covers 830 acres and is 4.2 miles long and 3,000 feet at its widest point.

For information on the Colorado River, see the entry for Colorado Bend State Park in this section.

Inks Lake is named for Roy B. Inks, a former mayor of the city of Llano and one of the original board members of the Lower Colorado River Authority who created the Highlands Lakes for hydroelectric power and flood control along the river above Austin.

Inks was born in Hoover's Valley in 1887, the second oldest in a large family. As a boy, he moved to Llano to live with Maggie and Lee Watkins, an aunt and uncle who had no children.

He worked as a traveling salesman for a wholesale grocery

business in the Hill Country until World War I when he enlisted in the U.S. Army. After the war, he retuned to his sales job and married Myrtle Moss of Llano in 1919.

Eventually he bought into a Ford dealership and became the principal owner soon after. One of his more flamboyant stunts to promote the Roy B. Inks Motor Company was driving a car up the steep slope on Enchanted Rock before it became a state park.

Inks also introduced motion pictures to the city of Llano at his Opera House theater. The Opera House also hosted basketball games, roller-skating, and Saturday night dances. He served several terms as mayor of Llano, but many of his business enterprises suffered greatly during the Depression.

Inks worked tirelessly to get what is now Inks Dam built on the Colorado River. At one point, he and other members of the Lower Colorado River Authority had to travel to Washington, D.C., to get formal authorization for the Highland Lakes project. He developed pneumonia on that trip in 1935 and while in a San Antonio hospital suffered a ruptured appendix, developed peritonitis, and died. He was forty-six years old.

Roy B. Inks

The LCRA then named the second dam in the chain for Inks, named the lake in his honor, and the Texas Highway Department named the new bridge over the Llano River for him as well.

Location: The park is located about twelve miles west of Burnet off Texas Highway 29. Open daily except for public hunts.

Amenities: Boating, boat rentals, camping, cabins, dump station, fishing, golf, hiking, park store, picnicking, restrooms, screened shelters, showers, swimming, water skiing, wireless Internet access.

Contact: Inks Lake State Park, 3630 Park Road 4 West, Burnet, TX 78611, 512-793-2223, www.tpwd.state.tx.us.

Kickapoo Cavern State Park

Kickapoo Cavern State Park is renowned for its bird watching and bat watching.

The park is at a crossroads of three different ecological zones—the Chihuahuan Desert, the Edwards Plateau of the far western Hill Country, and the South Texas Plains—offering a wide variety of plant and animal life. The unusual conglomeration of plant life, such as piñon pines growing next to cactus, attracts 240 species of birds. Among rare birds recorded here are the gray vireo, varied bunting, and Montezuma quail. The cavern is also home to one of largest breeding populations of endangered black-capped vireo.

But don't forget the caves. The park has fifteen known caves, all undeveloped. The largest, and the park's namesake, is about a quarter-mile long and has several interesting cave formations including the largest natural column in Texas, rising eight stories high.

One of the caves is home to approximately a half-million to one million Mexican free-tailed bats from mid-March through the end of October. When they emerge from their roosts in the evening, they are truly an impressive sight.

Acquired in 1986 and opened to the public in 1991, the park encompasses about 6,370 acres, and is open only for pre-arranged tours.

The park takes its name from the largest cave, Kickapoo Cavern, and the cavern was named for the Kickapoo Indians who continue to live in the general area.

The word "Kickapoo" derives from the Algonquian word *ki-ikaapoa*, meaning "the people who move around."

Although they have been settled for many generations along the Texas/Mexico border around Eagle Pass, the tribe originated in Michigan, around Lake Erie. Europeans first encountered them in the 1640s in the Green Bay area of Wisconsin. They were displaced to Illinois and eventually split into two groups with one group moving to the Sabine River in Texas. After 1836, the tribe split again with one band moving to Indian Territory (current Oklahoma) and the other to near Morelos, Coahuila, about forty miles south of the Rio Grande.

The Mexican Kickapoo raided into Texas for many years until Colonel Ranald Mackenzie of Fort Clark in Brackettville crossed the border in 1873 and captured an entire village, sending them north into Indian Territory. Only about 350 Kickapoo remained in Mexico.

By the 1960s, descendants of this small remaining band had created a squatter community under the international bridge at Eagle Pass. They resisted offers from the Mexican and American governments to move to remote reservations. In the 1980s, the tribe finally gained a small reservation near Eagle Pass. The Kickapoo now operate the Lucky Eagle casino on the Rio Grande.

Location: The park is located about twenty-two miles north of Brackettville. Access limited to scheduled tours.

Amenities: Biking, camping, hiking, restrooms, showers.

Contact: Kickapoo Cavern State Park, P.O. Box 705, Brackettville, TX 78832, 830-563-2342, www.tpwd. state.tx.us.

Landmark Inn State Historic Site

Sleep where history was made. At Landmark Inn State Historic Site, visitors may experience the romance and history of the Texas frontier in a comfortable, charming setting along the banks of the Medina River in Castroville.

The Landmark is a functioning bed and breakfast inn with ten rooms, but this unusual B-and-B will take you back into another time. Its rooms are furnished with antiques and have no telephones or televisions, and some share baths. All rooms do, however, have air conditioning. The building itself is more than one hundred years old, and other structures on the property, including a historic mill, may be examined.

Immigrants from the Alsace region of France settled Castroville in 1842 and many historic buildings remain. It was the first town established west of San Antonio in a region previously inhabited only by roving Apache and Comanche bands.

Landmark Inn State Historic Site

—Allan C. Kimball

The inn's property got its start in 1849 as a home and small store. After John Vance purchased it in 1853 and added a second story, the building was known as the Vance Hotel and Store. The next year, a dam was constructed across the river, and a grist mill and cotton gin were built.

Jordan T. Lawler bought the property in 1925, converting the mill to generate electricity. His sister, Ruth Lawler, a local school teacher and city judge, renovated the inn during World War II and renamed it the Landmark Inn.

The inn was a landmark almost since its beginning. It served as a popular general store for residents of Castroville and for travelers heading west. Among the travelers who stayed in the inn were James Longstreet, Abner Doubleday, Frederick Olmstead, and Robert E. Lee.

The store prospered when traffic increased on the San Antonio/El Paso Road. U.S. troops evacuating Texas at the beginning of the Civil War camped here, as did Confederate General Joe Shelby's Missouri cavalry on their way into Mexico after the Civil War.

During that war, the inn was an important way station for Southern cotton on its way to Mexican ports to avoid Union blockades along the Texas coast.

It was also an important stagecoach stop, and coaches and riders picked up and delivered mail there. In 1876, the first issue of the Castroville *Era* newspaper was published there. The on-site mill gave the city its first electric lights. And the inn's large bathhouse built in the courtyard was the only man-made bath between San Antonio and Eagle Pass for many years.

In 1974, Ruth Lawler donated the inn to state and TPWD operated it until it was transferred to the Texas Historical Commission in 2008.

Location: The park is located in downtown Castroville, about a half-hour west of San Antonio on U.S. Highway 90. Open daily 8 A.M. to 7 P.M., tours available.

Amenities: Fishing, historic site, lodging, restrooms.

Contact: Landmark Inn State Historic Site, 402 E. Florence Street, Castroville, TX 78009, 830-931-2133, www.landmarkinntx.com, www.thc.state.tx.us.

Longhorn Cavern State Park

If you hear someone tell you they're going to "get down" with some music at Longhorn Cavern, they mean it literally. This is one of the few places in the United States with underground concerts and where you can get married deep down in the ground. And they've been doing that sort of thing for many decades.

Summertime concerts aren't the only reason to visit Longhorn Cavern State Park. It's a bona fide historic site where gunpowder was secretly manufactured during the Civil War and was one of famed outlaw Sam Bass's favorite hideouts. And Comanche were hanging out down there about four hundred years before any Europeans found it.

One of the things that makes Longhorn Cavern unique among all Texas show caves is that it was formed mostly by flowing water, giving the walls a smooth, elegant appearance. In some rooms, you might swear you were in a marble hall. Fossil remains indicate that Ice Age animals also occupied the cavern. In the 1930s, the Civilian Conservation Corps built the stairs leading into the main entrance.

In addition to regular tours of the developed main cavern, special "wild cave" tours are offered where visitors crawl, climb and squeeze through small passages into areas not accessible on the regular tour.

Some of the larger underground rooms are also available for weddings and private parties.

In the 1920s, the cavern was a popular dance hall, restaurant, and speakeasy. One room was even used for theatrical performances and church ceremonies. In 1931, the state bought the property and the CCC developed it. It opened to the public in 1932. The cavern was designated a National Natural Landmark in 1971.

The Texas State Parks board gave the cavern its name, honoring the state's official large mammal.

Longhorn cattle are known for their diverse colors and exceptionally long horns—some can measure as much as 120 inches from tip to tip. The Texas longhorn is a hybrid breed resulting from a random mixing of Spanish stock and English cattle that Anglo-American frontiersmen brought to Texas from southern and midwestern states in the 1820s and 1830s.

Texas longhorns are, therefore, descended from the very first cattle to set foot in North America and are the only breed to evolve without human management. The longhorn can thrive in country where no other breed can live; subsist on weeds, cactus, and brush; range days away from water; and stay fit and fertile whether it's living in the scorching, parasite-infested tropics or in the arid, subzero winters of Montana.

The toughness and endurance of the longhorns made them well equipped for the long cattle drives in the years after the Civil War before railroads were common in the West. They usually lost very little weight on the drive.

Texas longhorns represent the romance of the Old West and are often raised for their beauty and intelligence.

The longhorn is also the mascot for University of Texas sports.

Location: The park is located nine miles west of Burnet, off U.S. Highway 281 on Park Road 4. Open daily but hours vary with the season and days of the week, so call ahead for times. Day use only.

Amenities: Hiking, exhibits, interpretive trail, park store, restrooms, tours.

Contact: Longhorn Cavern State Park, P.O. Box 732, Burnet, TX 78611, 830-598-CAVE, 877-441-CAVE (toll-free), www.longhorncaverns.com, www.tpwd.state.tx.us.

Lost Maples State Natural Area

Maple trees in Texas? They must be lost, maybe even lonely.

Lost Maples State Natural Area is brimming with bigtooth maple trees, a rare treat in the Lone Star State. The park is also renowned for its steep canyons, clear streams, grasslands, scattered springs, and abundant wildlife.

The Sabinal River flows through the heart of the 2,200-acre park, creating scenic limestone canyons typical of the Hill Country. Springs pop up all over the place, creating inviting pools with grassy banks and shade trees that are the perfect places to sit and enjoy nature, have lunch, or pitch a tent. While you're relaxing in one of these spots, you might spy an endangered golden-cheeked warbler or black-capped vireo or green kingfisher among dozens of other beautiful birds. And if you're feeling energetic, you have eleven miles of trails to choose from.

Texas Parks and Wildlife purchased from private owners in 1973-1974 and opened the park to the public in 1979. The park was named a National Natural Landmark in 1981.

Although located just a few miles from Garner State Park, one of the most popular parks in Texas, Lost Maples is one of the least visited, except when the maple leaves change in late fall to reds, yellows, and oranges rivaled only by those of the northeast.

The main canyon of the park is a true refuge. When the weather here became hotter and harsher and more arid after the last Ice Age, the canyon was a sheltering location where certain plants and animals that were once more widespread have been able to survive.

Among those plants are the relic maple trees that give the park its name.

Picnickers at Lost Maples State Natural Area
—Allan C. Kimball

Maples are trees that grow from 30 feet to 130 feet in height. They are distinguished by wide, deeply indented, three-to-five lobed leaves with sharp points that give the name to their genus *Acer*, a Latin word that means "sharp." Children love to spin maple seeds because they look like helicopter blades whirling as they fall. Until recently, the Lost Maples trees were thought to be a type of sugar maple, related to those famed in the northeast for their syrup, but new studies show they are a distinct form of bigtooth maple. Bigtooth maple leaves are serrated, hence the name.

The Sabinal River is sixty miles long and rises from springs around Lost Maples. The name derives from the Spanish *Rio Sabinas*, a slang Mexican term referring to the clusters of bald cypress trees growing along the river banks. The river was originally called *Arroyo del Soledad* or "Lonely Ditch."

Location: The park is located five miles north of Vanderpool on Farm Road 187. Open daily. The park can become very crowded with leaf peepers on weekends in late October through early November, and when parking capacity exceeds 250 cars, the park closes, so call ahead.

Amenities: Camping, dump station, hiking, nature trail, park store, restrooms, showers.

Contact: Lost Maples State Natural Area, 37221 FM 187, Vanderpool, TX 78885, 830-966-3413, www.tpwd.state.tx.us.

Lyndon B. Johnson State Park and Historic Site

For what could simply be a historic site, Lyndon B. Johnson State Park is amazingly diverse with scenic views, a nature trail, a museum, a living history farm, family recreation, and fields lush with wildflowers in the spring.

The 730-acre park in the tiny town of Stonewall honors Lyndon Baines Johnson, one of only two native Texans to become president of the United States. (The other is Dwight David Eisenhower. Please see information for Eisenhower Birthplace State Historic Site in the Prairies and Lakes section.) The park is located directly across from the LBJ Ranch along the Pedernales River.

Friends of then-President Johnson raised money to purchase the land across the river and the state accepted the property in 1965. The park was opened to the public in 1970.

The visitors' center contains Johnson memorabilia and interactive displays about the land and people who shaped the President. A film about LBJ shows regularly in the center's theater. A nature trail winds through the park and by roaming buffalo, white tail deer, longhorn cattle, wild turkey and other Hill Country wildlife. One of the other interesting attractions in the park is an almost hidden but imposing bronze statue of LBJ pointing across the Pedernales to his ranch.

The park also features a swimming pool, tennis court, and a baseball diamond. The park store offers a comprehensive variety of books relating to Johnson, the Presidency in general, Texas, and the Hill Country.

The Lyndon B. Johnson National Historical Park conducts bus tours of the LBJ Ranch, starting at the state park's Visitors Center.

Lyndon B. Johnson was born in Stonewall in 1908, the eldest of five children born to Samuel and Rebekah Johnson. Sam Johnson served in the Texas Legislature.

The Johnsons moved to nearby Johnson City in 1913 and in 1927, LBJ attended Texas State Teachers College (now Texas State University) in San Marcos and taught for a short period of time until becoming secretary to Congressman Richard M. Kleberg. In 1934, he met and married Claudia "Lady Bird" Taylor.

Johnson was elected to Congress in 1937 and served for

eleven years in the U.S. House. He was defeated in a 1941 race for the U.S. Senate, but when World War II began he joined the Navy and rose to the rank of lieutenant commander, seeing combat in the South Pacific.

LBJ ran for the Senate again in 1948 and won a narrow victory. He became Majority Leader in 1955. In that capacity, Johnson was instrumental in passing the first civil rights laws in eighty years. After becoming President he made passage of the landmark 1964 Civil Rights Act a cornerstone of his administration.

Lyndon B. Johnson
—Lyndon Baines Johnson
Presidential Library

He sought the Democratic nomination for President in 1960, but lost to Massachusetts Senator John F. Kennedy. JFK chose LBJ to be his running mate and the two were elected in a narrow race that year. When Kennedy was assassinated in Dallas in 1963, Johnson became President. He defeated Arizona Senator Barry Goldwater in a landslide victory in 1964 to win a term in his own right.

Johnson was plagued by the conduct of the war in Vietnam and by civil unrest at home. Faced with serious challenges within his own party, he withdrew from the 1968 presidential race that was eventually won by Republican Richard M. Nixon.

LBJ and Lady Bird retired to their ranch in Stonewall. He died on January 22, 1973. Lady Bird Johnson died on July 11, 2007. The couple is buried in the family cemetery in Stonewall, near LBJ's birthplace.

East of the Visitor Center is another unusual feature of the park, the Sauer-Beckmann Farm that takes visitors back to life in rural Texas in the early 1900s. Costumed interpreters carry out the day-to-day activities of a turn-of-the-century Texas-German farm family.

Johann and Christine Sauer, along with their four children, settled the property in 1869. By 1885, the family built several stone buildings near their original rock and log cabins. The Sauers had ten children, and one of them, Augusta Sauer Lindig, served as midwife at the birth of LBJ.

The Beckmann family acquired the property in 1900. A good cotton crop in 1915 allowed Emil and Emma Beckmann to build a new barn, add a room onto the old rock structure, and to construct porches connecting to a Victorian house covered with then fashionable pressed tin.

Edna Beckmann Hightower donated the farm acreage to the state in 1966 and the farm opened to the public as part of the LBJ park in 1975.

For information on the Pedernales River, see the entry below for Pedernales River State Park.

The Lyndon B. Johnson National Historical Park is located in Johnson City and the Lyndon B. Johnson Presidential Library is located on the campus of the University of Texas in Austin.

Location: The park is located two miles east of Stonewall on U.S. Highway 290. Ranch Road 1 goes around the park and along the banks of the Pedernales River. Open daily 8 A.M. to 5 P.M. Tours to the LBJ Ranch run from 10 A.M. to 4 P.M.

Amenities: Fishing, museum, nature trail, park store, restrooms, swimming pool.

Contact: Lyndon B. Johnson State Park and Historic Site, P.O. Box 238, Stonewall, TX 78671, 830-644-2252, www.tpwd.state.tx.us.

McKinney Falls State Park

Here's a bucolic park just thirteen miles from the state capitol, full of hike and bike trails, full of wildlife, and full of wildflowers in the spring.

Listen to the soothing sound of nature as water burbles along at the confluence of Onion and Williamson creeks and rushes over two falls on Onion Creek. The Upper Falls is near the Visitor Center and McKinney Falls is farther downstream. Cypress trees line Onion Creek, offering deep shade, and a visitor will also discover sycamore, oak, elm, hackberry, and pecan trees. Agarita, cactus, and mesquite abound.

Among the ruins are an old horse trainer's cabin, a homestead, and a water-powered gristmill. One trail passes by limestone shelters once used by nomadic Indians.

Santiago del Valle first owned the property and later Michel B. Menard acquired it, but neither ever lived on it. Thomas K. McKinney bought the land in 1839 and became its first resident in 1850. James Wood Smith bought the homestead in 1885. Smith's grandchildren, J. E. "Pete" Smith and Annie Smith, donated the property to the state in 1970. The park was opened to the public in 1976.

The 745-acre park is the former homestead of racehorse breeder Thomas F. McKinney, one of Stephen F. Austin's original 300 settlers in Texas.

McKinney was born in 1801 in Kentucky and moved with his family to Missouri in 1815. He arrived in Texas in 1824, running a trade business between Ciudad Chihuahua, Mexico, and San Antonio and Nacogdoches. He expanded his business interests across Texas in later years. In the early 1830s he became one of the co-founders of Galveston.

He opposed Texas independence, opposed its annexation to the United States, and opposed secession from the Union, but once each happened he worked tirelessly to support that government.

McKinney is considered the father of the Texas Navy, using

his own schooner to capture Mexican vessels in the Gulf. His firm was a primary source of money and supplies to the Texas army. He served as a senator from Galveston County in the first Texas Legislature.

In the early 1850s, McKinney moved to his property along Onion Creek. He served as a Travis County commissioner and represented the county in the 7th Texas Legislature. His businesses were ruined by the Civil War and he went broke. He died in 1873 after a long struggle with kidney disease. He is buried in the Oakwood Cemetery.

Location: The park is located 13 miles from downtown Austin off U.S. Highway 183. Open daily.

Amenities: Biking, camping, dump station, fishing, hiking, historic sites, park store, picnicking, restrooms, screened shelters, showers, swimming, wireless Internet access.

Contact: McKinney Falls State Park, 5808 McKinney Falls Parkway, Austin, TX 78744, 512-243-1643, www.tpwd. state.tx.us.

Pedernales Falls State Park

Pedernales Falls State Park is the perfect place for nature photography, wildlife and bird watching, hiking, horseback riding, fishing, camping—name it and you can do it here.

The heart of the park lies along the banks of the scenic Pedernales River, a clear stream flowing over gently sloping limestone to create the shallow but wide waterfall. What people think of as the waterfall is actually the end of the falls. Even though scenic overlooks will give you a bird's-eye view

Visitors scramble around at Pedernales Falls State Park
—Allan C. Kimball

*Who Is Mother Neff
and Why Is She a
Texas State Park?*

of this section of the river, only a high aerial view could show all of waterfall itself as the river flows through and over the sweeping limestone slabs. In this area, the elevation of the river drops about fifty feet over a distance of 3,000 feet.

These layers of limestone were tilted, then eroded more than 100 million years ago.

The 5,212-acre park has other falls, too. The Twin Falls are narrow waterfalls at the confluence of Bee Creek and Regal Creek.

Visitors may also swim and fish in the river, although swimming is limited to an area at least three miles downstream from the falls. Fish commonly caught in the Pedernales River include bass, carp, catfish, and perch.

Although the Pedernales River is the focal point of the park, other areas are just as interesting. More than fifteen miles of hike and bike trails, eight miles of backpacking trails, and twelve miles of equestrian trails wander over hills dotted with cedar and oak and woodlands, and provide access to more heavily-wooded areas of pecan, elm, sycamore, walnut, and hackberry trees. Ash, buttonbush, and cypress grow on the river banks.

The park was once the Circle Bar Ranch, owned by C. A. and Harriet Wheatley who raised cattle and goats. C. A. died in 1963 and Harriet sold the property to the state in 1970. The park opened to the public in 1971.

One thing to always bear in mind at Pedernales Falls is that the river can flash flood with little or no warning, transforming itself from a placid stream to a raging torrent in a few minutes. Sirens sound when the river reaches dangerous levels; when you hear them, leave the river area immediately.

The spring-fed Pedernales River flows for 106 miles from Kimble County to Lake Travis near Austin. The name *pedernales* is the Spanish word for the flint rocks that characterize the riverbed and was first used by Spanish explorers and missionaries in the mid-eighteenth century. Apaches made arrowheads from flint collected from pools near the base of the falls.

The word was originally pronounced "peh-der-NAH-less," but thanks to the way President Lyndon Johnson pronounced the name of his favorite river, a more common pronunciation today is "per-din-ALICE." When LBJ was waxing eloquent, he could draw out that first syllable considerably.

Location: The park is located nine miles east of Johnson City off Farm Road 2766. Open daily.

Amenities: Biking, camping, dump station, fishing, hiking, horseback riding, park store, picnicking, restrooms, showers, swimming.

Contact: Pedernales Falls State Park, 2585 Park Road 6026, Johnson City, TX 78636, 830-868-7304, www.friendsof pfalls.org, www.tpwd.state.tx.us.

South Llano River State Park

Frolic in one of the most pristine bodies of water in Texas at South Llano River State Park or stroll along the trails in the hills that overlook the river. South Llano is a small park of 525 acres—mostly along the river—but visitors can enlarge their experience by hiking the trails at the 2,200-acre Walter Buck Wildlife Management Area that is adjacent to the state park.

Because the river is spring-fed, its quality is excellent and maintains a nearly constant level. Canoeists and kayakers travel here knowing they will always have a wilderness experience and a good water flow over the mild rapids.

Being so remote—120 miles northwest of San Antonio and 145 miles west of Austin—the park offers a visitor a true taste of nature. Visitors report seeing axis deer, black buck antelope, fallow deer, kingfishers, colorful painted buntings, and rare black-capped vireos.

The park is also home to one of the oldest wild turkey roosts in the state and to protect them, the park closes the river bottom area from October 1 through March 31. However, relatively new observation blinds allow visitors to glimpse wild turkeys scampering from roost to roost.

The property was once a part of Walter S. Buck's ranch. His father, Walter W. Buck, bought the property from the James Thomas family and in 1910 moved his family here from Hillsboro in a horse-and-buggy.

Walter S. Buck never married, saying that his land here was his true love. He was particularly proud of the pecan trees and wild turkeys, often feeding the turkeys and wanting to ensure they would always have a safe place to roost in the midst of prime hunting territory in Texas, he donated the ranch to the state in 1977. A portion of that property opened as a state park in 1990; the largest portion became the wildlife management area next to the park. Buck died in 1982.

The South Llano River flows for fifty-five miles from north-western Edwards County to its confluence with the North Llano River near Junction. The Llano River then flows east for another one hundred miles to the Colorado River at Lake Lyndon B. Johnson near Kingsland.

When Spanish explorer Domingo Ramón discovered the river in 1711, he named it the *Rio de los Sanas*, after the Sana Indians, a Tonkawa tribe that lived nearby. The name *llano*, Spanish for "plain," came into use in the nineteenth century.

Location: The park is located five miles south of Junction on U.S. Highway 377. Open daily.

Amenities: Biking, camping, canoeing, dump station, fishing, hiking, picnicking, restrooms, showers, swimming.

Contact: South Llano River State Park, 1927 Park Road 73, Junction, TX 76849, 325-446-3994, www.tpwd.state.tx.us.

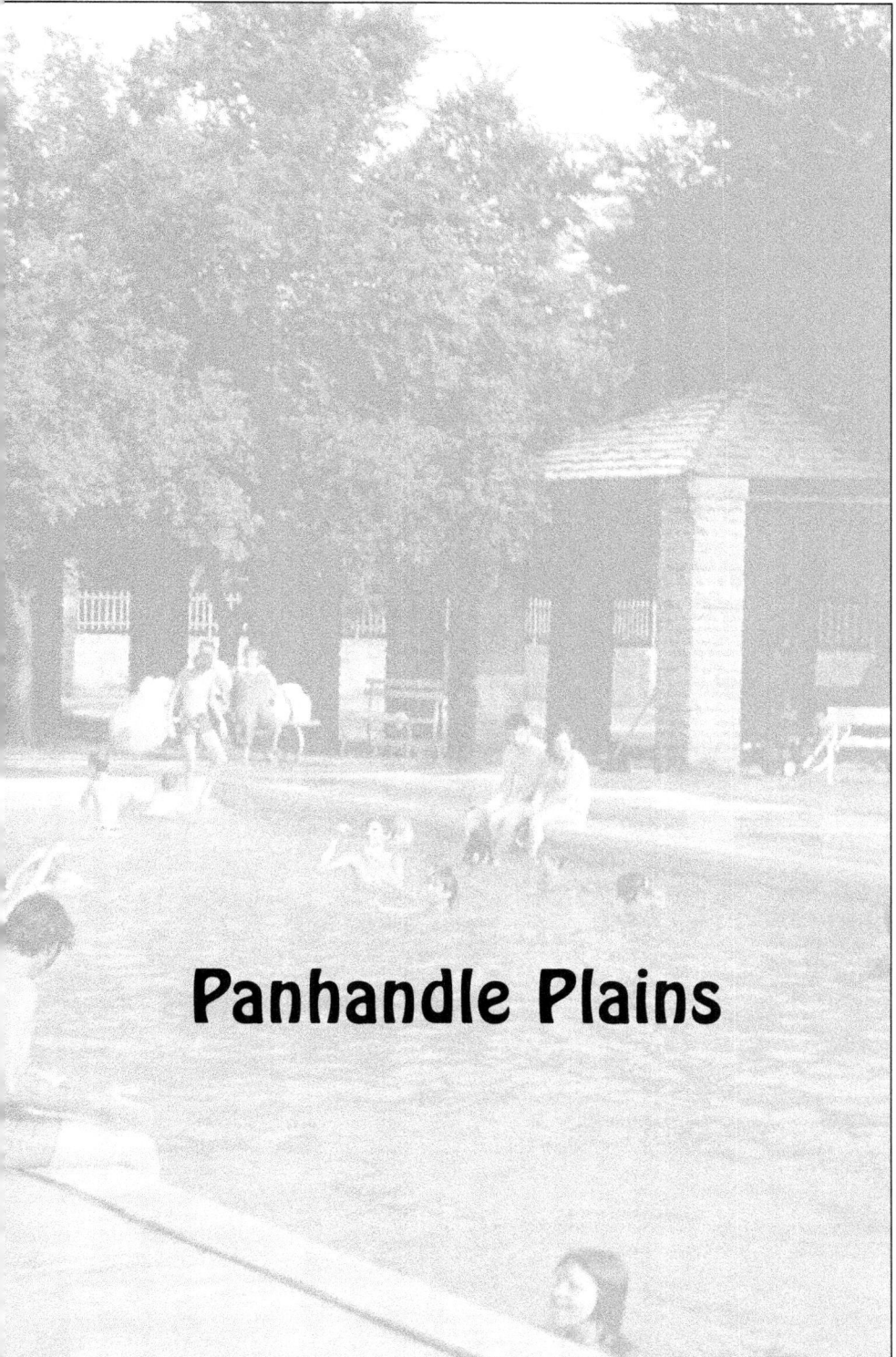

Panhandle Plains

Abilene State Park

At Abilene State Park you can have a picnic under pecan trees as the Comanche used to. The Comanche didn't have a swimming pool to frolic in, though, nor did they have a playground, restrooms, and showers.

But the park serves a similar purpose for visitors today as it did hundreds of years ago; it is a wooded oasis on the banks of Elm Creek in the midst of rolling plains. It just has more modern amenities. Certainly the fiercely competitive and nomadic Comanche would have appreciated the yurts with their soft beds and microwaves, and the basketball court.

In 1934, the Civilian Conservation Corps built a water tower and observation deck of rust-colored sandstone that now overlooks the swimming pool.

Armadillos, deer, fox, rabbits, roadrunners, and squirrels are among the wildlife a visitor may spot along the one-mile nature trail. Look up and spy cardinals and hummingbirds; and the state bird, the mockingbird, will let you know where it is with its distinctive cackle. Also, a portion of the official Texas longhorn herd and one buffalo make their home here.

The state acquired the 530-acre property from Abilene in 1933.

The park was named for the nearby city of Abilene that was incorporated in 1881. Abilene, Texas, was named for Abilene, Kansas. The cities had much in common since both were rowdy frontier towns on a broad plain and were major cattle shipping points.

Abilene, Kansas, got its name from the Bible. In 1858, city founder Timothy F. Hersey was trying to decide on a name for the town. His wife Sylvia picked up a Bible, allowing it to fall open wherever it might and the first passage she read was from Luke 3:1.

In the fifteenth year of the reign of Tiberius Caesar, when Pontius Pilate was governor of Judea, and Herod was tetrarch of Galilee, and his brother Philip tetrarch of the region of

Ituraea and Trachonitis, and Lysanias was tetrarch of Abilene . . .

In biblical times, Abilene was a district in Syria. The name *Abilene*—a Hebrew word meaning "plain"—caught their attention since the Kansas location was also a city on the plain.

Location: The park is located sixteen miles southwest of Abilene. Open daily; swimming pool open Memorial Day through Labor Day on Thursday through Sunday from 11 A.M. to 7 P.M.

Amenities: Biking, camping, dump station, hiking, fishing, park store, picnicking, playground, restrooms, screened shelters, showers, swimming pool.

Contact: Abilene State Park, 150 Park Road 32, Tuscola, TX 79562, 325-572-3204, www.tpwd.state.tx.us.

Swimming pool at Abilene State Park
—Jack Lewis/Texas Department of Transportation

Big Spring State Park

The Comanche made camp here, as did Spanish explorers, cattle drives, and immigrants moving west. Why? The spring found here was the only reliable water in a sixty-mile radius.

More than water attracts modern visitors. The view from the top of Scenic Mountain is breathtaking and other sightseeing opportunities abound. Big Spring State Park is located in an area where three ecological regions merge. To the north and east are the western Rolling Plains, to the south is the Edwards Plateau, and to the west is the Llano Estacado, the Staked Plains, also known as the High Plains. This mix provides the area with a wide variety of plant and animal life. A small prairie dog town lies in a valley on the south side of the park.

Attracted by the large source of spring water, Comanche and other Native American groups frequented the area in the past. Spanish explorers passed by as early as 1768.

The city deeded the 380-acre park to the state in 1934 and 1935, and it was opened to the public in 1936. The Civilian Conservation Corps built much of the original park facilities in 1934, including the pavilion, headquarters, a residence, pumphouse, and a restroom. The biggest CCC project was the three-mile drive that loops the mountain, following the limestone ledge capping the bluff.

The park was named for the city of Big Spring that was named for a gushing natural spring in a draw at the lower edge of the Llano Estacado. Over the years, heavy pumping by the railroad and the development of the city caused the spring to be depleted by the mid-1920s. It has since been rejuvenated with water diverted from Comanche Trail Lake.

Location: The park is located thirty-six miles east of Midland, off Farm Road 700 two miles southwest of Big Spring. Open daily from 8 A.M. to sunset.

Amenities: Hiking, park store, picnicking, playground, rest-rooms.

Contact: Big Spring State Park, 1 Scenic Drive, Big Spring, TX 79720, 432-263-4931, www.tpwd.state.tx.us.

Caprock Canyons State Park and Trailway

Visitors can still find the spirit of the buffalo at Caprock Canyons State Park. Descendents of Panhandle pioneer cattle-man Charles Goodnight's bison herd are protected here as the official Texas State Bison Herd. And prehistoric sites discovered here have offered up the relics of now extinct Ice Age bison bones and the hunters who stalked them.

The 15,315-acre park is one of the most rugged in Texas and one of the largest. It features spectacular landscapes, hoodoos, and waterfalls carved by erosion of the caprock, colorful cliffs and canyons and wooded glens, and abundant wildlife.

More than 175 species of birds, mule and white tail deer, bobcats, foxes, African aoudad sheep, and the occasional golden eagle call this oasis home. Bass and catfish are plentiful in the lake.

Springs in the area made this a popular site for several Native American cultures. A bison-kill Folsom age site more than 10,000 years old—one of only five such discovered in the U.S.—has been excavated near the park lake.

But the park has even more to offer with the Trailway, a sixty-four-mile rail-to-trail conversion, acquired by donation in 1992. The trailway stretches from the western terminus at South Plains up on top of the caprock escarpment to the eastern terminus of Estelline in the Red River Valley. This hike, bike, and equestrian trail stretches the park through Briscoe,

Salt deposits at Caprock Canyon State Park
—Stan A. Williams/Texas Department of Transportation

Floyd, and Hall counties crossing forty-six railroad trestles and running through the last active railroad tunnel in Texas. The railroad was built in 1887 and by 1890 the tiny town of Quitaque, where the park is now located, was a regular stage stop.

The park also has a forty-five-minute audio tour available for visitors.

The park property was bought by state in 1975, and opened to the public in 1982.

Caprock Canyons takes its name from the cap, or hard layer, underlying the Llano Estacado. It is not a rock layer in the usual sense, but is more like a hard layer that developed a few feet below the ground as highly mineral subsoil particles cemented themselves together to form a rock-like layer that resists erosion. Although the name caprock applies only to the formation itself, the expression is often used to mean the whole Llano Estacado.

The caprock escarpment was formed by erosion about one million to two million years ago. The escarpment forms a natural boundary line between the High Plains and the lower rolling plains of West Texas and stretches from the Panhandle into the Hill Country. It rises abruptly above the flat plains at two hundred, five hundred, or as much as one thousand feet. River often cut the east-facing wall to form canyons.

Prehistoric nomadic hunters, Apache, and Comanche lived in the region. Spanish explorer Vásquez de Coronado traveled through the area in 1541.

Llano Estacado is Spanish for "Staked Plains." The name comes from the fact that the plains are so flat and nondescript in this area that the first Spanish explorers staked out the land with flags so they could navigate with some degree of confidence.

Coronado wrote, "there was not a stone, nor bit of rising ground, nor a tree, nor a shrub, nor anything to go by" on the vast plain.

It is bound on the north by the southern escarpment of the Canadian River Valley and on the east by the Caprock Escarpment. The western boundary is the Mescalero Escarpment east of the Pecos River Valley of New Mexico. The southern end of the plateau lacks a distinct physical boundary as it blends into the Edwards Plateau that forms most of the central Texas Hill Country.

The Llano Estacado covers approximately 32,000 square miles, a larger area than all of New England. It is part of what was known to early explorers and settlers as the Great American Desert.

It's a matter of some confusion about how the city of Quitaque got its name.

One story claims that Charles Goodnight came up with the name, telling people it was an Indian word meaning "end of the trail."

A second story says that the name came from an Indian word for the two buttes in the area that resembled piles of horse manure.

A third story says the name came from the Quitaca Indians—a band of Wichita—and their name translated as "whatever one steals."

There is no real evidence for any version, so we may never know for certain. By the way, locals pronounce the name Quitaque as "kitty-kway."

Location: The park is located on Farm Road 1065 three-and-one-half miles north of Quitaque. Open Friday and Saturday 8 A.M. to 6 P.M., Sunday through Thursday 8 A.M. to noon and 1 P.M. to 5 P.M.

Amenities: Biking, boating, camping, dump station, fishing, guided audio tour, hiking, horseback riding, park store, picnicking, restrooms, showers, swimming. Horse rentals are available from a local concessionaire; call the park for more information.

Contact: Caprock Canyons State Park, P.O. Box 204, Quitaque, TX 79255, 806-455-1492, www.tpwd.state.tx.us.

Copper Breaks State Park

At Copper Breaks State Park the Rolling Plains expand into wide-open spaces once home to huge buffalo herds, Comanche and Kiowa. It's an arid land eroded by rivers and creeks into gullies and mesas and juniper breaks full of wildlife.

The wildlife visitors see here are typical of North Texas—bluebirds, cardinals, dove, hawks, meadow larks, mockingbirds, quail, roadrunners, armadillos, coyotes, deer, frogs, lizards, opossums, rabbits, turtles. You might even spy the prehistoric looking Texas horned frog (that some also call a "horny toad," but is actually a lizard). A portion of the official Texas State Longhorn Herd also calls Copper Breaks State Park home.

The 1,900-acre park also features two lakes, a swimming beach, a boat dock, a fishing pier, playgrounds, ten miles of trails, a nature trail, campsites, equestrian campsites, a group picnic pavilion, a meeting room, and an interpretive center. And the park explodes with the color of a wide variety of wildflowers in the spring.

The state purchased the property in 1970 and opened it to the public in 1974.

Small amounts of copper can be found in the area clay. The word "breaks" means "a broken place" or a "geological fault," and refers to the fractures and faults that define the limited waterways of the park.

Location: The park is located between the towns of Quanah and Crowell, off Texas Highway 6. Open daily.

Amenities: Biking, boating, camping, dump station, fishing, hiking, horseback riding, park store, picnicking, restrooms, showers, swimming.

Contact: Copper Breaks State Park, 777 Park Road 62, Quanah, TX 79252, 940-839-4331, www.tpwd.state.tx.us.

Fort Griffin State Historic Site

Get a feeling for what tough pioneer life was like on the vast Texas plains at Fort Griffin State Historic Site, once home to hard men, fast women, Buffalo Soldiers, bison, longhorn cattle, and more than a few tough times.

The fort was built in 1867 and deactivated in 1881. The fort once held command of the southern plains of Texas and saw the end of the great buffalo herds and the people who hunted them. It was a refuge for buffalo hunters, cattle drovers, settlers, stagecoaches, and wagon trains on the Texas frontier. Over the years, it was home to units of the 9th and 10th Cavalry and the 24th Infantry—black troopers called Buffalo Soldiers.

Soldiers from the fort made frequent expeditions onto the Llano Estacado searching for raiding bands of Comanche and Kiowa, and escorted mail and passenger stages across the plains. Fort Griffin also served as the primary supply center for the Red River Campaign of Colonel Ranald Mackenzie who drove Indians from the High Plains in the 1870s.

Located on 506 acres with 1,500 feet of river area, Fort Griffin is located on a bluff overlooking the town site of Fort Griffin and the Clear Fork of the Brazos River Valley. Ruins include a hand-dug well, a mess hall, a library, a store, an administration building, a cistern, a hospital, a powder magazine, the foundation of officers' quarters, the first sergeant's quarters, a restored bakery, and replicas of enlisted men's huts.

A portion of the official Texas State Longhorn Herd resides in the park.

The state acquired the property from Shackelford County in 1935 and the Civilian Conservation Corps built many of the park's facilities before it opened to the public in 1938. Fort Griffin was transferred to the Texas Historical Commission in 2008.

The town of Fort Griffin—also known as "The Flats"—grew up around the fort and became a haven for nearly every ne'r-do-well in the West such as Lottie Deno, Pat Garrett, John Selman, and John Wesley Hardin. Wyatt Earp first met Doc Holliday over a gambling table in the town.

The fort was named for General Charles Griffin, commander of the military Department of Texas during 1866 and 1867. He was born in 1825 in Granville, Ohio, and graduated from the U.S. Military Academy in 1847 with a commission as an artillery officer. He served as an instructor at the Academy from 1860 to 1861.

Griffin served for twenty-five years in the Army, from the Mexican War through the Civil War. He was honored for gallantry at the battles of Bull Run, The Wilderness, Weldon, and Five Forks, being promoted from major to major general. He also commanded divisions at the battles of Fredericksburg, Chancellorsville, and Gettysburg. He was one of the Union officers who accepted General Robert E. Lee's surrender at Appomattox.

In Texas, Griffin got deeply involved in Reconstruction politics and got Governor James Throckmorton removed from office for his lack of cooperation on civil rights for freedmen. Griffin's replacement for governor, Elisha M. Pease, then removed large numbers of other state and county officeholders.

Griffin was appointed to take over General Philip Sheridan's command of Fifth Military District when he contracted yellow fever in an epidemic that was sweeping Galveston. He died there in 1867.

Location: The park is located fifteen miles north of the city of Albany. Open daily 8 A.M. to 5 P.M.

Amenities: Fishing, hiking, living history re-enactments, picnicking, nature study.

Contact: Fort Griffin State Historic Site, 1701 N. U.S. Highway 283, Albany, TX 76430, 325-762-2492, www.thc.state.tx.us.

Fort Richardson State Park, Historic Site and Lost Creek Reservoir State Trailway

Fort Richardson State Park offers two distinct ways to be entertained, preserving history and featuring outdoor recreation.

Fort Richardson was established in 1867. It was the northernmost of a line of forts established after the Civil War. Troopers from the fort arrested Indians responsible for the Warren Wagon Train Massacre (sometimes called the Salt Creek Massacre) of 1871. Kiowa leaders Satanta and Big Tree were among those arrested and held at Fort Richardson. They became the first Indians tried in a Texas civil court. Soldiers here also fought the Comanche in Palo Duro Canyon under the fort's commanding officer, Colonel Ranald Mackenzie. The fort was abandoned in 1878.

The historic site includes seven of the original buildings that have been restored—the post bakery, the commissary, a guardhouse, the hospital, a morgue, officers' quarters, and a powder magazine. The officers' barracks and enlisted barracks are replicas; the officers' barracks houses the park's Interpretive Center.

The state acquired the 455-acre property from the city of Jackboro in 1968 and opened the park to the public the same year.

Part of the Rails-To-Trails program, the Lost Creek Reservoir State Trailway was opened in 1998. The ten-mile bike, hike, and equestrian trail runs adjacent to Fort Richardson and along Lost Creek. The trail offers a number of shaded areas under pecans and oak trees, wildlife viewing opportunities, and several locations to fish or swim in the creek or lake.

Fort Richardson was named for Major General Israel Bush Richardson who died in 1862 during the Civil War Battle of Antietam.

Richardson was born in 1815 in Fairfax, Vermont, and

graduated from the U.S. Military Academy in 1841. He saw action in the Seminole Wars, the Mexican War, and along the frontier. He resigned his commission in 1855 to become a farmer in Pontiac, Michigan, but returned to duty after organizing the 2nd Michigan Volunteers when the Civil War broke out.

Portraits of Richardson all show a dour man. His men called him either "Fighting Dick" or "Greasy Dick."

Location: The park is located one-half mile south of Jackboro on U.S. Highway 281. Open daily.

*Major General
Israel B. Richardson*
—Library of Congress

Amenities: Biking, camping, dump station, fishing, group picnic pavilion, hiking, historic site, horseback riding, military re-enactments, nature trail, park store, restrooms, screened shelters, showers, swimming, water/electric/sewer sites, tours.

Contact: Fort Richardson State Park, 228 Park Road 61, Jackboro, TX 76458, 940-567-3506, www.tpwd.state.tx.us.

Lake Arrowhead State Park

Lake Arrowhead's main attractions are fishing and water

sports on the 16,400-acre lake that gives the park its name. The park is surrounded by the Rolling Plains where visitors may also wander around on five miles of mostly flat trails.

The lake is a reservoir on the Little Wichita River with 106 miles of shoreline. It was built by Wichita Falls as the city's primary water supply. The state acquired the park's 524 acres from Wichita Falls in 1970 and opened it to the public the same year.

If you'd like to fish but didn't happen to bring a fishing pole, the park's Loan A Tackle Program lends fishing tackle to visitors.

An active prairie dog town and an eighteen-hole disc golf course make the park unique.

The name of Lake Arrowhead doesn't refer to any particular historical or cultural event that happened on or near the lake site, but just as a general reference to the Native Americans who lived in the area.

The Wichita River and the town of Wichita Falls draw their names from the Wichita Indians who lived in the area. The Wichita were key traders between the Comanche and Louisiana merchants.

Several stories try to explain the origin of the word "Wichita," but none have much evidence.

One story says the word is a corruption of the term French traders used to identify them: *Ousitas*. That word is supposed to be a corruption of a Wichita word meaning "scattered lodges."

Another story says the name comes from their word *wee-chi-tah* which means "waist deep" and refers to the band's crossing of the river that would take the tribe's name.

Yet another story says the word is taken from a Caddoan word, *Ouachita*, meaning "good hunting grounds."

None of these versions is accepted by the Wichita Indians who call themselves *Kitikiti'sh*, meaning "Raccoon Eyes," referring to the tattoos male tribal members made around their eyes.

Location: The park is located off Farm Road 1954, fourteen miles southeast of Wichita Falls. Open daily.

Amenities: Boat ramp, boating, camping, disc golf, dump station, fishing, hiking, horseback riding, park store, picnicking, restrooms, showers, swimming, water skiing.

Contact: Lake Arrowhead State Park, 229 Park Road 63, Wichita Falls, TX 76310, 940-528-2211, www.tpwd. state.tx.us.

Lake Brownwood State Park

Lake Brownwood is one of the oldest reservoirs in Texas, one of the oldest state parks, and it's remarkably the same today as it has always been.

The Civilian Conservation Corps built many of the structures in the early 1930s from timber and native rock found on the property. Their continued use gives visitors a timeless feeling. Add in the rustic beauty and tranquility of miles of shoreline where wildflowers, deer, ducks, armadillos, raccoons, squirrels, and birds can be observed in a natural setting. Fishing the lake will yield bass, catfish, crappie, and perch.

The park is one of only seven state parks that have cabins built by the CCC, and they offer scenic views of the lake. Plus they've been updated with air conditioning. Climb up the tower of the stone recreation building for a commanding 360-degree view of the lake, surrounding woods, and faraway hills.

Near the geographical center of Texas, the park is located at Lake Brownwood, a 7,300-acre reservoir created by damming Pecan Bayou, a tributary of the Colorado River. The park's 538 acres were acquired by the state in 1934 and opened to the public in 1938.

Pecan Bayou was named for the numerous pecan trees found along its banks.

The lake, nearby city, and county were named for Henry Stevenson Brown.

Brown was born in Madison County, Kentucky, in 1793. In 1810, he moved to St. Charles County, Missouri, where he traded via flatboats between Missouri and New Orleans. He also served as sheriff of the county. Brown fought in the War of 1812, and later came to Texas with his brother John Duff Brown, landing at the mouth of the Brazos River equipped to trade with Mexicans and Indians. In 1814, he married Margaret Kerr, daughter of James Kerr for whom Kerr County is named.

In 1825, John Brown was captured by a band of Waco Indians. Henry Brown gathered together a group of forty-two men who ventured into what was then Indian country in search of his brother. They found the main Waco village on the banks of the Brazos River and destroyed it, killing a large number of Indians. John Brown, however, was being held in another village and the rescue party did not find him. John Brown was given up for dead, but he escaped from the Wacos about a year later. Henry Brown, leading a group of Mexican soldiers, also destroyed the Waco band that had held John captive. Thereafter, John Brown was known as Waco Brown. The village that Henry Brown's volunteers destroyed is at the present site of the city of Waco.

Brown was a delegate from Gonzales to the Convention of 1832 at San Felipe. He died in Columbia, Texas, in 1834. Brown was never a resident of the county that would bear his name, but he was in the area for a short time searching for horses stolen by Indians.

Location: The park is located sixteen miles northwest of Brownwood off Texas Highway 279. Open daily; office open 8 A.M. to 5 P.M.

Amenities: Boating, camping, dump station, fishing, hiking, picnicking, restrooms, screened shelters, showers, swimming, water/electric/sewer sites, water skiing.

Contact: Lake Brownwood State Park, 200 State Highway Park Road 15, Lake Brownwood, TX 76801, 325-784-5223, www.tpwd.state.tx.us.

Lake Colorado City State Park

Lake Colorado City is a great place to fish because its water is usually warmer than usual thanks to the power plant on its shore. The water is fine for all sorts of other boating activities, too.

Limited-use cabins were recently built of sandstone and their reddish hue blends in perfectly with the surrounding landscape.

Lake Colorado City was built in 1949 on a tributary of the Colorado River by the Texas Electric Service Company to provide cooling water for the power plant, as a water supply for Colorado City, and for recreation. The power plant is the largest modern steam electric station in West Texas. The state leased the 500-acre park in 1971 from the utility company. It was opened to the public in 1972.

The lake is named for the nearby Colorado City that got its name from its location along the Colorado River. For details on the Colorado River, see the entry for Colorado Bend State Park in the Hill Country section.

Colorado City was once a boom town and called the "Mother City of West Texas." It started out as a camp for buffalo hunters, then as a Texas Ranger camp, and when the railroad arrived in 1881 the town's growth exploded. The city fell on hard times at the end of the decade as one disaster followed

another—drought destroyed the range, severe winters deci-
mated already weakened cattle, and Amarillo quickly grew as
a central cattle shipping point. The discovery of oil in the
1920s brought another boom, but the city never fully regained
its former glory.

By the way, locals pronounce the name of the city "Call-oh-
RAY-duh."

Location: The park is located eleven miles southwest of
Colorado City, off Interstate Highway 20. Open 8 A.M. to
10 P.M. daily.

Amenities: Boating, boat ramp, cabins, camping, dump station, fishing, hiking, lighted fishing pier, park store, picnicking, restrooms, showers, swimming, water skiing.

Contact: Lake Colorado City State Park, 4582 Farm Road
2836, Colorado City, TX 79512, 325-728-3931,
www.tpwd.state.tx.us.

Palo Duro Canyon Park

Palo Duro Canyon has one of the most dramatic landscapes
in all of Texas, including the imposing Lighthouse rock formation that visitors have to work hard to get to. The view looking down from the canyon rim isn't bad, either. In fact, if you
can look out over these terra cotta badlands of the second
largest canyon in America and not want to explore them, you
have no sense of adventure.

The park has about 40 miles of trails, including the 5.75-
mile roundtrip Lighthouse Trail that leads to a 75-foot high
sandstone pinnacle that is worth every drop of sweat to get

there. But the park also has 16 miles of scenic drives, enabling visitors to see much of the park without leaving air conditioning.

The canyon's diverse ecosystems mean a wide variety of plant and animal life can be found here, including the rare Texas horned lizard, rabbits, roadrunners, sheep, wild turkey, and diamondback rattlesnakes. A portion of the official Texas State Longhorn herd makes the canyon rim its home.

Palo Duro Canyon is about 120 miles long, 20 miles wide, and 800 feet deep. It was formed primarily by water erosion. The layers of rock exposed by the erosion—bright orange, red, brown, yellow, gray, maroon, and white—date back 250 million years.

One of the unique features of the park is the Pioneer Amphitheater where *Texas*, the official play of Texas has been performed from June through August each summer for more than forty years. The play depicts the history of the Texas Panhandle, concluding with a rousing display of the state flag carried on horseback with dramatic backlighting and a fireworks display. Visitors may even enjoy a Texas barbecue on the amphitheater's covered patio before the play.

The state acquired most of the park's 29,000 acres in 1933; 2,900 acres were added in 2008. From 1933 to 1937, the Civilian Conservation Corps sent six companies of men to the canyon to develop road access to the canyon floor and build cabins, shelters, park headquarters, and the visitor center. The park opened to the public in 1934.

Humans have lived in the sheltering canyon for at least 12,000 years. Prehistoric peoples hunted large herds of mammoth and giant bison here. Later, Apache, Comanche, and Kiowa frequented the canyon.

In 1874 Palo Duro Canyon gained notoriety as a major battle site during the Red River War when Colonel Ranald Mackenzie burned villages, destroyed tons of dried buffalo meat, and captured more than 1,400 Indian horses there. The Indians—Apache, Arapaho, Comanche, and Kiowa—were unable to escape the Army, surrendered and were sent to reservations in Oklahoma. The loss of life was very small on both sides, but the battle was significant because it ended the southern Plains Indians' resistance to encroaching white society.

From 1876 to 1890, most of the canyon belonged to the J. A. Ranch of famed cattleman Charles Goodnight. At one point, Goodnight ran more than 27,800 head of cattle in the canyon. Goodnight also realized that the buffalo were rapidly disappearing from the plains and established a breeding herd of buffalo. A rugged dugout once used by Goodnight is preserved at the park.

Spanish explorers who found eleven Indian villages there named the canyon in 1541. The phrase "Palo Duro" means "hard wood," referring to the abundant mesquite and juniper trees in the canyon.

Location: The park is located twenty-seven miles southeast of Amarillo, twelve miles east of the city of Canyon on Texas Highway 217. Open 8 A.M. to 10 P.M. March through October, 8 A.M. to 5 P.M. November through February. Busy season is during the summer.

Amenities: Biking, cabins, camping, dump station, guided horseback tours, hiking, horseback riding, museum, park store, picnicking, restrooms, showers.

Contact: Palo Duro Canyon State Park, 11450 Park Road 5, Canyon, TX 79015, 806-488-2227, www.tpwd.state.tx.us.

Possum Kingdom State Park

Frolic in the bluest, clearest water in Texas at Possum

Kingdom State Park in the rugged canyon country of the Brazos River Valley. And unlike most lakes in Texas, Lake Possum Kingdom's surrounding countryside is not flat but instead features the towering rocks of the Palo Pinto Mountains.

The park is adjacent to what some have called "The Great Lake of Texas," a deep reservoir that impounds 20,000 surface acres of water. It was the first reservoir built in the Brazos River basin. The lake is so clear that on a good day a visitor can see down for thirty feet.

In 1994 the rock band The Toadies had a popular song titled "Possum Kingdom," but the song was less about the lake than it was about a fictional killer stalking women on the lake's shoreline.

The Brazos River Authority constructed the lake in 1938 to 1941 by damming the Brazos River for flood control, irrigation, and power generation. The state acquired the 1,530 acres that make up the park in 1940 from the BRA and opened the park to the public in 1950. In the early 1940s, the Civilian Conservation Corps built some of the park's facilities.

For details about the Brazos River, see the entry for Brazos Bend State Park in the Gulf Coast section.

The dam is named for U.S. Senator John Morris Sheppard who fought to get federal funding for the Possum Lake project. Sheppard called the area a "veritable paradise for o'possums."

Sheppard was born in Morris County, Texas, in 1875, and his father John Levi Sheppard served in the U.S. House of Representatives from 1898 to 1902. In 1902, Sheppard was elected to the seat his father had held. He served ten years in the House, then was elected to the U.S. Senate in 1913.

Sheppard fought for passage of the Selective Service Act and for Lend-Lease in the months leading up to the U.S. entry into World War II. Just after passing the Lend-Lease law, he suffered a brain hemorrhage and died on April 9, 1941. General Douglas MacArthur later called Sheppard the first American casualty of World War II.

Ike Sablosky, a trader who came to Texas from Pennsylvania in 1906, first referred to the area as Possum Kingdom. He was a fur buyer and at the time the Palo Pinto Mountains were a haven for opossums that have very soft fur. Ike bought 'possum pelts from cedar choppers and hunters in the Palo Pinto area, labeling the hills a 'possum kingdom. The name became so popular that President Franklin Roosevelt, a good friend of Sheppard's, was fascinated by it and it stuck.

The fur traders trapped out many of the 'possums and they are nocturnal animals so current visitors are unlikely to see many of them today.

The opossum is the only marsupial native to North America—female opossums carry and nurse their young in a pouch.

Nicknamed a "living fossil," 'possums date back to the days of the dinosaur. They can grow as big as a large house cat or be as small as a mouse. The opossum has a white face, a fuzzy gray body, naked ears, and a prehensile tail that can wrap itself around objects. The common image of opossums hanging by their tails is kind of a myth—they do carry bundles of leaves and stems in their tails when building nests, and very young opossums have been observed hanging this way but the bodies of adults are too heavy for their tails to hold them.

When threatened, they will "play possum," giving the appearance and smell of being dead. This is an act they can perform for hours.

The word "opossum" is a corruption of an Algonquian word for the mammal, *wapathemwa*.

Location: The park is located seventeen miles north of Caddo on Park Road 33. Open daily.

Amenities: Boat ramp, boat rentals, cabins, camping, dump station, fishing, hiking, park store, picnicking, restrooms, showers, swimming, water skiing, wheelchair accessible.

Contact: Possum Kingdom State Park, P.O. Box 70, Caddo, TX 76429, 940-549-1803, www.tpwd.state.tx.us.

San Angelo State Park

You can't be bored at San Angelo State Park. Go hiking through the pecan and hackberry and mesquite breaks, pedal your mountain bike, go fishing, ride your horse, hunt for deer and wild turkey, go swimming, discover Indian petroglyphs, or hang out with longhorns or buffalos.

The park has more than fifty miles of developed multi-use trails and twenty miles of backpacking trails. Its location on O. C. Fisher Lake provides great fishing and all sorts of water sports. Archeological findings here indicate the area was occupied at least 18,000 years ago.

San Angelo State Park is located at the junction of four ecological zones—the High Plains to the north, the Hill Country to the south, the Rolling Plains to the east, and the arid Trans-Pecos to the west. Because of this, the park is home to a wide variety of plant and animal life, including 350 species of birds and 50 species of mammals. A portion of the Official State Longhorn Herd and some bison also call San Angelo home.

The U.S. Army Corps of Engineers created the reservoir in 1947 by damming the Concho River. It was named for U.S. Representative Ovie Clark Fisher who served in Congress for thirty-two years. He authored eight books about Texas history. Fisher was born in 1903 in Kimble County and died in Junction in 1994.

When Spaniards Hernán Martín and Diego del Castillo explored the area in 1650, they found large quantities of shells that contained freshwater pearls. The word *concho* means "shell" in Spanish and refers to the plentiful freshwater mussels that can be found in the river. The mussels produce iridescent gems of all sizes and colors, especially large purple ones called Concho Pearls.

The park, opened in 1995, gets its name from the city of San Angelo. The town grew up in the 1860s across the

Concho River from Fort Concho, which had been established in 1867. The frontier town was so rowdy that, reportedly, officers from the fort would not go into the town after dark.

San Angelo was at the junction of several streams and was surrounded by farms and ranches. During the cattle boom of the 1870s, thousands of longhorn cattle were watered and fed along the Concho River on their way to market. When the railroad arrived, the city became a major cattle-shipping point. It was incorporated in 1903. Goodfellow Air Force Base was established in San Angelo in 1940. The airfield was named in honor of San Angelo resident John J. Goodfellow, Jr., who was killed in 1918 while serving with the 24th Aero Squadron in France during World War I.

The town's name actually changed genders: It was first named Santa Angela (female) and became San Angelo (male) by the time it became the county seat. Bartholomew J. DeWitt, the founder of the town, named it for his wife Carolina Angela who died in 1866. By the time the city applied for a post office in 1883, the name had become San Angela in popular usage in the area but that name was rejected because it was ungrammatical—the Spanish word *san* is male and should not be used to modify a female name. So instead of changing the name back to the original Santa Angela, it was altered to San Angelo.

Location: The park is located on Farm Road 2288 in San Angelo. Open daily.

Amenities: Biking, boat ramp, cabins, camping, fishing, hiking, horseback riding, orienteering course, park store, playground, picnicking, restrooms, showers, swimming, tours, water skiing, wheelchair accessible.

Contact: San Angelo State Park, 3900-2 Mercedes, San Angelo, TX 76901, 325-949-8935 or 325-949-4757, www.tpwd.state.tx.us.

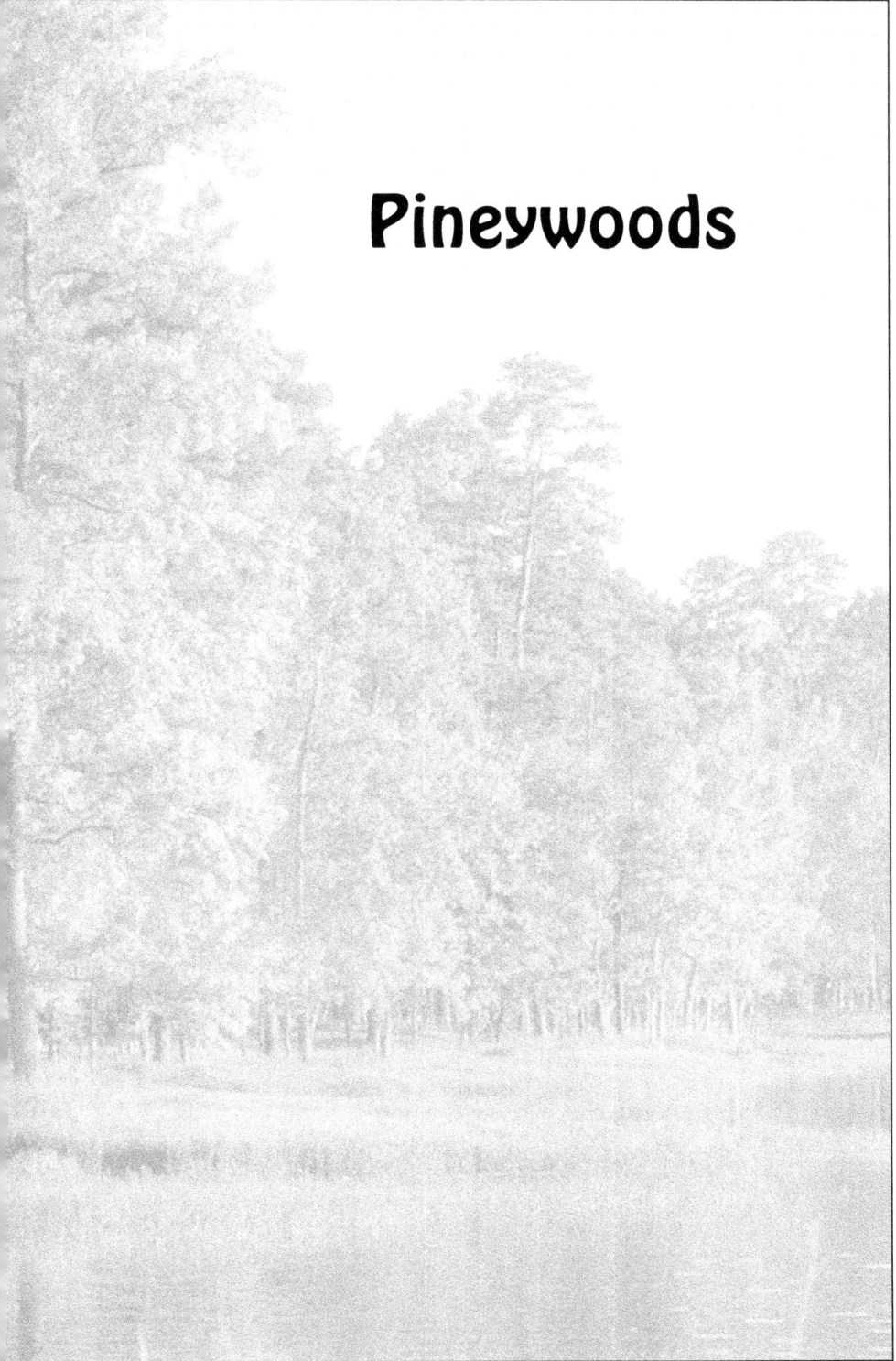

Pineywoods

Atlanta State Park

Located on Wright Patman Lake, the thickly wooded Atlanta State Park offers visitors fine fishing, excellent water sports, peaceful hiking and biking, and brilliant red and deep blue sunsets over the water.

The lake has 170 miles of shoreline and covers 20,300 surface acres. About five miles of hiking and nature trails surround the park.

Caddo Indians—non-nomadic farmers—once made this area their home and many archaeological sites have been discovered here.

The state acquired the park's 1,475 acres in 1954 in a lease from the federal government.

The lake was named in honor of Wright Patman, a longtime congressman from East Texas. The lake is owned by the U.S. government and operated the Army Corps of Engineers.

John William Wright Patman was born in Cass County, Texas, in 1893 and was involved in politics nearly his entire adult life. He served as assistant county attorney, in the Texas House of Representatives, as district attorney of the Fifth Judicial District, and in 1928 won a seat in the U.S. House representing the First Congressional District.

Patman was an outspoken critic of President Herbert Hoover's economic policies and authored the Veterans Bonus Bill that mandated immediate payment of the endowments promised to World War I veterans but never paid.

He served twenty-four terms in Congress and died in 1976.

The park was named for the nearby city of Atlanta, established in 1871 and named for the city of Atlanta, Georgia. Atlanta, Georgia, was incorporated in 1845 and drew its name from the Western and Atlantic Railroad that made the town a transportation hub of the Southeast by 1860.

The word "Atlantic" in the railroad's name refers to the

Atlantic Ocean, the second largest ocean on earth covering 31,800,000 square miles, touching the east coat of the Americas and the west coasts of Europe and Africa. The name means "the sea of Atlas."

In Greek mythology, Atlas was one of the Titans who revolted against Zeus and as his punishment was condemned to hold up the heavens on his shoulders. In works of art, Atlas is usually shown balancing a celestial globe on his back. The location of Atlas' task is often taken to be the Straits of Gibraltar, the gateway of the Mediterranean Sea into the Atlantic Ocean.

Location: The park is located eleven miles southwest of Texarkana off Farm Road 1154. Open daily.

Amenities: Biking, boating, camping, canoe rental, dump station, fishing, hiking, park store, picnicking, playground, restrooms, showers, swimming, water/electric/sewer sites, water skiing.

Contact: Atlanta State Park, 927 Park Road 42, Atlanta, TX 75551, 903-796-6476, www.tpwd.state.tx.us.

Caddo Lake State Park

Caddo Lake is not only one of the most atmospheric places in Texas, one of the most mysterious as you travel through it, but it's unique. It's the only natural lake within the state and remained that way until it was dammed on the Louisiana side for flood control in 1914.

A great flood, according to Caddo Indian stories, is what created the lake in the first place. Legend says that a Caddo chief ignored a warning to move his village to higher ground and the Great Spirit punished him by making the ground shake violently, filling the village site with water. Modern scientists agree, believing the lake was created when an earthquake in 1811 tore down trees and created a massive logjam on the Red River that backed up floodwaters. That logjam was still around in 1874 when the U.S. government finally destroyed what had become known as the Red River Raft.

Visitors to the park today might feel they are in the bayous of Louisiana rather than on a lake in Texas thanks to the abundance of bald cypress trees and hanging Spanish moss that imparts an almost mystical feel in the early morning light.

The lake is, in fact, a sprawling maze of picturesque bayous and sloughs covering 26,810 acres of cypress swamp. It's an angler's delight with more than seventy species of fish in its waters. On the shore, visitors will enjoy those cypress trees along with towering pine trees, American lotus and lily pads, American beautyberries, waterfowl, turtles, snakes, armadillos, white tail deer, raccoons, minks, beavers, and alligators.

Lily pads and cypress trees at Caddo Lake State Park
—Randy Green/Texas Department of Transportation

And where else do you get to paddle through Whangdoodle Pass or wander around Hog Wallow? Or visit the nearby city of Uncertain?

The 484-acre park was opened in 1934. The Civilian Conservation Corps made the park's original improvements between 1933 and 1937. Nine of their pine log cabins and their group recreation hall are in use today.

The lake was named for the Caddo Indians who once lived in the area. The word *Caddo* is a French abbreviation of *kadohadacho*, meaning "real chiefs" in the Caddo dialect. The band was one of 25 distinct but closely affiliated groups in the area. The Caddo groups lived in well-established settlements where they farmed beans, corn, and squash, and hunted bear and buffalo. Their largest cities were located along major streams like the Red, Arkansas, Little, Ouachita, and Sabine rivers.

The Caddo developed long-distance trade routes, using turquoise from New Mexico, copper from the Great Lakes, and marine shells from the Gulf Coast.

By the 1840s, most of the Caddo had moved to the Brazos River basin to get distance between them and the growing Anglo population. They were ultimately removed to a reservation in Indian Territory (present day Oklahoma) in 1859.

By the way, we have the Caddo to thank for the very word "Texas." One of the Caddoan bands, the Hasinai, referred to their confederacy as the *Tayshas*, meaning the "Friends" or the "Allies." Spaniard explorers wrote the word as *Tejas*, then applied it to the area north of the Rio Grande to the Red River.

Location: The park is located fifteen miles northeast of Marshall. Open daily.

Amenities: Boat ramp, boating, cabins, camping, canoe rentals, dump station, fishing, hiking, park store, picnicking, pontoon boat tours, restrooms, screened shelters, showers, swimming, wheelchair accessible.

Contact: Caddo Lake State Park, 245 Park Road 2, Karnack, TX 75661, 903-679-3351, www.tpwd.state.tx.us.

Caddoan Mounds State Historic Site

Walk to ancient mounds and imagine life here more than a thousand years ago. Learn about archaeological excavations and visit a museum full of information about a lost culture at Caddoan Mounds State Historic Site.

Caddoan Mounds was the home of mound building Caddo Indians who lived in the area for 500 years beginning about the year 800. The site has the remains of three large mounds. The largest is believed to be the oldest and about forty grass and cane-covered houses were built around it. A second mound near the center of the park is a rectangular platform and the third was used as a ceremonial burial mound.

Workers carried baskets loaded with soil on their backs to build the mounds, a slow and arduous process.

Researchers believe the mounds, especially the rectangular one, were aligned astronomically but have yet to figure out which celestial objects the Caddo used at the time. For details on the Caddo Indians, see the entry for Caddo Lake State Park above.

Replica hut at Caddoan Mounds State Historic Site
—O.C. Garza/Texas Department of Transportation

The 94-acre site was opened to the public in 1982. Caddoan Mounds was transferred to the Texas Historic Commission in 2008.

Location: The park is located about thirty-six miles west of Nacogdoches. Open Tuesday through Sunday, 8:30 A.M. to 4:30 P.M.

Amenities: Hiking, interpretive center, park store, restrooms.

Contact: Caddoan Mounds State Historic Site, 1649 Texas Highway 21W, Alto, TX 75925, 936-858-3218, www.thc.state.tx.us.

Daingerfield State Park

Slip away to a peaceful lake beneath the loblolly pines at Daingerfield State Park. Although the pine trees are the most notable trees in the Pineywoods of East Texas, the area contains a greater variety of trees than New England. A visitor will see most of them right here.

Daingerfield is also one of the few places in Texas that blazes with autumn colors. In the fall—if the weather has cooperated—maple, oak, and sweetgum trees produce dazzling shades of red and gold to contrast with the evergreen pines.

The park doesn't leave the fine foliage to the fall, either. In the spring, dogwoods, redbuds, and wisteria vines burst into bloom. In the open areas, bluebonnets, clover, and Indian paintbrushes add their own touches of color.

And in the summertime, that cool lake water is mighty inviting.

The state acquired the 507-acre park and its 80-acre lake

in 1935. The Civilian Conservation Corps built the original facilities (including newly renovated cabins), and the park was opened to the public in 1938.

The park is named for the nearby city of Daingerfield. In 1830, Captain London Daingerfield, a native of Nova Scotia, and a band of about one hundred men fought a bloody battle with Indians over the use of a spring here. Daingerfield was killed and when a town grew up near the spring in the 1840s, it was named in his honor.

Location: The park is located two miles east of Daingerfield off Texas Highway 49. Open daily.

Amenities: Boat rentals, boating, cabins, canoe and pedal boat rentals (March through October), dump station, fishing, group lodge, hiking, park store, picnicking, playground, restrooms, showers, swimming, tours.

Contact: Daingerfield State Park, 455 Park Road 17, Daingerfield, TX 75638, 903-645-2921, www.tpwd. state.tx.us.

Huntsville State Park

Have all sorts of fun at Huntsville State Park, the last outpost of the immense forest that covers much of the Eastern U.S.

The heavily wooded 2,084 acres of the park is in the midst of Sam Houston National Forest with loblolly and shortleaf pine trees typical of the East Texas Pineywoods. The park's hiking trails were built so wildlife and birds could be observed in a natural setting. Among the animals are deer and the occasional alligator. Among the birds are great blue herons, king-fishers, great egrets, and eight different types of woodpeck-ers—just a few of the 200 species found here. Camping and picnic areas surround Lake Raven, a 210-acre recreational reservoir, and the trees grow right to the water's edge.

The state acquired the property in 1937 and opened it to the public in 1938. A heavy flood damaged the area in 1940 and the park was idle for almost ten years afterwards. Finally, in 1956, the park was formally dedicated after many years of refining the property by harvesting trees, clearing brush, paving roads, and stocking the lake. The Civilian Conservation Corps built the park, including the dam creating Lake Raven; prisoners from Huntsville State Prison did much of the later work.

If you have any doubt about who the most important fig-ure in this neck of the woods is, you'll know for certain when you see the gleaming white statue of Sam Houston towering seventy feet over Interstate 45 on your way to the park.

Camping at Lake Raven in Huntsville State Park
—J. Griffis Smith/Texas Department of Transportation

Houston made his home in the city and he is buried there. Sam Houston University is located there. The national forest Huntsville State Park is in was named for Houston, and the name of the lake is taken from one of Houston's Cherokee names: The Raven.

Samuel Houston was born in 1793 in Virginia and moved to Tennessee in 1807 with his family. He ran away from home in 1809 and lived with a Cherokee Indian band until he turned eighteen. He joined the Army during the War of 1812 and fought with Andrew Jackson, receiving three nearly fatal wounds in the Battle of Horseshoe Bend. He and Jackson formed a life-long friendship.

He practiced law in Tennessee and was elected to the U.S. Congress in 1823 and in 1827 was elected governor of that state. In 1829 Houston married nineteen-year-old Eliza Allen but the marriage ended after only eleven weeks under mysterious circumstances. Neither side ever explained the reasons for the abrupt break-up. Houston immediately resigned his governorship and left for the Indian Territory to live again with the Cherokees who gave him a new nickname: Big Drunk. He later married Diana Rogers Gentry, an Indian woman of mixed blood, and they established a trading post near Fort Gibson.

In 1832 Houston left Indian Territory and his wife and crossed into Mexican Texas. He quickly got involved in the move for Texas independence and in 1835 he became the general in command of the Texas Army. On April 21, 1836, Houston's forces engaged Mexican dictator Antonio López de Santa Anna in the Battle of San Jacinto. Santa Anna was captured and Texas independence was secured.

Houston then became the first president of the Republic of Texas. In 1840 he married twenty-one-year-old Margaret Moffette Lea who was able to restrain his heavy drinking. They had eight children. When Texas joined the Union, Houston was elected to the U.S. Senate. He was elected governor of the state in 1859. When Texas seceded from the Union in 1860 despite protests from Houston, a strong

Unionist, he refused to take an oath of loyalty to the Confederacy and he was removed from office.

In 1862 Houston moved his family to Huntsville. He died there in 1863.

Huntsville is one of Texas' oldest cities, founded in 1836 as a trading post with the Alabama and Coushatta Indians. Today, the Alabama-Coushatta Reservation is in nearby Woodville. Huntsville, Texas, was named for the city of Huntsville, Alabama, the home of one of the town's founding families.

Huntsville, Alabama, was founded in 1810. It was named for John Hunt, a Revolutionary War veteran who first settled the area in 1805. Hunt was born in Virginia in 1750 and moved with his family to North Carolina in 1770. When the war began, Hunt enlisted and served as a private in Captain Charles Polk's Company of Light Horse from that state.

In 1779, Hunt was appointed a lieutenant in the state militia and served as a paymaster. In 1786, he was appointed the first sheriff of Hawkins County. He also served as a delegate from North Carolina to the Constitutional Convention in 1789. In the 1790s, he moved into Tennessee and founded the town of Tazewell, but he and other settlers were evicted in 1797. They took their claims to court and won, and in 1801 Hunt was named sheriff of the town where one of his duties was to whip creditors until they promised to go to work to pay their debts.

In 1804 Hunt began selling off his properties, went south, and settled around a big spring in Alabama, founding the community first called Hunt's Station and eventually Huntsville. He died in 1822 and was buried in an unmarked grave in Sively Cemetery, adjacent to the city dump.

Location: The park is located on Park Road 40 six miles southwest of Huntsville, off Interstate 45. Open daily.

Amenities: Biking, boating, camping, dump station, fishing, guided horseback tours, hiking, hydrobike rentals, park store, playground, picnicking, restrooms, screened shelters, showers, swimming, wheelchair accessible.

Contact: Huntsville State Park, P.O. Box 508, Huntsville, TX 77342-0508, 936-295-5644, www.tpwd.state.tx.us.

Lake Bob Sandlin State Park

Lake Bob Sandlin fits right in with other Pineywoods parks, offering a variety of outdoor recreation in a heavily wooded area around a popular lake. Its proximity to Interstate 30 makes it a popular destination for folks from the Dallas and Fort Worth areas seeking refuge from their urban Metroplex.

Foliage on the hickory, maple, and sweetgum trees turns to red and gold in the fall and the 9,400-acre lake has some of the best fishing in east Texas. A variety of birds and wildlife can be spotted here year round. Eagles may be seen during the winter.

Some archaeological evidence of Caddo Indians has been discovered in the park. Fort Sherman was established here in 1838 but no trace of the stockaded fort remain. The Fort Sherman cemetery is located within the park boundaries, however.

The state acquired the 640-acre property in 1979 and opened it to the public in 1987.

The park is named for the lake that was created when the dam was completed in 1978 by the Texas Utilities Electric Company that needed water to cool its lignite-fired power plant. The lake is named for Bob Murphy Sandlin, a prominent local civic leader who headed the drive for a fresh water supply for the region.

Sandlin was born in Louisiana in 1902 and eventually settled in Mount Pleasant, Texas, in 1937. He became a partner in a local auto dealership and eventually became its sole owner. He was involved in community affairs by serving on the city council, as president of the Chamber of Commerce, as a board member of several local financial institutions. Sandlin was also instrumental in the formation of both a poultry company and a steel company.

Unlike most reservoirs in the state that have some Army Corps of Engineers or state government involvement, Sandlin figured out a way for the lake to be created with private funds, getting commitments from TXU and the city of Mount Pleasant, then selling bonds on Wall Street.

Bob Sandlin died in 1988 but the Sandlin Chevrolet dealership continues to be run by his family.

Location: The park is located twelve miles southwest of Mount Pleasant off Farm Road 21. Open daily.

Amenities: Biking, boat ramp, boating, camping, fishing, hiking, park store, picnicking, playground, restrooms, screened shelters, showers, swimming, tours, wheelchair accessible.

Contact: Lake Bob Sandlin State Park, 341 Park Road 2117, Pittsburg, TX 75686, 903-572-5531, www.tpwd.state. tx.us.

Lake Livingston State Park

Lake Livingston State Park is a nice place to relax or take advantage of the recreational opportunities of its forest or lake. It's a popular respite for nature lovers from the sprawling Houston urban area.

Swamp rabbits and white tail deer are common sights in the park's distinct ecosystems of pine woodlands, hardwood bottomlands, and tallgrass blackland prairie. It's easy to hear and see woodpeckers and other forest birds in the park, including bobwhites and mourning doves, herons and egrets, eagles and ospreys, gnatcatchers and cuckoos, and a coot or two.

The 635-acre park is located on east shore of Lake Livingston, a project of the Trinity River Authority to supply water to the city of Houston. The lake is an 83,000-acre reservoir and, at thirty-nine miles long, it's the second largest lake within the borders of Texas. The state acquired the property in 1971 and opened it to the public in 1977.

The lake was named for the nearby town of Livingston that was established by Moses L. Choate in 1838. He named it for his hometown of Livingston, Tennessee. That town was established in 1833 and is named after Edward Livingston.

Edward Livingston was born in 1764 in Clermont, New York, and graduated from Princeton University. He practiced law in New York City in the late 1700s. From 1795 to 1801 he served in the U.S. House of Representatives from New York. He was elected mayor of New York City in 1801 while at the same time serving as U.S. attorney for that district. He resigned both offices in 1803 and moved to Louisiana the next year. He served in the state legislature, wrote the state's legal code, and used his influence to secure amnesty for pirate Jean Lafitte in return for his help in defense of New Orleans against attacking British forces during the War of 1812, and became a close friend of General Andrew Jackson.

Livingston then returned to the U.S. Congress, this time from Louisiana, serving in the House from 1823 to 1829 and in the Senate from 1829 to 1831.

He also served as U.S. Secretary of State under President Jackson from 1831 to 1833, and as ambassador to France from 1833 to 1835.

Livingston died in 1836 in New York. Among the other

places named for him are Livingston County, Illinois; Livingston Parish, Louisiana; Livingston County, Michigan; Livingston County, Missouri; and the city of Livingston, Guatemala.

Location: The park is located about six miles south of Livingston, seventy-five miles north of Houston, on U.S. Highway 59. Open daily.

Amenities: Activity center, Biking, boat ramp, boating, camping, fishing, hiking, horseback riding, park store, picnicking, playground, restrooms, screened shelters, showers, swimming, swimming pool, water/electric/sewer sites, water skiing.

Contact: Lake Livingston State Park, 300 Park Road 65, Livingston, TX 77351, 936-365-2201, www.tpwd.state. tx.us.

Martin Creek Lake State Park

Camp out on a small island in the middle of a lake at Martin Creek Lake State Park. Visitors not into such a primitive experience can still enjoy nature at one of the park's cabins, or on a boat pulling in more bass and catfish than you might imagine.

Fishing is excellent all year thanks to the lake water warmed by the nearby power plant.

People have been living here at least since 200 B.C. Caddo Indians lived here, as did Choctaw, Cherokee and Kickapoo Indians in later years; then came the Spanish explorers and, later, Anglo settlers. Visitors can still see the old roadbed of

Trammel's Trace, an Indian trail that became a major route for settlers moving to Texas from Arkansas.

In 1976, Texas Utilities donated the 287 acres on 5,000-acre Martin Creek Lake to the state, and the park opened to the public the same year. The lake was built to provide cooling water for a lignite-fired electric power plant.

The park is named for Martin Creek that was named for pioneer Daniel Martin. In 1833 he settled near the creek and he and neighbors built a small fort, then a town called Harmony Hill. The town's post office closed in 1905 after the city's decline in the wake of being bypassed by the railroad. A tornado destroyed much of what was left in 1906. Traces of the old roads can be seen in the park and are part of the hiking trails.

Harmony Hill was originally named Nip 'n' Tuck after an incident in which two hounds chased a fox down the main street. But that name gave way to its official name in 1856 because of the harmonious community relations of the early settlers.

Daniel Martin was born in 1781 in South Carolina. He fought in the Creek War of 1813 to 1814 alongside David Crockett. Martin, wife Eleanor, and their eight children came to Texas from Missouri in 1832, traveling over Trammel's Trace.

The family found an abandoned log cabin near the creek that now bears his name and moved in, becoming the first Anglo settlers in the area. Martin made a living by hunting, trapping and trading with local Indians. He died in 1851. The Martin family's homestead now lies under the lake.

Location: The park is located twenty miles southeast of Longview. Open daily.

Amenities: Boat ramp, boating, cabins, camping, dump station, fishing, hiking, park store, picnicking, restrooms, screened shelters, showers, swimming, water skiing, wheelchair accessible.

Contact: Martin Creek Lake State Park, 9515 County Road 2181D, Tatum, TX 75691-3425, 903-836-4336, www. tpwd.state.tx.us.

Martin Dies, Jr., State Park

Martin Dies, Jr., State Park is on the shore of a 16,000-acre reservoir, in the northern corner of the Big Thicket providing visitors with a wide diversity of recreational possibilities.

Nature and hiking trails meander through the bottomland forest, giving visitors a great chance to observe wildlife like bluebirds or deer, roadrunners or alligators. Sloughs around the lake invite canoeists to dip a paddle in their peaceful waters. And like many Pineywoods' parks, Martin Dies, Jr., is known for its fall foliage.

Fishermen at Martin Dies Jr. State Park
—Richard Reynolds/Texas Department of Transportation

The 705-acre park was acquired by the state in 1964 under a lease from the Army Corps of Engineers. It opened to the public in 1965.

The park is named for one of the driving forces behind getting the federal government to lease the land around the land for a park, Martin Dies, Jr. He was worried that the land was going to be purchased by a timber company and that they were going to start clearcutting an area he often rode horses through when he was younger.

Martin Dies, Jr.
—Texas State Archives

Originally, the park carried the prosaic name of Dam B State Park but Dies' colleagues in the state senate surprised him by passing a resolution in 1965 asking the Texas Parks and Wildlife Department to change the name to honor Dies.

"It was a rather embarrassing, but a very nice gesture on their part," he told the United Press, "but I doubt the Parks and Wildlife Department will pay any attention to the resolution."

They did.

Dies was born in 1921 in Hunt County, Texas, the eldest son of a U.S. Congressman. He joined the Navy and saw service in the South Pacific during World War II and saw combat in the Philippines, Okinawa, and the Battle of Leyte. Near the end of the war, he served as captain of the USS *Richard W. Seusens*.

Following the war, Dies graduated from Stephen F. Austin University and Southern Methodist University Law School. He joined the Lufkin law practice of his father, a former U.S. Congressman. In 1957, he was elected to the state senate and served there until 1967. He was known as "the gentle giant of the Texas Senate."

Dies also served as Texas secretary of state (1969-1971) and as chief justice of the 9th U.S. Circuit Court of Appeals (1971-1989). He died in Beaumont in 2001.

Location: The park is located seventeen miles east of Woodville. Open daily.

Amenities: Biking, boat ramp, boating, cabins, camping, canoeing, fishing, hiking, park store, picnicking, playground, restrooms, screened shelters, showers, swimming, wheelchair accessible.

Contact: Martin Dies, Jr. State Park, 634 Private Road 5025, Jasper, TX, 75951, 409-384-5231, www.tpwd.state.tx.us.

Mission Tejas State Park

Mission Tejas represents the first Spanish mission in East Texas, prompting contact with the Hasinai Indians, one of the bands in the Caddo confederacy. That contact eventually gave us the name of Texas.

The Hasinai, referred to their confederacy as the *Tayshas*, meaning the "Friends" or the "Allies." Spanish explorers wrote the word as *Tejas* and, believing it referred to a place rather than a group, eventually applied the word to the area north of the Rio Grande to the Red River.

The park is more than history. Hiking and nature trails wind through the Pineywoods. The trails are especially beautiful in late March when the dogwood trees bloom.

The Civilian Conservation Corps built the park in 1934 to commemorate the mission. Their structure is not a true replica of the mission, however. The parks department acquired the 364-acre property in 1957 from the Texas Forest Service.

Mission Tejas was established in 1689 at Nabadache, a Hasinai village near the Neches River. Spanish explorer Alonso De León gave the river its name in the 1680s for the Neches Indians, one of the Caddoan tribes he encountered there. That name is taken from the Caddo word *nachawi*, meaning the bois d'arc tree that grows along the river banks. Wood from the bois d'arc tree makes excellent bows. (*Bois d'arc* means "wood of the bow" in French.)

The mission was abandoned in 1693 after a drought and a smallpox epidemic, then reopened in 1716. But the missionaries were never able to convert many of the Hasinai. The isolation and lack of protection for the remote outpost made it difficult for missionaries to fulfill their work and was frustrating for soldiers whose job was to project Spanish power to the edge of French Louisiana. The mission was eventually moved in 1721, and again in 1731. The last move was to a site along the San Antonio River and became Mission San Francisco de Espada, now a part of the San Antonio Missions National Park in the city of San Antonio. (*Espada* means "sword" in Spanish.)

One of the oldest structures in the area, the Rice Family Log Home—built in 1828 and restored in 1974—is also in the park. The home served as a stopover for adventurers, immigrants, and local residents traveling the Old San Antonio Road.

Joseph R. Rice, Sr., was born in 1805 in Tennessee. Rice married Willie Masters, the daughter of one of the first Anglo settlers who brought his family to the area in 1828. Rice built a log home in the farming community known as Germany and the home became known as the Rice Stagecoach Inn.

Rice died in 1866; Willie Rice lived in the log home until her death in 1886.

Over the years, the Rice family made many modifications to the home, moving it short distances twice. In 1963 it was being used as the family garage. After Nancy Rice donated the log home to the state in 1973, Texas Parks and Wildlife moved the structure to Mission Tejas State Park and restored it in 1974.

Freedmen gave the community the name of "Germany," referring to a pioneer German family named Grounds or Groundt that lived in the area. The Grounds Cemetery is still in the community.

Location: The park is located twenty-two miles northeast of Crockett, off Texas Highway 21. Open daily; office hours 8 A.M. to 5 P.M.

Amenities: Camping, dump station, fishing, hiking, museum, picnicking, playground, restrooms, showers, tours.

Contact: Mission Tejas State Park, 120 Park Road 44, Grapeland, TX 75844, 936-687-2394, www.tpwd.state.tx.us.

Starr Family State Historic Site

Tour a historic East Texas plantation at the Starr Family Home State Historic Site where visitors may also get a taste of Victorian luxury at the spacious Rosemont Cottage Bed and Breakfast.

The site preserves the 150-year history of the stately home, known to the family as Maplecroft. Maplecroft is typical of many large homes built in Texas after the Civil War, reflecting a shift away from the Greek Revival style to Victorian design. It was built in 1870 to 1871.

The name of the mansion comes from the maple trees found in the area combined with the Old English word "croft" that means a field.

James Harper Starr and his wife Harriet moved to Marshall from Nacogdoches in 1870. At that time, Marshall was the third largest city in the state.

Starr was born in 1809 in New Hartford, Connecticut, and his family moved to Ohio in 1815. While he was teaching school near Columbus, Starr taught himself medicine and in 1830 became a member of the first class of the Reformed Medical Society of the United States of America. He moved to Georgia in 1832 to practice medicine.

Starr and his wife Harriett moved to Nacogdoches, Texas, in 1837 with several other Georgians. Under President Sam Houston, Starr became president of the Texas Land Commission that year. In 1839, he was appointed the treasurer of the Republic of Texas under President Mirabeau B. Lamar.

After a year as treasurer, Starr became a land agent. In 1868, he formed James H. Starr and Son, a land and banking agency in Marshall, one of the first banks in Texas. He moved his family there in 1870. He died in 1890. Starr County, Texas, is named for him.

Rosemont was part of the estate Starr bought in 1870 and served as the family's first home while his son, James Franklin Starr, built Maplecroft. The three-room cottage is located in the northeast corner of the site and is within walking distance of downtown Marshall. The three-acre site at the cottage offers privacy to guests. The walls are papered with roses.

The home is listed in the National Register of Historic Places. The three-acre site was given to the state in 1976. The Starr family continued to occupy the estate until it became a state park in 1985. It was opened to the public in 1986. The Starr Family State Historic Site was transferred to the Texas Historical Commission in 2008.

Marshall is named for U.S. Chief Justice John Marshall. Marshall was born in 1755 in Germantown, Virginia. He served in the Virginia House of Delegates and in 1796 was one of three diplomats sent to France. He was elected to the U.S. House of Representatives in 1799 then appointed secretary of state by President John Adams in 1800. In 1801, Adams named Marshall chief justice of the Supreme Court. During his tenure, he helped establish the Supreme Court as the final authority on the U.S. Constitution. Marshall served as chief justice until his death in 1835.

Location: The site is located at the corner of Travis and South Grove streets in Marshall. Open Tuesday through Sunday 10 A.M. to 4 P.M.

Amenities: Bed and breakfast inn, guided tours.

Contact: Starr Family State Historic Site, 407 West Travis Street, Marshall, TX 75670, 903-935-3044, www.thc. state.tx.us.

Texas State Railroad

Ride through the scenic Pineywoods and hardwood creek bottoms on a steam train that's been rolling since the 1890s at the Texas State Railroad.

The experience of returning to an earlier era of travel is given in a 4½-hour, 50-mile roundtrip between the cities of Palestine and Rusk. The depots at each city are examples of Victorian charm, surrounded by parks with lakes and streams and campgrounds, picnic areas, and various concessions.

Inmates from the Texas state prison system began building the Texas State Railroad in 1881, using the line to transport hardwood that was used as fuel for furnaces at the Rusk Penitentiary. The smelter at the prison supplied the state with iron products that were used in building the capitol in Austin.

In 1913, the prison stopped using the rail line and in 1921 regular rail service was discontinued and the line was leased to the Texas & New Orleans Railroad. Texas Southeastern Railroad leased the line in the early 1960s and operated it until 1969.

In 1972, the state turned the railroad over to the Parks and Wildlife Department and prison inmates were again brought in to help with the creation of the parks. The official Texas State Railroad and Palestine and Rusk state parks were opened in 1976 as part of the Bicentennial Celebration.

The Texas State Railroad and both Palestine and Rusk state parks were transferred to American Heritage Railways in 2007.

The city of Palestine was founded in 1846 and named for Palestine, Illinois, the hometown of Daniel Parker who was a local pastor. For more details on Daniel Parker, see the entry for Fort Parker State Park in the Prairies and Lakes section.

Palestine, Illinois, was named for the biblical Palestine. Palestine refers to the area between the Jordan River and the Mediterranean Sea, including all or part of modern Jordan, Israel, Lebanon, and Syria.

Palestine's location at the center of trade routes linking three continents made it a place where religious and cultural influences from Africa, Asia, and Europe

Steam locomotive at Texas State Railroad
—James Wright Steely/
Texas Department of Transportation

melded. It also became a natural battleground for groups wanting to dominate that important area. It continues to be a focal point of diverse cultures, three major religions, and strife.

The city of Rusk was founded in 1846 and was named for Thomas Jefferson Rusk of Nacogdoches. Rusk was born in South Carolina in 1803 and began a law practice in Georgia in 1825. He made large investments in gold mines. One day he discovered that managers of the company embezzled all the funds and, as so many criminals did at that time, were gone to Texas. Rusk pursued them to Nacogdoches but never recovered the money.

Rusk was enamored of Texas and decided to stay. He served as a major general in the Texas militia, signed the Texas Declaration of Independence, served as chief justice of the Republic of Texas Supreme Court, and was elected to the U.S. Senate when Texas became a state, serving alongside Sam Houston.

Rusk was serving as president pro tem of the Senate when his wife Polly died from tuberculosis. Despondent over her death and ill from a tumor in his neck, Rusk committed suicide in 1857. Rusk County is also named in his honor.

Location: The railroad and its depots are located six miles east of Palestine and three miles west Rusk, both on U.S. Highway 84. Trips leave either depot at 11 A.M. and return at 3:30 P.M. with a ninety minute lunch layover at each depot.

Amenities: Concessions and restrooms on each train. Camping, gift shops, restrooms, showers at each park.

Contact: Texas State Railroad, P.O. Box 166, Rusk, TX 75785, 903-683-2561, www.texasstaterr.com

Tyler State Park

Pedal a mountain bike, paddle a canoe, camp out, hike through the woods, fish for bass or catfish or perch, enjoy the beautiful wood and stonework buildings, spy wildlife like bobcats and coyotes, or enjoy the blooms of dogwood and redbud trees at Tyler State Park.

The 985-acre park includes a 64-acre lake and more than a dozen trails through the dense forest that grows right up to the water's edge.

The state acquired the property in 1934 and 1935. The Civilian Conservation Corps made the park's original improvements. The park opened in 1939.

The park is named for the adjacent city of Tyler, established in 1846. In the 1920s, the city's rose industry developed into a major business and by the 1940s more than half the U.S. supply of rose bushes was grown within ten miles of Tyler. The annual Rose Festival attracts more than 100,000 visitors each year. The city was named for John Tyler, the 10th president of the United States honoring his support for admitting Texas to the Union.

John Tyler was born in 1790 in Charles County, Virginia. He studied law and became politically active when quite young, serving in the Virginia legislature (1811-1816), in the U.S. House (1817-1821), as governor of Virginia (1825-1827), and in the U.S. Senate (1827-1836).

Whig presidential nominee Harrison had been a war hero at the battle of Tippecanoe and when Tyler was chosen as the

John Tyler

vice presidential nominee, the campaign slogan became "Tippecanoe and Tyler, too!"

Tyler was the first vice president to rise to the top office in the nation on the death of the president. President William Henry Harrison served a mere thirty days in office, becoming ill at his inauguration in 1841. Fiercely independent, Tyler refused to bow to either the Whig or Democrat parties and lost his bid for re-election to James K. Polk.

During his tenure, Tyler oversaw a reorganization of the U.S. Navy, fostered scientific discovery and documentation, and brought the Second Seminole War to an end.

Tyler strongly supported Southern rights but was firmly opposed to secession. In 1861, he presided over the Washington Peace Conference, a failed try to bring a compromise solution to the problems between North and South. When that attempt failed, he served in the Confederate House of Representatives. Tyler died in 1862.

Location: The park is located two miles north of Tyler off Farm Road 14. Open daily. The park fills up quickly in October during the city of Tyler's Rose Festival.

Amenities: Biking, bicycle and boat rentals, boating, camping, dining hall, dump station, hiking, fishing, park store, picnicking, playground, restrooms, screened shelters, showers, swimming.

Contact: Tyler State Park, 789 Park Road 16, Tyler, TX 75706-9141, 903-597-5338, www.tpwd.state.tx.us.

Village Creek State Park

Village Creek is one of the most popular flat-water streams

for canoeing in all of Texas, traveling through the heart and soul of the Big Thicket.

The park provides an overnight facility for those paddling through, or visitors just in the mood for carnivorous plants, colorful birds, wild animals, beautiful flowers, snakes, and swamps. The park has so few roads that the only way to really experience it is to canoe or hike through it. In the summertime, the thrum of cicadas is so loud it's almost overwhelming. And if you're camping, you will almost always fall asleep to the knock-knock-knock-knock of several woodpeckers—maybe even the growling rumble of an alligator.

The state acquired the 1,090-acre property in 1979 and the park opened in 1994.

The Big Thicket is so named because it is a pine and hardwood forest wilderness so impenetrably dense, over such a large area, that early pioneers usually avoided it, rarely trying to settle here. Today, much of the area is a part of the Big Thicket National Preserve.

The park's name comes from Village Creek, a free flowing stream that rises near the Alabama-Coushatta Indian Reservation near Woodville and meanders southeasterly for 69 miles to its junction with the Neches River. The creek takes its name from the nearby town of Village Mills. Village Mills was first called, originally enough, just Village in the 1880s. By 1883, the Village Mill Company operated here, shipping lumber sawed at its mills out of the region. The mill closed in the 1930s.

Location: The park is located ten miles north of Beaumont. Open daily.

Amenities: Biking, cabins, camping, canoeing, dump station, fishing, hiking, park store, picnicking, playground, restrooms, showers, swimming, tours wheelchair accessible.

Contact: Village Creek State Park, P.O. Box 8565, Lumberton, TX 77657, 409-755-7322, www.tpwd.state.tx.us.

Prairies and Lakes

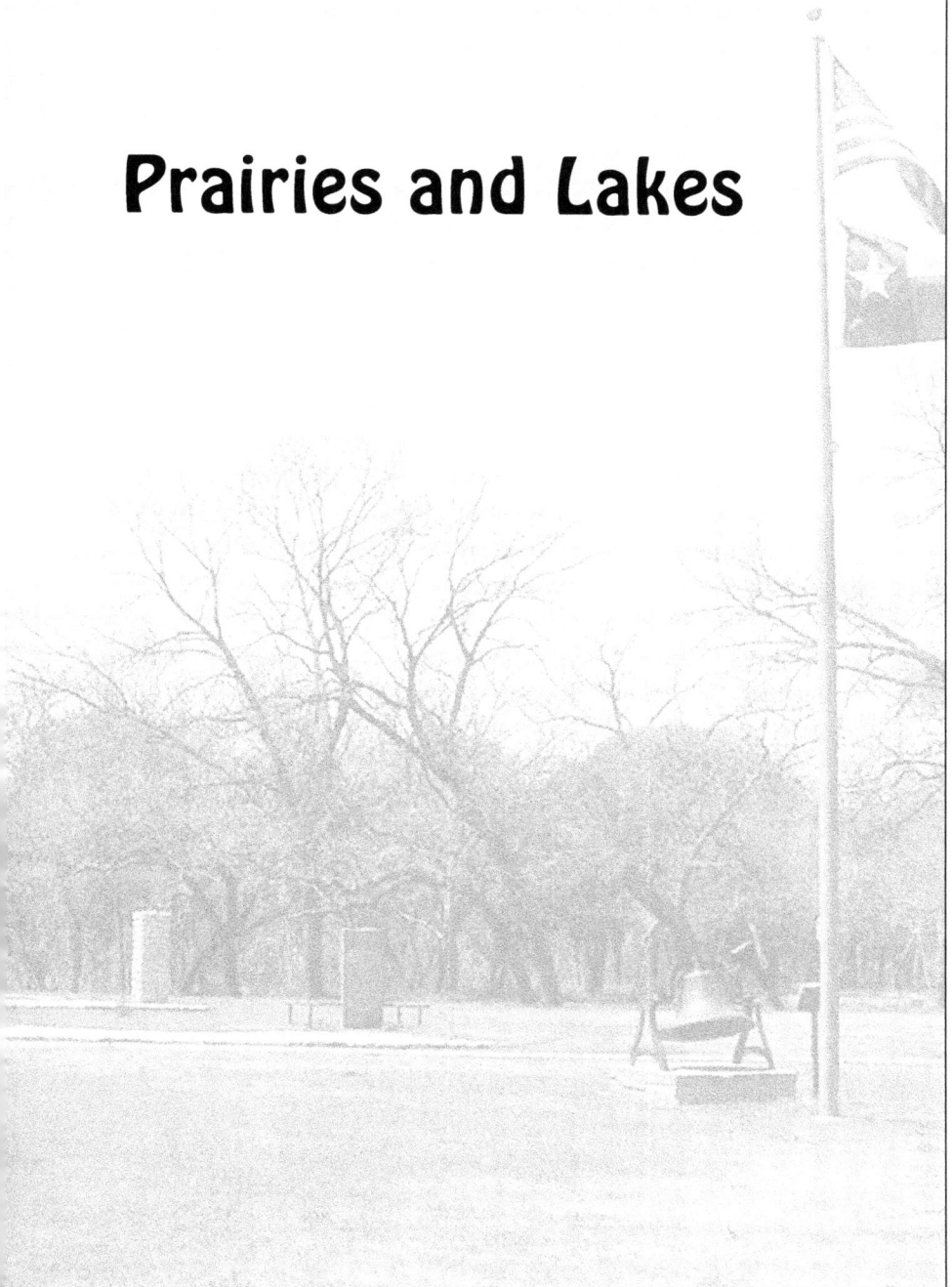

Acton State Historic Site

Acton is the smallest historic site in the state. It's twelve feet wide and twenty-one feet long and visitors won't find much to do there. Why? Because the entire site is a grave.

Elizabeth Crockett, Texas hero David Crockett's second wife, is buried here. Because David Crockett (1786-1836) died at the Alamo, his heirs were eligible for a land grant after Texas won its independence, but Elizabeth Crockett didn't claim her grant until 1853 when most choice land was already claimed. Then she had to give a surveyor half of the land she did get for locating a tract for her, leaving her family with 320 acres.

The monument honoring her at the site was erected in 1911. Atop the monument is a statue of Elizabeth, shading her eyes and gazing at the horizon as if looking for her husband, a rather appropriate gesture since during the twenty-one years of their marriage he was seldom home. One of David's most famous quotes—"You may all go to Hell, and I will go to Texas"—was directed at Tennessee voters after he lost re-election to Congress and not, as far as we know, towards Elizabeth.

Elizabeth Patton was born in Buncomb County, North Carolina, in 1788, and married David Crockett in Lawrence, Tennessee, in 1815. It was the second marriage for both of them. David's first wife, Polly, died leaving him two sons and a daughter, and Elizabeth's first husband, James Patton (her first cousin), was killed while serving in the Creek War, leaving her with a son and a daughter. James Patton died while serving alongside David at the Battle of Horseshoe Bend. As James lay dying, he asked David to deliver his personal effects to Elizabeth. After Polly Crockett died, David spent a great deal of time wooing Elizabeth and succeeded.

Elizabeth Crockett died in Acton in 1860.

The cemetery is located in the town of Acton. The town's

first merchant, C. P. Hollis, came up with the name in honor of a former sweetheart, a Miss Acton.

The park was transferred to the Texas Historical Commission in 2008.

Location: The park is located about seven miles southeast of Granbury on Farm Road 167. Open daily.

Amenities: Historic site.

Contact: Acton State Historic Site, 512-463-6323, www.thc. state.tx.us.

Bastrop State Park

Discover the beautiful Lost Pines of Texas at Bastrop State Park in a rustic setting that can be either luxurious or simple.

You can camp out under the tall trees sleeping on a soft floor of fragrant pine needles, bike along the twelve-mile picturesque ride between Bastrop and Buescher parks, relax in the swimming pool, fish in or paddle on the lake, go for a scenic drive, have a picnic, spend a night or two in the fully equipped cabins, or play a round of golf at the park's eighteen-hole course.

The Lost Pines area is a loblolly pine forest isolated from the main body of East Texas pines by about one hundred miles of post oak woodlands. These pine-oak woods cover about seventy square miles of rugged hills and are filled with wildlife.

Bastrop State Park covers 5,926 acres. The state acquired the property from the city of Bastrop and private owners from 1933 to 1935 and the park opened in 1937. Additional property was acquired in 1979. The Civilian Conservation Corps made the park's original improvements.

The park is named for the nearby city of Bastrop, seat of Bastrop County. Stephen F. Austin founded the city in 1827 when he located a colony of one hundred families on the site. Austin gave the city its name, honoring his longtime friend and fellow land empresario, Felipe Enrique Neri, Baron de Bastrop.

Neri was born Philip Hendrik Nering Bögel in Dutch Guiana in 1759 and moved with his parents to The Netherlands in 1764. He later served as tax collector for the Dutch province of Friesland. In 1793, he was accused of embezzlement of tax funds and fled the country with a reward on his head.

Bögel then changed his name and awarded himself the title of Baron of Bastrop. Just where "Bastrop" was, no one ever knew. By 1795 he was in Louisiana, then moved to Texas and settled in San Antonio in 1806 where he started a freighting business.

Neri was popular enough to become deputy mayor of the city. In 1820 he interceded on behalf of Moses Austin's second request to bring Anglo colonists into Mexican Texas, and he was appointed commissioner of colonization with authority

Cabin built by Civilian Conservation Corps at Bastrop State Park.
—Bob Parvin/Texas Department of Transportation

to issue land titles. In 1823, he obtained permission to found a German colony in the area that would become the city of Bastrop but the effort failed.

He was chosen as a representative to the Coahuila y Texas state legislature in 1824. During Neri's tenure, he was responsible for establishing a port at Galveston. He died penniless in Saltillo in 1827 and his fellow legislators donated funds for his funeral.

Location: The park is located thirty miles southeast of Austin on Texas Highway 21. Open daily.

Amenities: Biking, cabins, camping, dining hall, dump station, fishing, golf course, hiking, park store, picnicking, restrooms, showers, swimming pool, wheelchair accessible, wireless Internet.

Contact: Bastrop State Park, P.O. Box 518, Bastrop, TX 78602-0518, 512-321-2101, www.tpwd.state.tx.us.

Bonham State Park

Bonham State Park is a microcosm of the entire region with its rolling hills, prairie grasslands, small lake, and woodlands. It's significantly quieter than the sprawling Metroplex of Dallas and Fort Worth that dominates the region, however.

Fish, swim, paddle a canoe, take a hike, camp out, or just sit back and relax.

Don't mistake the park for Lake Bonham. That's a different, and much larger, lake north of the city. The 65-acre lake in the park doesn't have a name.

The Civilian Conservation Corps built the 261-acre park in

the early 1930s. The state acquired the land from Bonham and it was opened to the public in 1936.

The park is named after the nearby city of Bonham that began in 1836 and was originally named Bois D'Arc after the tree that grows abundantly in the area. The city was renamed in 1844 to honor Alamo defender James Bonham.

James Butler Bonham was born in 1807 in Edgefield County, South Carolina. Although he attended South Carolina College, he never graduated because he led a protest against poor food served at the college's boardinghouse and he and a number of other students were expelled.

He studied law and began a practice in 1830. Ever the maverick, Bonham caned an opposing lawyer for insulting his female client and when told to apologize by the judge, Bonham threatened to tweak the judge's nose. He was sentenced to ninety days for contempt of court. He left South Carolina and was practicing law in Montgomery, Alabama, in 1834. In 1835 he organized a volunteer company, the Mobile Grays, and left for Texas, offering their services to General Sam Houston. He arrived at the Alamo with James Bowie on January 19, 1836.

James Butler Bonham
—Cushing Memorial Library and Archives, Texas A&M University

Bonham was a second cousin of Alamo commander William B. Travis and Travis used Bonham as a messenger who frequently made his way through enemy lines surrounding the old church. He left the Alamo in late February to seek reinforcements, then returned to the garrison just in time for the Mexican siege that ended in the deaths of all defenders on March 6, 1836. According to Mexican accounts, Bonham was one of the last to die. He and ten others manned two twelve-

pound cannons in the chapel area that were eventually destroyed by shot from an eighteen-pound Mexican cannon. The
survivors were bayoneted.

Interestingly, the city of Bonham is the county seat of
Fannin County, which was named for James Fannin, the Texas
Army commander who failed to come to the Alamo's aid after
Bonham's urging.

The Texas Centennial Commission erected a statue in his
honor on the courthouse square in Bonham.

Location: The park is located four miles southeast of Bonham,
sixty miles northeast of Dallas. Open daily.

Amenities: Biking, boating, camping, dump station, fishing,
group camping with dining hall, hiking, picnicking, playground, restrooms, showers, swimming.

Contact: Bonham State Park, 11363 Park Road 24, Bonham,
TX 75418-9285, 903-583-5022, www.tpwd.state.tx.us.

Buescher State Park

Buescher State Park may be relatively small at barely
1,000 acres but it joins up with Bastrop State Park to provide
a variety of leisure activities in the westernmost edge of Texas'
pine forest.

A small, stocked lake offers fishing. Hikers enjoy seven and
one-half miles of shaded trails. Campers can choose between
tent sites, screened shelters, or air-conditioned cabins. A recreational hall has a full kitchen and air conditioning.

A twelve-mile scenic park road that is used by bicyclists,

hikers and motorists connects Buescher with Bastrop State Park.

The Civilian Conservation Corps made the original park improvements. The state acquired some of the property from the city of Smithville and the Buescher family donated the remainder in the 1930s. The park opened to the public in 1940.

The park is named for the Buescher (pronounced "Bisher") family, a prominent family in the area for many generations. In the 1880s, Henry Buescher operated a store and saloon at a junction on the Galveston, Harrisburg, and San Antonio railroad line and a community grew up around the store. He was born Adolph Heinrich Buescher in 1810 in Hanover, Germany. The town that was later named Buescher was originally called Ax Handle Junction because of Buescher's propensity to settle arguments with an ax handle. He died in 1882. The town declined in the 1920s when a flood destroyed a trestle over the Colorado River and the rail line was rerouted, and later closed down. By the 1980s, the town had disappeared.

Henry's son, Emil Buescher, was born in 1864 and donated 318 acres to the state for the park. Buescher built the Smithville Electric Light, Water and Power Company, and a sewage plant. He died in 1931. In 1933, his widow Elizabeth and three sons donated another 318 acres.

Location: The park is located two miles northwest of Smithville off Texas Highway 71. Open daily.

Amenities: Biking, cabins, camping, canoeing, dump station, fishing, hiking, park store, picnicking, playground, recreational hall, restrooms, screened shelters, showers, wheelchair accessible.

Contact: Buescher State Park, P.O. Box 75, Smithville, TX 78957-0075, 512-237-2241, www.tpwd.state.tx.us.

Cedar Hill State Park

Want to see what the Metroplex looked like before it got all metropolitan? Visit Cedar Hill State Park, just a few minutes from downtown Dallas. This is a 1,826-acre urban preserve at 7,500-acre Joe Pool Lake—a lake with more than 100 miles of shoreline.

Water recreation is the main attraction here, but so is biking. The Dallas Off Road Bicycle Association built more than fifteen miles of biking trails that cross varying terrain. Then there's the 355 campsites. And since the park used to be a farm, the Penn Farm Agricultural Center gives visitors a glimpse into farming from a century ago.

The state acquired the property in 1982 and it was opened to the public in 1991.

Born in 1804 in Murray County, Georgia, John Anderson Penn came to Texas from Illinois in 1854 to farm in the rugged cedar-covered hills of southwest Dallas County. He later returned to Illinois where he died in 1871.

In 1859 his son, John Wesley Penn, built several structures for what would become a 1,100-acre farm. The family lived on and operated the farm until 1970. The remnant of that farm is now Cedar Hill.

John Wesley Penn was born in Saint Clair County, Illinois, in 1833. He and his wife Lucinda had five children. He died in 1888 from a rattlesnake bite.

The park's central attraction, Joe Pool Lake, is a reservoir that was proposed by U.S. Congressman Pool in the 1960s, but construction didn't begin until 1981 and was completed in 1986.

Joe Richard Pool was born in Fort Worth in 1911 and attended the University of Texas and Southern Methodist University School of Law. He served as a special investigator with the U.S. Army during World War II, and in 1953 through 1958 served in the Texas House of Representatives.

He served in the U.S. House from 1963 until his death in Houston in 1968.

Location: The park is located ten miles southwest of Dallas. Open 8 A.M. to 10 P.M. daily.

Amenities: Biking, boat ramp, boating, camping, fishing, hiking, park store, picnicking, playground, restrooms, showers, swimming, water skiing, wheelchair accessible, wireless Internet.

Contact: Cedar Hill State Park, 1570 Farm Road 1382, Cedar Hill, TX 75104, 972-291-3900, www.tpwd.state.tx.us.

Cleburne State Park

Cleburne State Park is in a thickly wooded valley of springs, framed by white, rocky hills—a refreshing change from the thick traffic of the Metroplex just a few miles to the north.

The park's 528 acres surround a 116-acre spring-fed lake, offering good fishing and the perfect place to cool off in the summer. The park also offers five and one-half miles of scenic bike trails with diverse terrain. And it's a great place to bask in bluebonnets and other wildflowers in the spring.

The park area was a regular campground for Comanche Indians raiding from the plains into Mexico.

The state acquired the property from the city of Cleburne and private owners in 1935-1936. The Civilian Conservation Corps built the earthen dam that impounds the lake, roads, and other improvements, and several buildings. The park was opened to the public in 1938.

The park is named for the nearby city of Cleburne, founded in 1867. The city was named in honor of General Patrick Cleburne, under whom many of the settlers had fought during the Civil War.

Patrick Ronayne Cleburne was born in County Cork, Ireland, in 1928, the son of a physician. He wished to follow in his father's occupation, but failed the medical entrance exam and enlisted in the 41st Regiment of Foot of the British Army.

On his discharge, he came to America with two brothers and a sister and settled in Arkansas in 1850 to practice law.

At the beginning of the Civil War, Cleburne became a colonel of the First Arkansas volunteers, then was promoted to brigadier general in 1862. He saw combat at Shiloh, during the Kentucky Campaign, and at the Battle of Mufreesboro. In 1863, he was promoted to the rank of major general. He distinguished himself at the Battle of Ringgold Gap in North Carolina, using a small force so successfully that it is still studied in military tactics classes today.

Major General Patrick Ronayne Cleburne
—Library of Congress

He was killed in action in 1870 during an assault on Union breastworks at Franklin, Tennessee.

Cleburne was a proponent of using slaves to fight in Confederate forces, offering them freedom in return for service. He even took his proposal a step further, saying "we [should] guarantee freedom within a reasonable time to every slave in the South who shall remain true to the Confederacy in this war."

Location: The park is located about thirty-five miles southwest of Fort Worth and ten miles southwest of Cleburne, off U.S. Highway 67. Gates open 7 A.M. to 10 P.M. daily.

Amenities: Biking, boat ramp, boating, camping, dining hall, dump station, fishing, hiking, picnicking, playground, restrooms, screened shelters, showers, swimming, water/electric/sewer sites, wheelchair accessible.

Contact: Cleburne State Park, 5800 Park Road 21, Cleburne, TX 76033, 817-645-4215, www.tpwd.state.tx.us.

Confederate Reunion Grounds State Historic Site

Visit the site where Confederate veterans gathered for many decades to remember fallen comrades and to support widows and orphans of the Civil War. In addition to taking in a little history, the site has a hiking trail and visitors can paddle a canoe or kayak along the Navasota River to Fort Parker State Park.

Attractions include several historic buildings, an eight-sided 1893 dance pavilion, a Civil War cannon, and two scenic footbridges over a creek.

In 1889, twenty-four years after the end of the Civil War, veterans of the Confederacy in Limestone and Freestone counties gathered on the banks of the Navasota River and formed the Joseph E. Johnston Camp No. 94, United Confederate Veterans. That meeting was the first in a series of annual reunions that ran for fifty-seven years.

In 1965, the group was chartered as a nonprofit corporation and in 1983 the corporation donated the grounds to the state. The site was transferred from the parks department to the Texas Historical Commission in 2008.

The Navasota River rises in southeastern Hill County and flows southeast for 125 miles to a confluence with the Brazos River. Local Indians called the river the *Nabasoto*. Early Spanish explorers recorded the name, but it is unknown what the name means or which tribe named it.

Joseph Eggleston Johnston was born in 1807 in Prince Edward County, Virginia, and graduated from the U.S. Military Academy in 1829. He served during the Seminole War and the Mexican War and in 1860 was appointed quartermaster general of the U.S. Army. He resigned that post in 1861 to join the Confederate Army where he rose to the rank of full general and commanded the Army of Northern Virginia. Robert E. Lee took over that command when Johnston was severely wounded in the Battle of Seven Pines.

He later commanded the Army of Tennessee. From 1879 to 1881, Johnston served in the U.S. Congress and was commissioner of railroads from 1887-1891. He died in Washington, D.C., in 1891.

Location: The park is located about eight miles southwest of Mexia. Open daily 8 A.M. to 5 P.M.

Amenities: Fishing, hiking, restrooms.

Contact: Confederate Reunion Grounds State Historic Site, Farm Road 2705, Mexia, TX 76667, 254-716-3730, www.thc.state.tx.us.

Cooper Lake State Park

Visitors will find lots of choices at Cooper Lake. Take in the scenery by boat, on foot, or horseback. Camp out in the woods or choose one of the shelters or fully appointed cabins. Watch for bald eagles or white pelicans, deer, or beaver. Take in the panoramic views. Boat or fish on the lake. The park even has two separate units to choose from.

The gradual slopes of the Doctors Creek Unit are located on the northeast side of the lake with 6.2 miles of shoreline. The steeper hills of the South Sulphur Unit are located on the south side of the lake. This unit is the larger of the two and has the widest variety of amenities, from equestrian trails to a volleyball court to two lighted fishing piers to a five-mile hike and bike trail. Together the two units cover 3,026 acres.

Cooper Lake covers 19,300 acres and was created in 1991 for flood control, recreation, and as a water supply for towns in the area. The state acquired the property on a lease from the Army Corps of Engineers in 1991 and the lake opened to the public in 1992. The park was dedicated in 1996.

The Doctors Creek unit is named for nearby community of Doctors Creek that began in 1882 but has since disappeared. The creek was named for medicinal herbs that Caddo Indians gathered from the area.

The South Sulphur unit is named for the South Sulphur River that the lake impounds and for the city of Sulphur Springs that takes its name from local springs that have a high mineral content, most prominently sulfur.

Sulfur is a yellow, nonmetallic element occurring in sedimentary and volcanic deposits. Liquid sulfur can be ignited and burns with a deep blue flame. *Sulfur* means "burning stone" in Latin.

Cooper Lake is named for the nearby town of Cooper. Cooper was founded in 1870 and named for L. W. Cooper of Houston, one of the sponsors of the bill to organize Delta County in 1870.

Leroy W. Cooper was born in Guillemette County, Georgia, in 1822 and moved to Texas in 1856. He was a member of the Texas Legislature and later served as a district court judge. He died in 1900.

Location: The Doctors Creek Unit of the park is located three miles east of Cooper off Texas Highway 154. The South Sulphur Unit is located fourteen miles northwest of Sulphur Springs off Texas Highway 71. Open daily 8 A.M. to 10 P.M.

Amenities: Biking, boat ramp, boating, cabins, camping, dump station, fishing, hiking, horseback riding, park store, picnicking, playground, restrooms, screened shelters, showers, swimming, water skiing, wheelchair accessible.

Contact: Cooper Lake State Park, Doctors Creek Unit, 1664 Farm Road 1529 South, Cooper, TX 75432, 903-395-3100; South Sulphur Unit, 1690 Farm Road 3505, Sulphur Springs, TX 75482, 903-945-5256, www.tpwd. state.tx.us.

Dinosaur Valley State Park

Step back in time and literally step into the footprints of dinosaurs at Dinosaur Valley State Park. The park has some of the best-preserved tracks in the world.

It seems that about 113 million years ago, several pleurocoelus dinosaurs went traipsing through the muck of an ancient coastline, leaving behind these tracks. The pleurocoelus was a plant-eater with a huge, elephant-like body, a long tail, and a tiny head on a long neck. They were followed by acrocanthosauruses, thirty-eight-foot-long predators with razor-clawed three-toed feet.

Visitors will also find two fiberglass, life-sized models of dinosaurs near park headquarters. The tyrannosaurus rex stands forty-five feet tall, the apatosaurus's head reaches up seventy feet. They were built for the Sinclair Oil Company's exhibit for the New York World's Fair in 1964-1965.

The park isn't just about dinosaurs. Hike and bike trails meander through the oak and juniper trees, the river invites fishing and swimming, and a separate one-hundred-acre area is set aside for equestrian use (bring your own horse).

The tracks were discovered here in 1908 and many were removed for display at the American Museum of Natural History in New York. But thousands of tracks remain today to fascinate people of all ages. The tracks are located in the bed of the Paluxy River, so they are not always visible—in the dry summer is the best time to see them. If they're not visible, visitors can see replicas at the visitor center where the store also sells lots of dinosaur souvenirs.

The state acquired the 1,525 acres from private owners in 1968 and opened the park in 1972.

The Paluxy River flows for 29 miles through southwestern Hood County. No one is certain where the name originated and the name itself seems to have been a point of confusion over the years. First called Pulltight because of the difficulty travelers had in crossing the river, the name was variously recorded in later years as Poloxey, Paluxie, Baloxey, and, finally, Paluxy.

Dinosaur replicas at Dinosaur Valley State Park
—Allan C. Kimball

The park is, of course, named for the dinosaur tracks found here.

Dinosaurs were reptiles that walked with their legs directly under their bodies, compared to modern reptiles most of which tend to have their legs sprawled to the sides. While most of these reptiles were land dwellers, some—mosasaurs—were marine lizards while others—pterosaurs—flew. Now extinct, they roamed the earth in the Mesozoic Era between 230 million and 65 million years ago. They ranged in size from about a foot long to one hundred feet long. The name means "terrible lizard" in Latin.

Location: The park is located four miles west of Glen Rose on Park Road 59. Open daily 8 A.M. to 10 P.M.

Amenities: Biking, camping, dump station, fishing, hiking, horseback riding, park store, picnicking, restrooms, showers, swimming, wheelchair accessible.

Contact: Dinosaur Valley State Park, P.O. Box 396, Glen Rose, TX 76043, 254-897-4588, www.tpwd.state.tx.us.

Eisenhower State Park

In the 1950s, Americans proclaimed, "I like Ike," overwhelmingly electing Dwight "Ike" Eisenhower to two terms as president. North Texans today proclaim the same thing in similar numbers, referring to Eisenhower State Park.

The 424-acre park is located on the southeast shore of the 89,000-acre Lake Texoma. The lake is one of the most popular attractions in North Texas with plenty of room for powerboats, fishing boats, sailboats, and water skiers. Swimmers can splash away in a protected cove while hikers can enjoy four and one-half miles of trails with excellent views of the lake. ATV and mini-bike aficionados have ten designated acres to roam around in.

Fishing for bass and catfish in the lake is among the best in the nation—blue catfish caught here have won several international records, including one that topped out at more than 118 pounds.

The Eisenhower Yacht Club is located within the park. It's a privately operated full-service marina with a repair shop, boat rentals, and a sewer pump-out station. It also sells bait, boating supplies, camping supplies, some clothing, fuel, some groceries, and snacks.

The state acquired the property in 1954 on a lease from the Department of the Army. It was opened to the public is 1958.

Lake Texoma gets its name from the fact that it lies in two states, Texas and Oklahoma.

Dwight D. Eisenhower
—U.S. Navy Photo/Dwight D.
Eisenhower Presidential Library

The park was named for Dwight D. Eisenhower, the 34th president of the United States. For details on Eisenhower, see the entry for Eisenhower Birthplace State Historic Site below.

Location: The park is located about sixty miles north of Dallas, about five miles northwest of Denison, off Texas Highway 91. Open daily.

Amenities: Biking, boat ramp, boating, camping, dump station, fishing, hiking, park store, picnicking, restrooms, screened shelters, showers, swimming, water skiing, wheelchair accessible.

Contact: Eisenhower State Park, 50 Park Road 20, Denison, TX 75020-4878, 903-465-1956, www.tpwd.state.tx.us. Eisenhower Yacht Club, 903-463-3999, www.eisenhoweryachtclub.com.

Eisenhower Birthplace State Historic Site

Didn't know that Dwight Eisenhower was the first president of the United States born in Texas? That's OK. Neither did he.

Known during his presidential campaign as "The Man From Abilene," Eisenhower thought he was born in Abilene, Kansas, where he was raised. His family moved from Denison to Abilene when he was eighteen months old and that's where he thought he was born until he was a teenager when he learned he was born in Texas. But even then he didn't know the whole story because when he applied to West Point, he listed his birthplace as Tyler, Texas. He didn't discover he was born in Denison until 1946 when he was in his fifties.

One of the nice things about visiting Eisenhower Birthplace is that Ike himself, in that unassuming voice he had, will welcome you, because a recording Eisenhower made for this site in 1958 while he was still president plays at the visitor center. The birthplace contains family possessions and period antiques of a late nineteenth century working family. The Visitor Center is filled with hundreds of items relating to Eisenhower and his place in America and the world, both as a general leading the largest army in history and as President.

Outside the Visitor Center stands a statue of the grandfatherly general in a typical pose, hands on hips, and wearing the ever-present hip-length jacket that is still known by his name.

Appropriately enough, since Eisenhower's father worked for the railroad, an abandoned rail track at the park has been turned into a hiking trail.

A statue of Dwight D. Eisenhower overlooks his home at Eisenhower Birthplace State Historic Site

—Allan C. Kimball

The state acquired the six-acre property in 1958 from the Eisenhower Birthplace Foundation, and it was opened as a historical park in 1959. The site was transferred to the Texas Historical Commission in 2008.

Dwight David Eisenhower was actually born David Dwight Eisenhower, but his mother soon switched the names around to avoided confusion with his father. The only one of David and Ida Eisenhower's seven children born in Texas, Ike was born in this two-story frame house at Lamar Avenue and Day Street in Denison in 1890.

As a child, he earned money by selling tamales based on his mother's recipe, three for a nickel. He later worked at creamery to help put his brother Edgar through college.

Ike was appointed to the U.S. Military Academy at the age of twenty. He was a good student, but earned demerits for smoking and improper "whirling" on the dance floor. Acknowledged as a gifted athlete, his football career at West Point ended when he suffered a broken knee in a game against Jim Thorpe's Carlisle Indians. On his graduation in 1915, he had a second lieutenant's bars and a transfer to Fort Sam Houston in San Antonio.

In his early career, he served in Panama, with General John Pershing in Washington, D.C., with General Douglas Mac-Arthur in the Philippines, and graduated at the top of his class at the Command and General Staff School.

During World War II, Eisenhower earned promotions quickly and, although he had never seen front-line combat in his entire career, was named Supreme Commander of Allied Forces in Europe in 1943, then became a five-star general of the army in 1944. He planned and supervised the Normandy invasion in 1944 that led to the defeat of Germany and the end of the war in Europe eleven months later. After the war, he served as the supreme commander of NATO.

One of the most popular heroes to emerge from World War II, Eisenhower was elected the 34th President of the United States in 1952, and was re-elected in 1956. One of his first accomplishments was to end the Korean Conflict in 1953.

During his tenure, Alaska and Hawaii were admitted to the Union—the last territories to be admitted.

All Americans continue to enjoy one of his pet projects: the Interstate Highway system that he began in 1956.

He proposed the first civil rights laws since the Civil War, signing them into law in 1957 and 1960, and dispatched the 101st Airborne Division of the Army to enforce school integration in Little Rock, Arkansas, in 1957. He also created the National Aeronautic and Space Administration (NASA) in 1958. Although a lifelong soldier, he warned about the "unwarranted influence . . . of the military-industrial complex" in his farewell address.

He retired to Gettysburg, Pennsylvania, and died in 1969. He is buried in Abilene.

Location: The park is located in Denison. Open Tuesday through Saturday 9 A.M. to 5 P.M., Sunday 1 P.M. to 5 P.M.

Amenities: Hiking, museum, restrooms.

Contact: Eisenhower Birthplace State Historic Site, 609 S. Lamar Avenue, Denison, TX 75021, 903-465-8908, www.thc.state.tx.us.

Fairfield Lake State Park

Hikers love Fairfield Lake State Park. A six-mile trail connects to a nine-mile trail, making a continuous fifteen-mile trailway that runs from one end of the park to the other, most of it adjacent to the 2,400-acre lake. Bikes and horses also use this trail. A two-mile nature trail and one-mile bird watching trail offer other opportunities.

Fairfield Lake State Park has some hot fishing, too. That's because the waters of Fairfield Lake are warm (up to 107 degrees in the summer) since they cool an electric power plant, and that means excellent winter fishing. The 2,400-acre lake is stocked with red drum and a state record inland red drum of 36.83 pounds and 44 inches was caught here. The fishing is so good that the park hosts tournaments every weekend from November through February. And those warm lake waters extend the swimming season.

Visitors can watch bald eagles frequently diving into the lake for their favorite tilapia during the winter months. Ospreys do the same all year long.

Conveniently located, Fairfield's 1,460 acres are just a few miles from Interstate 45, ninety miles south of the Dallas/Fort Worth Metroplex, 150 miles north of Houston and sixty miles west of Waco.

The park is situated on the lake's southern and southwestern shores. The dam creating the lake was built on Big Brown Creek in 1969 to provide a reservoir for cooling an adjacent power plant and for recreation. The state acquired the park property in 1971-1972 by lease from Texas Utilities and it was opened as a state park in 1976.

Big Brown Creek begins three miles southwest of the city of Fairfield and flows northeast for thirteen miles. The water in the creek is generally brown since it crosses rolling prairies made up of clays and sandy loams.

The lake was named for the city of Fairfield that was founded in 1851. The town was named Fairfield in honor of the home of many of the settlers: Fairfield, Alabama.

Fairfield, Alabama, is located in Jefferson County and was named for the city of Fairfield, Connecticut, home of one of the founders.

Fairfield, Connecticut, is located on a shore of Long Island Sound and was originally called *Uncoway* after a Paugussett Indian name for the area that meant "place beyond." The settlers wanted a more Anglicized name and settled on Fairfield for the hundreds of acres of salt marsh that bordered the coast, land the Paugussett had already cleared and culti-vated.

The town's founders wanted a community of like-minded people and those who were not approved by the Town Meeting were warned to leave town. Anyone disobeying community rules was shown the highway.

Location: The park is located six miles northeast of Fairfield off Farm Road 3285. Open daily.

Amenities: Biking, boat ramp, boating, camping, dump station, fishing, hiking, horseback riding, lighted fishing pier, park store, picnicking, playground, restrooms, showers, swimming, water skiing.

Contact: Fairfield Lake State Park, 123 State Park Road 64, Fairfield, TX 75840, 903-389-4514, www.tpwd.state.tx.us.

Fanthorp Inn State Historic Site

Ride in a replica of an 1850 Concord stagecoach and walk through a historic inn more than 150 years old that served as a stagecoach stop at Fanthorp Inn.

The inn provided lodging for a number of prominent men over the years: Texas Presidents Sam Houston and Anson Jones, Confederate President Jefferson Davis, Confederate generals Robert E. Lee and Stonewall Jackson, and U.S. Presidents Zachary Taylor and Ulysses Grant.

In 1847, food and lodging at the inn cost $1 a day. In the 1850s, $1.50 would get a visitor two meals, stabling and food for his horse, and sleeping space. Accommodations were quite different in those days when travelers usually slept two to a bed and some on the floor, and used a common washroom. Any connection to personal hygiene and health was at least a half-century away.

The site is preserved today as it was in the 1850s, with original plank flooring, original glass panes in the windows, and original mantel and fireplace and mantel clock. Several items belonging to the Fanthorp family are on display, including two wardrobes, a Masonic ceremonial sword, and a walking stick with an engraved silver handle. The house is completed with period antiques. Stagecoach rides are given on the second Saturday of each month.

The state bought the property from a Fanthorp descendant in 1977, and it was opened to the public in 1987.

Fanthorp was born about 1790 in Lincolnshire, England. He sailed for America and arrived in Texas in 1832. That year, he petitioned Stephen F. Austin for permission to settle in Grimes County and bought 1,100 acres. When he made the land request, he identified himself as a widower and that he had left a son in England. Fanthorp built the cedar log house in 1834 after his marriage to Rachel Kennard. The house was at the crossing of mail routes between Houston and Springfield and Nacogdoches and San Felipe, and immediately began to be used as an inn by travelers.

Fanthorp was appointed postmaster of the county by the provisional Texas government in 1835. Two years later, he opened a general store at the inn, and in another couple of years was selling home lots in the area. In 1851, he was agent for the U.S. mail coaches operating between Houston and Austin.

Fanthorp and his wife Rachel died of yellow fever in 1867, and soon after that their daughter Mary closed the inn but continued to live there.

Location: The park is located about thirty miles southeast of Bryan/College Station off Texas Highway 90 in the town of

Anderson. Open Saturday and Sunday 9 A.M. to 3:30 P.M., open Wednesday through Friday for group tours.

Amenities: Museum, restrooms, wheelchair accessible.

Contact: Fanthorp Inn State Historic Site, P.O. Box 296, Anderson, TX 77830, 936-873-2633, www.thc.state. tx.us.

Fort Boggy State Park

Listen to a chorus of frogs or the slap of a beaver's tail, paddle a kayak, roam through a tunnel of sweet gum trees at Fort Boggy State Park. The park's location about midway between Dallas and Houston, near Interstate 45, makes it a popular escape to nature.

The small lake in the midst of post oak and hickory woodlands attracts many migratory waterfowls. Wood ducks call the park lake and nearby Boggy Creek home year round.

In early 1840, settlers gathered in an area north of the Old San Antonio Road between the Navasota and Trinity Rivers and immediately were raided by two different tribes, the Keechi and the Kickapoo. The settlers built a palisaded fort for protection from the Indians. The fort had upright logs set into the ground, was seventy-five yards square, and enclosed two blockhouses and eleven dwellings that housed seventy-five families by 1841. Texas President Mirabeau B. Lamar authorized formation of a military company to man the fort that began to be known as Fort Boggy because of its proximity to Boggy Creek.

A few years later, Indian attacks decreased and the need for the fort lessened and it fell into disrepair, but settlers—including many African-Americans—continued to farm in the area until at least the 1930s.

Not only are there no remains of the fort today, no one is certain where it was located. Prison inmates made many improvements to the park in the late 1990s. Eileen Crain Sullivan donated the park's 1,847 acres in 1985. The park opened to the public in 2001.

Boggy Creek, a spring-fed stream, rises in northern Colorado County and flows southwest for seven miles. It was named for the marshy condition of the creek bottom.

Location: The park is located about four miles south of Centerville. Open Friday through Sunday 8 A.M. to sunset.

Amenities: Biking, boating, fishing, hiking, picnicking, swimming, restroom, wheelchair accessible.

Contact: Fort Boggy State Park, 4994 Texas Highway 75 South, Centerville, TX 75833, 903-344-1116, www. tpwd.state.tx.us.

Fort Parker State Park

Fort Parker State Park is a beautifully wooded spot on the Navasota River just a few hour's drive from the metropolitan areas of Austin, Dallas, or Houston. Fish, bike, hike, or paddle a canoe or kayak on the small lake. In the spring, take pictures of your children surrounded by bluebonnets and other Texas wildflowers.

The park has become a popular place for family reunions and church groups. Its group recreation hall has a dining hall and four barracks that will sleep up to 96 people.

The park's 1,458 acres includes a 700-acre lake. The city of Mexia and three landowners donated the land for the park in 1935. It opened to the public 1941. The Civilian Conservation Corps built all the park's recreational facilities in the late 1930s, and built a dam across the Navasota River in 1939, creating Fort Parker Lake.

For information on the Navasota River, see the entry for the Confederate Reunion Grounds State Historic Site above.

The park was named for Fort Parker, a settlement three miles away that was established in 1833. Fort Parker was named for Elder Daniel Parker.

Parker was born in Culpeper County, Virginia, in 1781. He moved to Georgia then Tennessee and then Illinois where he served as a state senator in 1822. In 1833, he came to Texas and brought his Pilgrim Predestinarian Regular Baptist Church with him. In 1835, he was elected to represent Nacogdoches County at the General Council of the Texas provisional government. He was also elected to the Texas Congress in 1939 but he was barred from taking his seat because ordained ministers were Constitutionally ineligible. He died at his home in 1844.

Daniel Parker

Daniel's younger brothers Silas M. Parker and James W. Parker built the fort. The fort was a collection of cabins that had outer walls integrated into a surrounding stockade that had small holes in it for defenders to shot through.

James W. Parker was born in 1797 in Franklin County, Georgia. He moved to Texas in 1833. In 1835, he brokered a treaty with hostile Caddo and Comanche Indians and later that year traveled to San Felipe to consult on the Texas Declaration of Independence. In 1845, James was elected justice of the peace in Houston County where he died in 1864.

Silas M. Parker was born in 1802 in Franklin County, Georgia. He served in the Black Hawk War in 1832 and moved to Texas the following year. The fort was the site of a Comanche raid on May 19, 1836, during which Silas was killed and his nine-year-old daughter Cynthia Ann Parker and six-year-old son John Parker were captured.

Cynthia Ann Parker was born in 1825 in Crawford County, Illinois, and came to Texas with her family in 1833. At some point after her capture, she married Peta Nocona and had two sons and a daughter by him. He was killed in the battle with Texas Rangers that led to her rescue.

On December 18, 1860, Texas Ranger Sul Ross attacked a Comanche hunting party and captured three Indians. One of them had blue eyes—Cynthia Ann. Her uncle, Isaac Parker, took her home. After so many years among the Comanche, she was never reconciled to living back in white society and made several attempts to run away to her Comanche family. She died in 1871.

One of her sons, Quanah Parker, was the last of the great Comanche chiefs. He was born in 1845 in what is now Oklahoma and his name means "Perfume." He was the leader of the Comanche band that lost what is known as the Red River War to Colonel Ranald Mackenzie. (For more details on that, see the entry for Palo Duro Canyon State Park in the Panhandle section.)

After surrendering and going to the Fort Sill Reservation in Oklahoma to live, Quanah Parker worked tirelessly to bring his two heritages together, was elected deputy sheriff in Lawton, and became a wealthy man and one of the best known Indians of his day. He died in 1911 and was buried in full Comanche regalia and a large amount of money. His grave was later robbed for the cash. He and his mother, Cynthia Ann, are buried at Fort Sill.

Rachel Parker Plummer, James Pratt Plummer, and Elizabeth Kellogg were also captured that day. James Parker made three forays into Comanche territory to rescue his relatives, but all three expeditions failed.

Rachel Plummer, James's daughter, was returned in 1838 and died in 1839. Kellogg was bought by Delaware Indians and returned to her family. John Parker and James Pratt Plummer were recovered in 1843.

Like his sister, John Parker grew to adulthood with the Comanche. His adoptive family later abandoned him on the Llano Estacado when he became ill with smallpox. After he was rescued, he refused to return to either Texas or the Comanche but went to Mexico where he married the woman who nursed him back to health. He became a rancher and served in a Mexican company in the Confederacy during the Civil War. After the war, he returned to Mexico where he died in 1915.

More information on the Parker family and a reconstruction of the actual fort may be discovered at nearby Old Fort Parker, operated by the city of Groesbeck.

Location: The park is located seven miles south of Mexia on Texas Highway 14. Open daily 8 A.M. to 10 P.M.

Amenities: Biking, boat rental, boating, camping, dump station, fishing, hiking, park store, picnicking, restrooms, screened shelters, showers, swimming.

Contact: Fort Parker State Park, 194 Park Road 28, Mexia, TX 76667, 254-562-5751, www.tpwd.state.tx.us. Old Fort Parker, RR3 Box 746, Groesbeck, TX 76642, 254-729-5253, www.tpwd.state.tx.us.

Lake Mineral Wells State Park and Trailway

Lake Mineral Wells State Park has something for just about

everybody: boating, camping, fishing, hiking, horseback riding, rock climbing, and swimming.

Lake Mineral Wells is located along Rock Creek, an area that was home to the Comanche and other Indians. After white settlers arrived in the 1850s, warfare with the Comanche continued until the late 1870s.

The park is named for the lake that is named for the nearby city.

James Alvis Lynch settled in the area in 1877 and a few years later drilled a well because he was tired of hauling water from the Brazos River. Lynch was born in 1827 in Lexington, Missouri, and moved with his family to Texas in 1861. He laid out the site for the city of Mineral Wells in 1881. He died in 1920.

His wife Armenia suffered from rheumatism, but after drinking the "funny-tasting" water from the new well she wasn't bothered by the infliction any more. The curative power of the water was touted far and wide and the area quickly became a health resort: Mineral Wells.

The city of Mineral Wells grew until it needed more water than the local water supply could handle, so plans were made for another reservoir. In 1922, Rock Creek was impounded to create Lake Mineral Wells. The lake was no longer necessary after the city found a better water source in 1963, leading to its donation and 1,095 acres of surrounding land in 1975 to the Texas Parks and Wildlife Department. The U.S. government transferred more land to the state for use in the park. The park was opened in July 1981.

The Lake Mineral Wells State Trailway was opened in 1998. The twenty-mile trail begins in central Parker County and travels westward to downtown Mineral Wells, and is connected to the park. The trail has four trailheads—in Garner, in Mineral Wells, in the state park, and near Weatherford.

The trailway, located on a railroad bed, winds through remote farm and ranch lands and its rolling hills are full of wildlife and birds. The grades of the trail are relatively flat and gentle, making it popular for bikers, hikers, and horseback riders of all ages and abilities.

Location: The park is located four miles east of Mineral Wells on U.S. Highway 180. Open daily 6 A.M. to 10 P.M.

Amenities: Biking, boat rental, boating, camping, dump station, fishing, hiking, horseback riding, park store, picnicking, restrooms, rock climbing, screened shelters, showers, swimming, wheelchair accessible.

Contact: Lake Mineral Wells State Park and Trailway, 100 Park Road 71, Mineral Wells, TX 76067, 940-328-1171, www.tpwd.state.tx.us.

Lake Somerville State Park and Trailway

Lake Somerville State Park offers a multitude of recreational opportunities in two separate units and an inviting trailway that connects the two.

Horses are welcome at either the Birch Creek or Nails Creek units. Water lovers are welcome on the lake where they can paddle around or fish, swim, or water ski. And the trailway connects the two units with thirteen miles of trails suitable for biking, birding, hiking, horseback riding, nature study, and photography.

Birch Creek rises six miles southwest of Caldwell in Burleson County and flows southeast for ten miles. It was named for the abundant number of river birch trees along its banks.

Nails Creek rises in south central Lee County, two-and-one-half miles west of Giddings, and flows northeast for twenty-five miles.

The U.S. Army Corp of Engineers completed the Somerville reservoir in 1967 for flood control, water supply, and recreation. It covers 11,630 acres with a shoreline of 85 miles. The state leased the park property from the federal government in 1969 and opened it to the public in 1970.

Lake Somerville was named for the nearby city of Somerville. A community grew up when the Gulf, Colorado and Santa Fe Railway built its Galveston/Caldwell spur through the area in 1880. It was incorporated as Somerville in 1913 and named for Albert Somerville, the first president of the GC&SF that was formed in 1873. Somerville had also been mayor of Galveston in 1871-1872. His company started a railroad tie manufacturing facility in the area—it is still operating and produces more than one million ties a year.

Location: The Birch Creek unit is located on the north shore of Lake Somerville, about fifteen miles northwest from

Lake Somerville State Park
—Gay Shackelford/Texas Department of Transportation

Somerville. The Nails Creek unit is located on the east shore of Lake Somerville, about twenty miles northeast from Giddings. Open daily.

Amenities: Biking, boating, camping, dump station, fishing, hiking, horseback riding, park store, picnicking, restrooms, showers, swimming, water skiing.

Contact: Birch Creek Unit, Lake Somerville State Park, 14222 Park Road 57, Somerville, TX 77879-9713, 979-535-7763, www.tpwd.state.tx.us. Nails Creek Unit, Lake Somerville State Park and Trailway, 6280 Farm Road 180, Ledbetter, TX 78946-7036, 979-289-2392, www.tpwd.state.tx.us

Lake Tawakoni State Park

Less than an hour east of Dallas is Lake Tawakoni State Park where visitors can enjoy water recreation, fish, or hike through an ecosystem that's hard to find anywhere close.

The park's forty acres of native tallgrass prairie is rare in East Texas and serves as a habitat for some of the 215 bird species sighted here. Explore some of it on five and one-half miles of hiking trails.

The park's 376 acres has 5.2 miles of shoreline along the south shore of the lake. The 36,700-surface-acre lake has a shoreline of about 200 miles and was built to provide a water supply for surrounding communities and the city of Dallas. The state acquired the property in 1984 in a lease with the Sabine River Authority that operates the reservoir.

The reservoir impounds the Sabine River. For details on the Sabine, see the entry for Sabine Pass Battleground State Historic Site in the Gulf Coast section.

The lake is named for the Tawakoni Indians who occupied the area in the eighteenth century. The Tawakonis were a Wichita group originating in what is now central Kansas. They lived along the Brazos River in an area roughly bounded by Waco and Palestine and were included in treaties made by the Republic of Texas in 1843 and those made by the U.S. in 1837 and 1856.

Though they were skilled raiders, their numbers went into a sharp decline and they became less and less of a threat to settlers who kept forcing them to move. For a time, the Tawakonis lived around Fort Belknap in Young County then, in 1859, moved into the Indian Territory of present-day Oklahoma to the Wichita Reservation at Anadarko.

The name *Tawakoni* comes from a Wichita word meaning "river bed among red hills," signifying the land they occupied. For more information on the name "Wichita," see the entry for Lake Arrowhead State Park in the Panhandle Plains section.

Location: The park is located fifty miles east of Dallas, twenty-five miles south of Greenville. Open daily 7 A.M. to 10 P.M.

Amenities: Boating, camping, dump station, fishing, hiking, picnicking, restrooms, showers, swimming, water skiing.

Contact: Lake Tawakoni State Park, 10822 Farm Road 2475, Wills Point, TX 75169, 903-560-7123, www.tpwd.state.tx.us.

Lake Whitney State Park

Fishing may be the most popular activity at Lake Whitney State Park, but visitors will find lots of room to zip around the lake in a boat or on skis or even fly in to the park's own airstrip.

The 1,280-acre park's open meadows have enough space for the 2,000-foot, unlighted landing strip that area flying groups often take advantage of. And, of course, those meadows explode with colorful wildflowers in the spring.

Forested areas surrounding the meadows provide habitats to a variety of wildlife like white tail deer, rabbits, and foxes. Hiking trails offer abundant opportunities to also look for the nearly 200 bird species identified here.

The park is on the east shore of 23,500-acre Lake Whitney—the fourth largest lake in Texas—with 225 miles of shoreline and that means good swimming and all sorts of water recreation.

The state acquired the property in 1954 in a department of the Army lease and was opened to the public in 1965.

The park was named for the lake that was named for the nearby town of Whitney. Whitney was founded in 1876 when the Houston and Texas Central Railroad came through the area. The town was named for Charles A. Whitney of New York, a major stockholder in the railroad company and a brother-in-law of tycoon J. P. Morgan. He died in 1882.

Whitney's nephew Richard was a heavy gambler and at one time was president of the New York Stock Exchange. In 1938, Richard was caught embezzling funds, was convicted and sent to prison, owing some $6.5 million. His actions led to major reforms for the NYSE.

Location: The park is located eighteen miles west of Hillsboro on Farm Road 1244. Open daily 8 A.M. to 10 P.M.

Amenities: Airstrip, biking, boat ramp, boating, camping, dining hall, dump station, fishing, hiking, park store, picnicking, playground, restrooms, screened shelters, showers, swimming, water/electric/sewer sites, water skiing, wheelchair accessible.

Contact: Lake Whitney State Park, Box 1175, Whitney, TX 76692, 254-694-3793, www.tpwd.state.tx.us.

Lockhart State Park

A round of golf, a picnic on a scenic hilltop location, a refreshing swim in the pool, a competitive game on the sand volleyball court—it's not an exclusive country club, it's Lockhart State Park.

The park also has one and one-half miles of hiking trails, a recreation hall that's perfect for group gatherings like family reunions or weddings, a lake to fish for bass or catfish or sunfish, and plenty of wildlife and birds.

The state acquired the 264-acre property from private owners between 1934 and 1937. The Civilian Conservation Corps built the improvements, including the nine-hole golf course and several native stone buildings, between 1935 and 1939. The park was opened in 1948.

The park is named for the nearby city of Lockhart that was established in the 1830s. The city was named for Byrd Lockhart who, in 1831, received the land that would become the townsite in return for survey work done for the Mexican government.

Lockhart was born in Virginia in 1782. A widower, he moved to Texas from Missouri in 1826 with his mother, sister, and two children. He made his living as a surveyor and worked the lands around Gonzales. In 1827, he opened a road from San Antonio through Gonzales to Matagorda Bay. In 1831, José Antonio Navarro appointed him surveyor to DeWitt's Colony.

When the Texas Revolution began, Lockhart acted as a scout and eventually raised volunteers for a ranging company in Gonzales and Milam. He served in the Alamo until just before the final siege when he was sent out with some of his men to get supplies for the garrison. Because Lockhart and his men were delayed in Gonzales buying cattle, they missed being massacred at the Alamo. He continued to serve in the Texas Army as a captain of scouts. He died in 1839.

Location: The park is located about two miles southeast of Lockhart, off Farm Road 20. Open daily.

Amenities: Camping, dump station, fishing, golf course, hiking, park store, picnicking, playground, recreation hall, restrooms, showers, swimming pool, water/electric/sewer sites.

Contact: Lockhart State Park, 4179 Park Road 10, Lockhart, TX 78644, 512-398-3479, www.tpwd.state.tx.us.

Meridian State Park

Enjoy a quiet lakeside retreat in the wooded hills near Waco at Meridian State Park.

The park's 505 acres are heavily wooded with cedar and oak, providing habitat for a variety of wildlife and birds, including the rare golden-cheeked warbler in the spring. The small lake is popular for bass, bream, catfish, and crappie.

Swim in the lake or traipse around the hiking trail that circles it, checking out fossils found in the limestone outcroppings.

The Civilian Conservation Corps built a rock and earth dam on Bee Creek to form the park's 72-acre lake. Meridian was the first state park to benefit from CCC workers who arrived just three months after authorization by Congress. The state acquired the land from private owners between 1933 and 1935. It was opened to the public in 1935.

Bee Creek rises four miles west of Meridian and flows south for nine miles. It was named for wild bees found along its banks.

The park was named for the nearby town of Meridian. The town lies on the 9th meridian, considered the dividing line between the prairies of the eastern U.S. and the plains of the west.

Location: The park is located about three miles southwest of Meridian off Texas Highway 22. Open daily 8 A.M. to 10 P.M.

Amenities: Biking, boating, cabins, camping, dump station, fishing, hiking, picnicking, restrooms, screened shelters, showers, swimming.

Contact: Meridian State Park, 173 Park Road 7, Meridian, TX 76665, 254-435-2536, www.tpwd.state.tx.us.

Monument Hill and Kreische Brewery State Historic Site

Picnic on the lawn of the historic Kreische House, tour the ruins of one of the first breweries in the state of Texas, and pay respects to early Texas patriots at Monument Hill and Kreische Brewery State Historic Site.

The natural features of the forty-acre park are interesting as well. The bluff at Monument Hill marks the boundary between the upland post oak woodlands and the Fayette prairie environments. Along this bluff, plant and animal communities of the woodlands and the prairie coexist in an isolated colony.

The state acquired the tomb at Monument Hill in 1907 and transferred it to Texas Parks and Wildlife in 1948. In 1956, the archbishop of San Antonio and the citizens of Fayette County donated additional land. The Kreische Brewery and Home were added in 1977. The park opened in 1983.

The tomb at Monument Hill contains the remains of Texians who died in the Battle of Salado under Captain Nicholas M. Dawson and those from the ill-fated Mier Expedition who were executed after a macabre lottery.

In 1842, Dawson was in commanded of a fifty-three-man company of volunteers from Fayette County that marched from La Grange in support of Colonel Matthew Caldwell who was fighting Mexican forces at Salado Creek. Dawson's men were outnumbered and quickly surrounded. Dawson attempted to surrender but was shot down and thirty-six of his men were killed with fifteen taken prisoner while two escaped. The prisoners were marched to Mexico and only nine survived to return to Texas.

Dawson was born in Woolford, Kentucky, in 1808 and moved with his family to Tennessee then to Texas in 1834. He enlisted in the Texas Army and fought in the Battle of San Jacinto as a second lieutenant. When Mexican General Adrián Woll invaded Texas in 1842, Dawson raised a company of volunteers. He died that year in a battle that became known as the Dawson Massacre. His remains and those of thirty-five others were buried along with casualties from the Mier Expedition in a vault on Kreische Bluff, later renamed Monument Hill.

In 1842 the Mier Expedition was the last raiding party from Texas into the disputed area south of Nueces River during the days of the Republic of Texas.

In late December, troops under Captain William S. Fisher reached the city of Mier, Mexico, and attacked. They met with fierce resistance from a superior armed force. Fisher, already wounded, surrendered after being warned if he didn't, all his men would be captured and executed.

The captured Texians were initially sentenced to execution anyway but the decree was reversed and the prisoners were marched toward Mexico City. They staged an escape but most were recaptured and interred at El Rancho Salado. General Antonio López de Santa Anna ordered all the men executed but Francisco Mexía, governor of the state of Coahuila, refused to obey and modified the order in what is known as the Black Bean Episode.

In early 1843, the 176 captured Texians were forced to draw a bean from a pot—a white bean meant life, a black bean meant death. Seventeen men were executed; the remainder were marched to Mexico City. Some of the survivors later escaped, some died in captivity.

Their remains were recovered during the Mexican War and transferred to La Grange where they were buried in a vault on Kreische Bluff.

In 1936, during the Texas Centennial, a forty-eight-foot monument was built on the bluff to commemorate the Dawson and Mier men.

Heinrich L. Kreische was born in Saxony, Germany, in 1872 and came to Texas in 1846. He was a master stonemason and built the Fayette County jail and the third courthouse in La Grange.

Sometime after 1860, Kreische changed his occupation from stonemason to beer maker, building a large brewery near his home and by the late 1870s his company was the third largest in the state. His ads proclaimed, "Bluff beer is good," and the slogan for the brewery was *Frisch Auf!*—Refresh! Look Alive!

Although Kreische maintained the gravesite on the bluff, he and his family made repeated requests to have it moved because they were also selling beer on the bluff and they didn't think the two mixed well. In 1905 the Texas Legislature authorized buying the land from the family but the family insisted the graves be moved. The state then took possession of the site through a condemnation procedure.

Kreische was crushed by a wagon loaded with stone in 1882. The brewery closed shortly after his death.

Location: The park is located one mile south of La Grange. Open daily 8 A.M. to 5 P.M.

Amenities: Guided tours, historic exhibits, nature trail, park store, picnicking, restrooms.

Contact: Monument Hill and Kreische Brewery State Historic Site, 414 State Loop 42, La Grange, TX 78945, 979-968-5658, www.tpwd.state.tx.us.

Mother Neff State Park

Enjoy the park that started it all—Mother Neff State Park, the first official state park of Texas.

Picnic or camp in the shade of tall pecan trees. Hike over a network of trails that cut through the park. Fish in the Leon River, framed by rugged limestone hills covered with old cedars and oaks.

Wildflowers cover the 259-acre park in the spring as migrating songbirds pass through. More color delights visitors in the fall when sumacs turn bright red. White tail deer seem to be almost everywhere as are hawks overhead.

In the 1930s, the Civilian Conservation Corps restored the park to its historical setting and built the group pavilion, the Rock Tabernacle and its hand-hewn pews, and other stone buildings.

The Leon River rises in Eastland County and flows southeast for 185 miles. Spanish explorers named the river for Alonso De León in 1721. (For information on De León, see the entry for Guadalupe River State Park in the Hill Country section.)

In 1916, Isabella Neff donated six acres of land for a public gathering place. After her death, her son Governor Pat Neff created Mother Neff Memorial Park. Governor Neff saw the need for a state parks system and worked to create one for Texas. In 1923, during his second term, the Texas Legislature created the State Parks Board. In 1963, the State Parks Board was merged with the Texas Game and Fish Commission to create the Texas Parks and Wildlife Department. In 1934, Pat Neff donated another 250 acres and Frank Smith donated another three acres. The park was opened to the public in 1937.

Pat Morris Neff was born in Coryell County in 1871, attended Baylor University and earned a law degree from the University of Texas. He practiced law in Waco, served in the

Picnic pavilion at Mother Neff State Park
—Allan C. Kimball

Texas House from 1899 to 1905, the last two as speaker, the youngest in history at the time.

Neff was elected governor in 1921 on a prohibitionist platform and in 1922 sent a National Guard unit and Texas Rangers

Tonkawa cave at Mother Neff State Park
—Allan C. Kimball

to the town of Mexia to control bootlegging, gambling, and prostitution in that oil boom town. He was re-elected that year.

One of Neff's unusual actions as governor was to pardon a murderer after he heard him sing. While on an inspection tour of the state prison, Neff heard Huddie Ledbetter perform, went back to the governor's mansion and issued the man a pardon. Ledbetter was convicted of murder and sentenced to thirty years in prison in 1918, but served only six years of that punishment thanks to Neff who recognized the talent of a man who would become known as Leadbelly, a folk and blues legend.

In 1932, Neff became president of Baylor University where he served until 1947. He infuriated many university trustees when he invited President Harry Truman to visit Baylor to receive an honorary degree—the teetotaling trustees didn't approve of Truman's drinking and loose interpretation of Baptist doctrine. Neff died in 1953.

Isabella Eleanor Shepherd Neff was born in 1830 in Roanoke, Virginia, and grew up to teach school. She married Noah Neff there in 1854 and a few days later they moved to Texas. Their trip took fifty-two days, but she was later to quickly point out that they didn't drive their carriage on Sundays.

The couple built a log cabin on Coryell County in an area still used by Tonkawa Indians. They raised cotton and twelve children on their farm, and saw thousands of cattle driven by on the Chisholm Trail, offering coffee and a piece of pie to eager cowboys. Noah died in 1882 when Pat Neff was eleven years old. Isabella Neff's hospitality—to the cowboys and for her opening up a

Isabella Eleanor Shepherd Neff
—The Texas Collection
of Baylor University

portion of the family farm for public gatherings—led to her nickname of Mother Neff. She moved into the Governor's Mansion after her son was elected and she died there in 1921.

Location: The park is located sixteen miles southeast of Gatesville on Texas Highway 236. Open daily 8 A.M. to 5 P.M.

Amenities: Camping, dump station, fishing, hiking, picnicking, playground, restrooms, showers.

Contact: Mother Neff State Park, 1680 Texas Highway 236, Moody, TX 76557-3317, 254-853-2389, www.tpwd.state.tx.us.

Palmetto State Park

Palmetto State Park resembles the tropics more than the surrounding brush country thanks to its location on the beautiful San Marcos River and its four-acre oxbow lake.

Three miles of hiking trails meander through the 270-acre park, giving visitors a close-up glimpse of the more than 600 plant species, 350 species of animals, and 240 species of birds that call Palmetto home. It's a unique place. A visitor won't find prickly pear cactus growing much further east than here, nor palmettos much further north, nor hickory trees much further south.

Camping out, visitors will be treated to cicadas thrumming and fireflies flitting about in the deep twilight. And a popular canoe and kayak trip is to put in the San Marcos River fourteen miles upriver in Luling and paddle down to the park.

A historic pump forces artesian water into a cistern atop a

tower for release into a swampy woodlands along a nature trail. This system, built by the Civilian Conservation Corps helps offset the loss of the swamp's moisture that has been happening because of increased water-well drilling and pumping for both growing agriculture and housing developments. That water tower, by the way, is gorgeous in its own right.

The state acquired the land from private owners and the city of Gonzales between 1934 and 1936. It was opened to the public in 1936. The CCC built many of the park's buildings in the 1930s.

The area was originally called Ottine Swamp, a combination of the names of early pioneers Adolph Otto and his wife Christine. They operated a cotton gin along the river in 1879.

The San Marcos River rises at Aquarena Springs in the city of San Marcos and flows southeast for seventy-five miles. Spanish explorer Alonso De León gave the river its name, discovering it on the feast day of Saint Mark in 1689.

The park was named for the tropical dwarf palmetto plant

A trail at Palmetto State Park
—John Suhrstedt/Texas Department of Transportation

found there. Reaching between three to six feet tall, the dwarf palmettos are a low-growing member of the palm family (sabal minor) that normally occurs in the moist forests of East Texas and Louisiana. The large population of the plants in the park is isolated far west of its normal range.

Location: The park is located about nine miles southeast of Luling off U.S. Highway 183. Open daily.

Amenities: Camping, dump station, fishing, group pavilion, hiking, park store, picnicking, playground, restrooms, showers, swimming, water/electric/sewer sites, wheelchair accessible.

Contact: Palmetto State Park, 78 Park Road 11 South, Gonzales, TX 78629-5180, 830-672-3266, www.tpwd. state.tx.us.

Purtis Creek State Park

Exceptional fishing and shady campsites are the main attractions at Purtis Creek State Park. The park's 355-acre lake was designed specifically for fishing and stocked with trophy-sized bass. Largemouth bass are plentiful (catch-and-release only), as are large catfish and crappie (keepers).

Caddo and Wichita Indians once roamed here and visitors may find petroglyphs carved into nearby rock walls indicating the area was a good hunting area. All that abundant game drew Anglo settlers in the 1880s.

The state acquired the park's 1,582 acres from private owners in 1977 and opened the park in 1988.

Most of the land came from the Homer L. Smith family

who requested the park be named for their father. That request was not honored. Some property owners like Lottie P. Fagg, refused to sell but the state declared eminent domain and took the land without further negotiation.

Purtis Creek rises in southwestern Van Zandt County and flows southwest for nine miles.

Purtis Creek was named for ... well, no one seems to know. Neither historical societies in Henderson or Van Zandt counties have any information, nor do the state archives, TPWD archives, nor the park itself. A man named J. R. Burtis was a druggist in the town of La Rue in 1929 and the creek's name might be a misprint of his name, but no proof exists of that. If anyone has any information, please contact the author through the publisher of this book and it will be included in the next edition.

Location: The park is located about three miles north of Eustace. Open daily.

Amenities: Boat rental, boating, camping, dump station, fishing, hiking, park store, picnicking, playground, restrooms, showers, swimming.

Contact: Purtis Creek State Park, 14225 Farm Road 316, Eustace, TX 75124, 903-425-2332, www.tpwd.state.tx.us.

Ray Roberts Lake State Park

Backpacking along a scenic trail, birdwatching, horseback riding, or a wide variety of water sports—Ray Roberts Lake State Park has something for everyone who loves the outdoors.

The park's 5,849 acres are in a narrow strip of wooded terrain bordering the Blackland Prairies of north central Texas on the shore of 30,000-acre Ray Roberts Lake. The park consists of several different units and is also surrounded by wildlife management areas, wetlands, waterfowl sanctuaries, and a twenty-mile greenbelt corridor that connects Ray Roberts Lake with Lake Lewisville.

The Greenbelt Corridor trail meanders along the heavily wooded banks of the Elm Fork of the Trinity River. Anglers, bikers, birdwatchers, canoeists, equestrians, hikers and other outdoor enthusiasts can access the corridor at one of three trailheads.

The Isle du Bois Unit has boat ramps, equestrian and walk-in campsites, a swimming beach, a lighted fishing pier, and a park store. *Isle du Bois* means "island of the woods" in French and refers to the forested islands seen in the lake. (By the way, locals pronounce the name "Zilla Boy.")

The Johnson Unit has boat ramps, campsites, several miles of hike and bike trails, and a park store. It was named for nearby Fort Johnson, which was named for Colonel Francis W. Johnson. He was commander of the Texas Army at the capture of San Antonio on December 10, 1835.

Francis White Johnson was born in 1799 near Leesburg, Virginia. His family moved to Tennessee in 1812. He later lived in Illinois and Missouri where he worked in several businesses. In 1826 he caught malaria delivering produce down the Mississippi River and on the advice of a physician moved to Texas. He was considered a firebrand in favor of war with Mexico and in 1835 he was indicted by the Mexican government for treason but never arrested. In 1836, a superior Mexican force surprised him and a company of fifty men and all except Johnson and four others were killed or captured. When he later heard of Houston's retreat in the face of the advancing Mexican Army, Johnson quit the revolution in disgust. After the revolution, he settled along the Trinity River in San Jacinto County. Johnson's wife Rozelia divorced him in 1842 and he traveled around the U.S. trying to sell Texas lands, then prospected for precious metals in the West. When his ex-wife's new husband divorced her in 1847, Johnson reclaimed her. In 1861 he turned up penniless in Indianapolis, Indiana, but returned to Texas in 1871, living in the Austin area as a recluse. He was researching Texas history in Aguascalientes, Mexico, in 1884 when he died. He is buried in the State Cemetery in Austin.

The Jordan Unit is home to the Lantana Lodge, which offers fine dining and luxurious accommodations. The lodge is located on a high ridge overlooking the lake and has fifteen docks, a boat launch, along with twenty-seven miles of equestrian trails and ten horse stalls. The Jordan Unit is named for Jordan Creek that rises a mile south of Whitesboro and flows south for thirteen miles.

The Sanger Unit is home to a full-service marina with boat ramps, boat rentals, a fishing barge, and a courtesy dock. The Sanger Unit is named for the city of Sanger, which was founded by the Santa Fe Railroad in 1886. It was named for Alexander Sanger and his family who owned stores in Waco and Dallas.

Sanger was born in 1847 in Germany and came to the U.S. in 1865 and moved to Corsicana, Texas, in 1872, helping found a retail business, the Sanger Brothers. He moved to Dallas later that year to open a branch of the company there. Pioneers in the dry goods business in Texas, Sanger Brothers was the premier department store in North Texas.

He became president of the company, helped organized the first synagogue in Dallas, and worked to get railroads to pass through Dallas. He served on the Dallas City Council, established the Dallas Public Library, and helped organize the Dallas Fire Department and the State Fair of Texas. Sanger died in Dallas in 1925.

The state acquired the property in 1984 on a lease from the Department of the Army. It was opened as a park in 1993.

Ray Roberts Lake was created in 1984 to provide water to the cities of Dallas and Denton by impounding the Elm Fork of the Trinity River. The Elm Fork rises in east Montague County and flows southeast eighty-five miles to a confluence with the West Fork to form the Trinity River. It's named for the elm trees found along its banks. The Trinity River flows 423 miles from the Elm and West confluence in southwestern Kaufman County to the Gulf Coast. Spanish explorer Alonso De León named the river in honor of the Christian Holy Trinity in 1690.

The lake was named for U.S. Congressman Ray Roberts. Herbert Ray Roberts was born in Collin County in 1913 and attended Texas A&M, North Texas State, and Texas universities, and later served on the staff of U.S. House Speaker Sam Rayburn of Texas.

During World War II, Roberts served as a lieutenant commander in the U.S. Navy in both the European and Pacific theaters, and was recalled to duty for the Korean Conflict. He reached the rank of captain in the Naval Reserve.

Roberts served in the Texas Senate from 1955 to 1962 and was elected to the U.S. House of Representatives in 1962 to fill the vacancy caused by the death of Rayburn. He served in Congress until 1981. He died in Denton in 1992.

Congressman H. Ray Roberts
—Texas State Archives

Location: The park is located twelve miles northeast of Denton off Interstate 35. Open daily.

Amenities: Biking, boat ramp, boating, camping, dump station, fishing, hiking, horseback riding, marina, park store, picnicking, playground, restrooms, roller blading, showers, swimming, wheelchair accessible, wireless Internet.

Contact: Ray Roberts Lake State Park: Isle du Bois Unit, 100 PW 4137, Pilot Point, TX 76258-8944, 940-686-2148; Johnson Branch Unit, 100 PW 4153, Valley View, TX 76272-7411, 940-637-2294; Jordan Unit, Farm Road 1192, Pilot Point, TX 76258, 940-686-0261 or 866-LANTANA; Ray Roberts Greenbelt Corridor, 100 PW 4137, Pilot Point, TX 76258, 940-686-2148; Sanger Unit, 1399 Marina Circle, Sanger, TX 76226, 940-458-7343; www.tpwd.state.tx.us.

Sam Bell Maxey House State Historic Site

At the Sam Bell Maxey House, visitors can take a trip to post Civil War Texas when an indoor toilet was a status symbol. In fact it was the first running-water toilet in the city of Paris—Paris, Texas, that is.

This fashionable home quickly became the small town's social center. Visitors can enjoy the landscaped grounds, impressive architecture, and grand spaces that showcase a collection of furnishings, clothing and letters from generations of the Maxey family.

The elegant, historic house almost didn't survive. It was one of the few structures which survived the terrible Paris Fire of 1916 that destroyed nearly the entire city.

The historic site is named for Civil War general and U.S. Senator Sam Bell Maxey. Maxey and his wife Marilda moved into this High Victorian Italianate style home in 1868. It was remodeled in 1911 and members of the Maxey family lived in the house until 1966. That year, the family donated the home to the Lamar County Historical Society. In 1971, the Society donated the home to the city of Paris and in 1976 the city transferred the property to Texas Parks and Wildlife. The house was listed in the National Register of Historical Places in 1971. In 1980, the house was restored and furnished to reflect the almost one hundred years of continuous use by Maxey's family and opened to the public that year.

Samuel Bell Maxey was born in Tompkinsville, Kentucky, in 1825 and graduated from the U.S. Military Academy—where he roomed with Thomas "Stonewall" Jackson—in 1846. He fought with the 7th Infantry in the Mexican War with fellow West Point classmate Ulysses S. Grant. He saw action and was commended for valor in the battles of Cerro Gordo, Contreras, Churubusco, and Molino del Ray. After the war, he returned to Kentucky and studied law with his father, Rice Maxey, but when that practice began to fail, Maxey and his father moved their families to Texas in 1857.

Sam Bell Maxey
—Texas State Archives

Maxey practiced law in Paris and was county district attorney until 1861. When Texas seceded from the Union, he joined the Confederate Army as a captain and was later commissioned a brigadier general. He was elected to the Texas Senate that year but because he was now in charge of a regiment, he sent his father to Austin to serve his term.

Maxey served with the 9th Texas Infantry in Tennessee and Mississippi then, from 1863 through 1865, he was commander of the Indian Territory District. After his soldiers captured a 170-wagon Union supply train in 1864, he was promoted to major general.

After the war he returned to Paris and built the house on Church Street. Being a high-ranking Confederate officer,

Maxey needed a presidential pardon to regain full citizenship rights. His old friend General Grant helped secure the pardon in 1867 so that Maxey could resume his legal career and political careers.

Maxey was elected to the U.S. Senate in 1875 and served through 1887. He died in 1895 in Eureka Springs, Arkansas, where he had gone for treatment of a gastrointestinal disease. He is buried in Paris.

By the way, Paris, Texas, is named for Paris, France, and it has a replica of the Eifel Tower downtown. The main difference between the two distinctive towers? The Texas one is capped by a gigantic red cowboy hat.

Location: The park is located in downtown Paris. Open daily 8 A.M. to 5 P.M.

Amenities: Historic site, park store, restrooms.

Contact: Sam Bell Maxey House State Historic Site, 812 South Church Street, Paris, TX 75460, 903-785-5716, www.thc.state.tx.us.

Sebastopol House State Historic Site

Visit a prime example of limecrete construction in the mother of concrete cities at Sebastopol House State Historic Site in Seguin.

That the home has survived more than one hundred years is a testament to its structural integrity. Builders combined gravel, lime, sand, and water to form limecrete bricks. Because the process was quick and because water, sand, lime and gravel are very common all around the Seguin area, limecrete construction was affordable and became quite popular. Seguin—pronounced "Suh-geen"— once had nearly one hundred limecrete structures, and Sebastopol House is the best surviving example in the American southwest.

Although we may think of concrete homes as very old-fashioned today, at one time they were on the cutting edge of technology. In an 1854 visit, famed architect Frederick Law Olmstead was amazed that a small Texas town would be using such advanced building techniques less than twenty years after their introduction in the U.S.

Sebastopol House was abandoned in the 1960s and was nearly demolished, but the Seguin Conservation Society bought the home in 1961. The Society sold it to Texas Parks and Wildlife in 1976. After restoration to its 1880 appearance, the house opened as a state historic site in 1989. Antique roses and three-hundred-year-old Live Oaks surround the home. The grounds are available for rent for gatherings such as parties, receptions, reunions, and weddings.

In 1856, Colonel Joshua W. Young built this unusual split-level, T-shaped home in the Greek Revival style then popular in the south. Young's widowed sister, Catherine LaGette, and her seven children originally occupied the home. Young was born in 1811 in Wilmington, North Carolina. He settled in Seguin in 1847, and died there in 1897.

Dr. John E. Park was a physician and chemist who had several patents on concrete use long before Portland cement was invented. He was born in Georgia in 1815 and moved to Seguin in 1847. He is credited with introducing the formula for limecrete. Park built the city's first schoolhouse in 1850. He died in 1872.

Sebastopol was named for a Russian naval base during the Crimean War. Why it got the name has yet to be determined.

The Battle of Sebastopol was made famous in Alfred Lord Tennyson's famous poem *The Charge of the Light Brigade*. The siege of that seaport took place in 1854, just as Young began construction on the house.

Now part of the Ukraine, Sebastopol has been occupied at

least since 421 B.C. when Greeks established a colony there. In 1783, Russia annexed the Crimea and built the naval base and commercial port on the Black Sea. British and French armies laid siege to Sebastopol from October 1854 to September 1855 before it fell. With much of the Russian navy destroyed at Sebastopol, the war ended in early 1856. After the war, the severely damaged town was rebuilt. It came under siege again in 1942 by German forces and was nearly destroyed. After World War II, the city was again rebuilt.

Location: The park is located at 704 Zorn Street in Seguin. Open Friday through Sunday 9 A.M. to 4 P.M.

Amenities: Historic site, picnicking.

Contact: Sebastopol House State Historic Site, P.O. Box 900, Seguin, TX 78156-0900, 830-379-4833, www.tpwd. state.tx.us.

Stephen F. Austin State Park and San Felipe State Historic Site

Mother Neff State Park may be where the Texas parks system began, but Stephen F. Austin State Park is where Texas itself began.

This park is draped in history, but it also provides an array of recreational options ranging from hiking along five miles of trails through the pecan bottoms to fishing in the Brazos River to playing a round of golf.

The park is 663 acres, which the San Felipe de Austin Corporation donated to the state in 1940. The park opened the same year.

Stephen F. Austin is considered the "Father of Texas" because he brought the first 297 Anglo colonists—the "Old 300" as they became known—to Texas and was instrumental in the Texas Revolution and establishment of the Republic of Texas.

Stephen Fuller Austin was born in 1793 in Virginia. Five years later, his father Moses, a lead miner, moved the family to Missouri and established the town of Potosi. Austin later went to school in Connecticut, then attended Transylvania University in Kentucky. In search of business prospects, Stephen Austin wandered through Arkansas and Louisiana while Moses Austin was in San Antonio applying for a grant of land and permission to settle 300 Anglo families in Mexican Texas.

Moses Austin died in San Antonio and Stephen Austin immediately went to the city in 1821 to continue his father's quest. Governor Antonio María Martínez authorized Austin to continue and Austin searched for

Stephen F. Austin

land between the San Antonio and Brazos rivers for the colony. But the provisional government, set up after Mexican independence, reneged on the agreement, so Austin headed to Mexico City to plead his case. A new system for immigrants was passed into law, and as an "empresario," Austin would get 67,000 acres of land for each 200 families he brought in. He was also authorized to charge twelve-and-one-half cents per acre sold to each family for his services. His colonists settled in a broad area between the Lavaca River in the west to the San Jacinto River in the east, but their unofficial capital was a community called San Felipe de Austin along the Brazos River around the area the park is now in.

Austin had complete civil and military authority over the colonists until 1828. They elected their own officials to conduct business and hold courts. As leader of the militia, Austin also led campaigns against Indians. He consistently strived to keep the colonists away from controversy and out of Mexican political intrigue, advising them to "play the turtle; head and feet within our own shells."

But the number of Anglo colonists grew quickly, many coming in with the help of other empresarios, and many of them began clamoring for relief from perceived wrongs by Mexican government. The Convention of 1832 convened in San Felipe to inform the government of the needs of the Texians. But the petition was not presented to Mexico City, possibly through maneuvers by Austin trying to force his colonists to keep a low profile and not draw the attention of the government.

Another convention was called in San Felipe in 1833 and this time Austin traveled to Mexico City to present the colonists' requests for reform, including making Texas its own Mexican state. General Antonio Lopéz de Santa Anna, dictator of Mexico, not only refused but had Austin arrested and jailed. He was eventually freed in 1835.

By the time Austin returned to San Felipe, Texians were calling for another convention and some were calling for independence. Shortly thereafter, war began and Austin was chosen to command volunteers in the Gonzales area. He was then selected as a commissioner to the United States—his main job was to secure loans and volunteers, munitions and equipment for the Texian insurgents.

He returned to Texas in 1836, hoping the U.S. would annex Texas immediately after Texas won its independence. That didn't happen. He ran for president of the Republic but lost to Sam Houston. He did accept the office of secretary of state, however, but he died in office in 1836 at the age of forty-three.

The city of Austin and Austin County are also named for him.

San Felipe State Historic Site is the location of the township of San Felipe de Austin, the seat of government of the Anglo-American colonies in Mexican Texas. From 1824 to 1836, San Felipe was the social, economic, and political center and has become known as the "Cradle of Texas Liberty." The conventions of 1832 and 1833 and the Consultation of 1835 were held here, meetings that eventually led to the Texas Declaration of Independence. The town was the home of Stephen F. Austin and other famous early Texans; home of *The Texas Gazette*, the first Anglo newspaper in 1829; home of the postal system of Texas; and the place where the Texas Rangers began.

Citizens burned the settlement's original buildings in 1836 during the Runaway Scrape when General Sam Houston retreated from Mexican forces until the decisive Battle of San Jacinto.

The park features an obelisk and a bronze statue commemorating Austin's achievements, a replica of Austin's log house, and a monument on the site of the town hall. The historic site was transferred to the Texas Historic Commission in 2008.

Felipe de la Garza, governor of the Eastern Interior Provinces, proposed the town's name of San Felipe de Austin to honor both Austin and the governor's own patron saint. Saint Philip the Apostle was a native of Bethsaida in Palestine and was originally a follower of John the Baptist until Jesus urged him to "Follow me." Tradition says he was a shy, sober-minded man. He was martyred around 80 A.D. in Egypt by being crucified upside down. His remains are now in the church of Saints Peter and Paul in Rome. He feast day is celebrated on May 3. The name "Philip" is derived from the Greek word *philippos*, which means "lover of horses."

Location: The park is located forty-five miles west of Houston off Farm Road 1458 on Park Road 38. The historic site is located just past the park entrance. Open daily.

Amenities: Biking, camping, dump station, fishing, golfing, group dining hall, hiking, park store, picnicking, playground, restrooms, screened shelters, showers, tours, water/electric/sewer sites, wheelchair accessible.

Contact: Stephen F. Austin State Park, P.O. Box 125, San Felipe, TX 77473-0125, 979-885-3613, www.tpwd. state.tx.us. San Felipe State Historic Site, Farm Road 1458, San Felipe, TX 77473, 512-463-6323, www.thc. state.tx.us.

Washington-on-the-Brazos State Historic Site

Enjoy nature and learn about history in the birthplace of Texas: Washington-on-the-Brazos State Historic Site.

Located on the Brazos River, the town of Washington was the site of the 1836 General Convention, which would decide the fate of Texas. While the Alamo was under siege in San Antonio, Texians here signed the Texas Declaration of Independence. The Star of the Republic Museum, a replica of Independence Hall, and the site's Visitor Center showcase more than 20,000 artifacts to provide visitors with a clear view of how Texas came into existence.

Groups may reserve the Conference Center, a group meeting facility, and two picnic pavilions here. The picturesque park is also a favorite spot for picnics and birdwatching.

But history remains the central attraction and the replica of Independence Hall serves as the focal point for the park. Although a great military defeat at the Alamo and a great military victory at San Jacinto overshadow what happened in the pecan groves along the banks of the Brazos River, what happened here determined the future of Texas.

This was where Texians risked their lives on March 2, 1836 (now a state holiday), to sign the Texas Declaration of

Independence. If the revolution had failed, all the names on the Declaration would have just been a list of fifty-nine traitors to round up and hang. The document is more a list of grievances than an eloquent, philosophical appeal like the American Declaration of Independence is. Among those grievances were that Mexico forced citizens to convert to Catholicism, arrested citizens without cause, refused to allow trials by jury, refused to establish a system of public education, incited "the merciless savage," and was governed by a military despot "in an unknown tongue."

The Star of the Republic Museum is one of the premier historical museums in Texas. Artifacts here illustrate the story of Texas from Native Americans through 1846, after the Republic became the 28th state to join the union. Exhibits in the 10,000-square-foot museum rotate often, so return visits

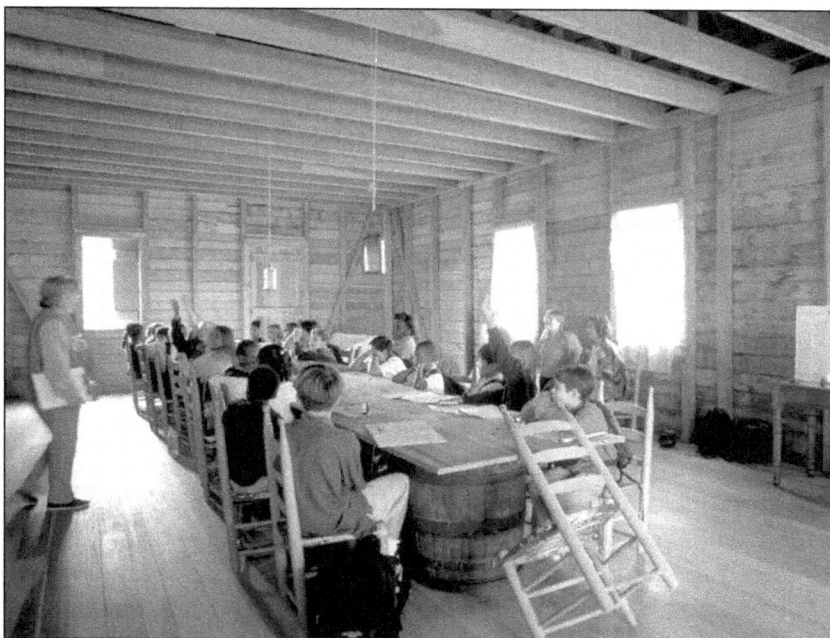

Students at Independence Hall, Washington-on-the-Brazos State Historic Site
—J. Griffis Smith/Texas Department of Transportation

always offer something new. Many of the exhibits are interactive and hands-on.

The museum is housed in a distinctive two-story, star-shaped building with an observation deck that provides a panoramic view of the park and the river.

Visitors may also enjoy Barrington Living History Farm at the park. It's a recreated nineteenth century farm along with Barrington, the home of Anson Jones—last president of the Republic—that was moved here in 1936 as part of the Texas centennial celebration.

The 293-acre park also includes the townsite of Washington, a major political center in early Texas that was founded in 1821 and was the first capital of the Republic. It grew steadily during the Republic, but declined rapidly when the railroad passed it by in the 1860s.

In 1899, school children in Brenham collected money and placed a monument at Washington-on-the-Brazos to commemorate the signing of the Texas Declaration of Independence. That stone obelisk now stands in front of Independence Hall. By the turn of the century, nothing was left of the town.

The state acquired the land from private owners in 1916 and it was transferred to the State Parks Board in 1949. The museum opened in 1970. More land was acquired in 1976 and 1996. The museum is now controlled by Blinn College in Brenham and it was named a Smithsonian Affiliate in 2008.

For more details on the Brazos River, see the entry for Brazos Bend State Park in the Gulf Coast section.

Anson Jones was born in 1798 in Great Barrington, Massachusetts. He wanted to become a printer but was talked into becoming a physician. He had his medical license in 1820 but practices in several towns in New York and Pennsylvania failed. He even tried Venezuela for two years. In 1832, he renounced medicine and became a commission merchant in New Orleans, but failed at that, too, although he did manage to survive cholera and yellow fever epidemics that ravaged the city.

Broke and despondent, Jones drifted to Texas. He opened a medical practice in Brazoria in 1833 and finally succeeded.

When the Texas Revolution began, he joined up, serving as a judge advocate and surgeon, but insisted on retaining the rank of private.

Jones helped establish the first Masonic Lodge in Texas in 1835 and was chosen its first grand master. He was elected to the Texas Congress and was later appointed minister to the United States by President Sam Houston. When he was recalled in 1839, he was elected to the Texas Senate. In 1841, Jones served as Houston's secretary of state. He was elected President in 1844, but Jones lost popularity when he waffled on the issue of whether Texas should be annexed by the U.S. He was burned in effigy, endured threats to overthrow his government, and was nearly removed from office by the Convention of 1845. Although he did retain his title, his duties became largely ceremonial and in 1846 when Texas became a state, Jones retired to his Barrington estate near Washington-on-the-Brazos. He committed suicide in Houston in 1858.

Jones named his home Barrington after his Massachusetts home, Great Barrington. That town was named for British War Minister Lord Barrington. Viscount William Wildman Shute Barrington (1717-1793) was also a member of Parliament, treasurer of the navy, chancellor of the exchequer, and postmaster general.

George Washington

Washington, Texas, was known as Washington-on-the-Brazos to distinguish it from the city it was named after, the capital of the United States, which was named after America's first president, George Washington.

George Washington was born in Westmoreland County, Virginia, in 1732 and began work as a surveyor when he was sixteen years old. He was a tall, thin, quiet man who loved farming the Mount Vernon estate in Virginia he inherited from his older brother Lawrence, loved playing billiards and cards, and riding his own race horses.

Washington served in the French and Indian War, eventually becoming a colonel commanding all Virginia troops. When he was elected to the Virginia House of Burgesses in 1758, he resigned his commission. In 1774, he was elected to the Continental Congress, sitting in sessions dressed in a full uniform although he professed to oppose independence for the colonies. After the fighting between Americans and British at the battles of Concord and Lexington in April of 1775, Congress named Washington commander of all colonial forces. His first victory was to drive the British from Boston in March 1776.

Although other victories eluded him for a long time, he kept his army in the field and harassed British regulars until the right battle presented itself. That was in Yorktown in 1781 when the American army combined with French forces to defeat General Charles Cornwallis and win independence for the colonies from England.

He was chosen unanimously as president of the Constitutional Convention in 1787 and elected by an overwhelming margin as the first President of the United States in 1779. He served two terms, refusing to yield to general pressure to run for a third—establishing the traditional two-term limit that wasn't broken until Franklin D. Roosevelt during World War II. The two-term limit became official with the 22nd Amendment to the Constitution in 1951.

Washington is the only president to actually take command of troops in the field in his role as commander-in-chief of America's armed forces. In 1794, a tax on distilled spirits led to armed protests known as the Whiskey Rebellion. The U.S. had no standing army at the time, but Washington requested militia from several states. He took command and marched them into the rebellious areas. The protesters dispersed without fighting.

He even commanded troops after he left office. When war with France was threatened in 1798, Washington's retirement was interrupted by his appointment by President John Adams to again command the U.S. Army. Adams was able to avoid the war.

Washington rode one of his favorite horses in the cold and snow of December 1799, and returned home very ill. He was treated in the manner of the day—bleedings and applications of a poultice of dried beetles—but died at his Mount Vernon home two days later. Modern physicians believe he died as a result of his medical treatment and not the cold.

Location: The park is located eight miles southwest of Brenham on Farm Road 1155. The park is open daily from 8 A.M. to sundown; the Visitor Center is open 9 A.M. to 5 P.M.; the museum is open daily from 10 A.M. to 5 P.M.

Amenities: Guided tours, hiking, historic site, museum, park store, picnicking, restrooms, self-guided audio tours, wheelchair accessible, wireless Internet.

Contact: Washington-on-the-Brazos State Historic Site, Box 305, Washington, TX 77880-0305, 936-878-2214, www.tpwd.state.tx.us. Star of the Republic Museum, P.O. Box 317, Washington, TX 77880, 936-878-2461, www.starmuseum.org.

South Texas Plains

Bentsen-Rio Grande Valley State Park

Birds of many different feathers flock to Bensten-Rio Grande Valley State Park. That's because it's the headquarters of the World Birding Center, home to more than 325 species of birds and more than 250 species of butterflies—many of them found nowhere else in the United States.

Among the unusual birds seen here are the grooved-billed ani, rose-throated becard, black-bellied whistling duck, paraque, tropical parula, and masked tityra. The park is also one of the last natural refuges in Texas for cats such as the jaguarundi and ocelot.

Witness hawk migrations, enjoy bird walks and natural history tours on 760 acres of riparian woodland built up layer by layer by centuries of flooding on the Rio Grande. This rich and fertile land is a key migratory stopover.

The World Birding Center—created in 2004—uses the expertise of the Texas Parks and Wildlife Department, the U.S. Fish and Wildlife Services, and nine Rio Grande Valley communities working together to expand awareness about this ecological treasure that ranges from dry chaparral brush to verdant riverside thickets, from freshwater marshes to coastal wetlands.

In addition to Bentsen-Rio Grande Valley State Park, other sites in the World Birding Center are the Edinburg Scenic Wetlands, Estero Llano Grande State Park, Harlingen Arroyo Colorado, Old Hidalgo Pumphouse, Quinta Mazatlan, Resaca de la Palma State Park, Roma Bluffs, and the South Padre Island Birding and Nature Center.

Rio Grande means "Big River" in Spanish and refers to the third longest river in the United States, a 1,865-mile long river that also forms the 1,250-mile border between Mexico and Texas from El Paso to the Gulf of Mexico near Brownsville. The first person to call the river by this name was Spanish explorer Juan de Oñate in 1598 when he arrived in what is now

El Paso. He may have taken the idea for the name from local Pueblo Indians who called it the *Posoge*, which means "big river."

Technically, the Rio Grande Valley in Texas lies all along its 1,250 miles but when the term is used in the state it applies to a much smaller area, an economic region centered on Cameron, Hidalgo, Starr, and Willacy counties from the mouth of the river upstream for about one hundred miles. Thanks to the river and its delta, this area has excellent agricultural lands. In the 1940s, irrigation spurred an explosion in agriculture, especially in citrus fruits and winter vegetables, and crops grown here are one of the main businesses in Texas.

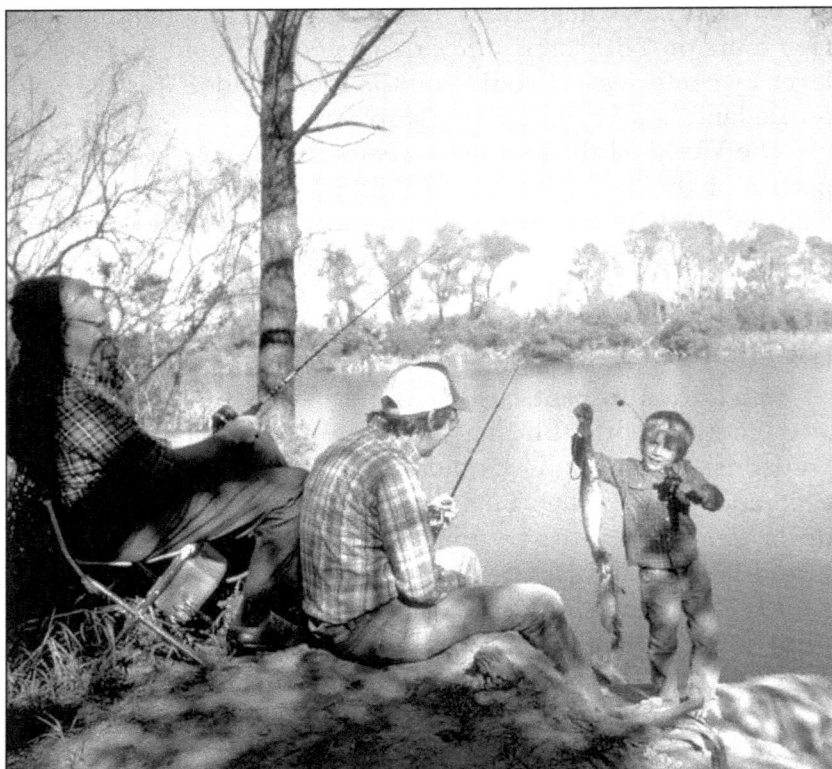

Fishing along the river at Bentsen Rio Grande Valley State Park.
—Jack Lewis/ Texas Department of Transportation

The Bentsen family donated the property to the state in 1944. It officially opened to the public in 1962.

The park was named for Lloyd Millard Bentsen, Sr., known in the area as "Big Lloyd" to distinguish him from his son, Lloyd, Jr. (1921-2006), who was a U.S. Congressman (1949-1955), U.S. Senator (1971-1993), a Democratic vice presidential candidate in 1988, and secretary of the treasury (1993-1994).

Big Lloyd was born in 1894 in South Dakota. He served in the U.S. Army Signal Corps during World War I, and then moved with his parents and his family to a farm near Mission, Texas. The Bentsens became prime developers in Hidalgo County with a nursery-seedling and farming businesses. Big Lloyd later also became a principal in several area banks and an insurance company. Despite significant fortunes in land and money, and being one of the best-known people in the Valley, Big Lloyd was renowned for his unassuming ways, usually wearing jeans and boots and often traveling on a motorcycle.

In 1959, he was promoted to major general in the Texas State Guard. Later in life, Big Lloyd became concerned with preserving the natural environment of the Valley and donated land that became the park. He died in 1989 in an automobile accident.

Location: The park is located about six miles southwest of Mission. Open 7 A.M. to 10 P.M. daily. Busy season is in September and October.

Amenities: Biking, bird blinds, boating, butterfly garden, camping, fishing, hiking, observation tower, park store, picnicking, restrooms, showers, tours, wheelchair accessible, wireless Internet.

Contact: Bensten-Rio Grande Valley State Park, 2800 S. Bentsen Palm Drive, Mission, TX 78572, 956-584-9156, www.worldbirdingcenter.org.

Casa Navarro State Historic Site

Visit the home of one of the top Tejano patriots of Texas, a man who lived here under five different flags.

José Antonio Navarro lived out the later years of his life in an adobe home in San Antonio. During his life, he saw governments come and go, living under the rule of Spain, Mexico, the Republic of Texas, the United States, and the Confederate States.

Navarro was born in 1795 in San Antonio. He and his wife Margarita de la Garza had seven children. One son, Angel Navarro, graduated from Harvard University and became a Texas attorney and a state senator.

Navarro was a merchant, rancher, one of only two native-born Texans to sign the Texas Declaration of Independence, served on the committee that wrote the Texas Constitution, and was a member of the State Constitutional Convention. He served as a member of Texas legislatures under Mexico, the Republic of Texas, and the State of Texas, and

Jose Antonio Navarro
—Texas State Archives

served on the San Antonio City Council. He was a tireless defender of Tejano (Mexican Texans) rights, especially the validity of Mexican land grants made prior to the establishment of the Republic of Texas. During the Constitutional Convention, Navarro argued successfully to have the word "white" stricken from the section that gave voting rights to the "free white population" of Texas. Although modern Texans rarely know his name, he was one of the most influential men in Texas from 1810 to 1865.

Over the years, Navarro owned a number of properties in San Antonio and ranch land in Atascosa and Guadalupe counties. He acquired the Laredo Street property in 1832. He died in 1871 in this home.

Casa Navarro means "Navarro House" in Spanish. The original complex had three structures of limestone, caliche block, and adobe brick. The homestead was built in 1848 and is furnished today with period antiques, has copies of Navarro's writings, and is the only site in the Alamo City interpreting the Mexican history and heritage of Texas.

The home remained in the family for several years, and was purchased by the San Antonio Conservation Society in 1962 to preserve it from demolition. It was placed on the National Register of Historic Places in 1972. The Conservation Society donated it to the Texas Parks and Wildlife Department in 1975. Casa Navarro State Historic Site was transferred to the Texas Historical Commission in 2008.

Location: The park is located in downtown San Antonio, two blocks from Market Square. Open Tuesday through Sunday 9 A.M. to 4 P.M.

Amenities: Museum, park store, restroom.

Contact: Casa Navarro State Historic Site, 228 E. Laredo Street, San Antonio, TX 78207, 210-226-4801, www.thc.state.tx.us.

Choke Canyon State Park

Winter is not observed at Choke Canyon. The park is a year-round playground with two separate units on the shores of a 26,000-acre reservoir. Being only sixty miles from the Gulf of Mexico, mild weather in the area invites all sorts of water recreation nearly all year and the fishing is considered excellent for alligator gar, bass, catfish, crappie, and sunfish.

On shore, the lake attracts a variety of wildlife to the dense thickets, including white tail deer, wild turkey, javelina, rattlesnakes, and alligators. Nature trails winding through mesquite groves offer excellent bird watching opportunities, including the crested Mexican eagle.

The U.S. Bureau of Reclamation and Corpus Christi dammed the Frio River in the 1970s to create a supplemental water supply for the city and surrounding area. The state acquired the property in 1981 in an agreement among the bureau, the city, and the Nueces River Authority.

Choke Canyon was named for an area along the Frio River where steep banks of rocks form what dam builders call a natural "choke" in the river during floods.

The Frio River flows for two hundred miles southeast from Uvalde County to a confluence with the Nueces River near the city of Three Rivers. The word *frio* is Spanish for "cold" and refers to the river's cool temperatures, even in the heat of summer, making the river a popular tourist destination along much of its length.

The South Shore Unit of the park got its name because it is along the southern and eastern shores of the lake. The Calliham Unit of the park derives its name from the nearby town of Calliham. After the city was moved three miles south, Choke Canyon Reservoir inundated the original townsite.

The community of Calliham got its name from Joseph

Thomas Calliham, a rancher and owner of the townsite. He was born in 1841 in Saint Landry Parish, Louisiana, and moved to Texas after the Civil War to farm and raise cattle and sheep. He died in 1922 in the town that bears his name.

Location: The South Shore Unit of the park is located three and one-half miles west of Three Rivers. The Calliham Unit is located twelve miles west of Three Rivers. Both units are on Texas Highway 72. Open Sunday through Friday 8 A.M. to 5 P.M., Friday and Saturday 8 A.M. to 10 P.M.

Amenities: Biking, boat ramp, boating, camping, dining hall, dump station, fishing, gymnasium, hiking, horseback riding, picnicking, playground, restrooms, screened shelters, showers, swimming, water skiing, wheelchair accessible.

Contact: Choke Canyon State Park, P.O. Box 2, Calliham, TX 78007, 361-786-3868, www.tpwd.state.tx.us.

Estero Llano Grande State Park

Explore the Estero Llano Grande's many trails, boardwalks over the wetlands, pavilions, and observation decks. The park has a well-deserved reputation as a can't-miss birding destination—it boasts more than five hundred species—and is the largest wetlands environment in the World Birding Center network.

In the summer when water is at a premium in other places throughout South Texas, wading birds and shore birds flock here. Migrating waterbirds almost always schedule a stopover at the park's narrow lake. It's a bird-watcher's paradise. Even in the middle of the day, a visitor is going to see and hear birds here. Sometimes, visitors will spot tropical birds that are rarely, if ever, found in the U.S., like the northern jacana that recently drew birders from all over North America and Europe.

The park is at the intersection of two major migratory flyways—the Central and the Mississippi—so it gets not only wintering birds but all the ones just passing through.

At the geographic center of the Rio Grande Valley, this 179-acre refuge in Weslaco also attracts a wide array of wildlife with its shallow lakes, woodlands, and thorn forest. And don't go for a dip in the lake unless you like swimming with alligators.

Estero Llano Grande wasn't a case of preserving a wilderness habitat, but of creating one. The Texas Parks and Wildlife Department, Ducks Unlimited, and several other groups worked for six years to re-vegetate a sorghum field and dry lake with native trees and shrubs to create a wetlands habitat common to the Rio Grande Valley. It opened in 2006.

For information on the World Birding Center, see the entry for Bentsen-Rio Grande Valley State Park in this section.

Estero llano grande means "big wet place on the plain" in Spanish, referring to relatively flat wetlands that mark the park and the body of water along the south side of the park.

Location: The park is located on International Boulevard in Weslaco. Open 8 A.M. to 5 P.M. daily.

Amenities: Biking, hiking, observation decks, park store, picnicking, restrooms, tours, wheelchair accessible.

Contact: Estero Llano Grande State Park, 154A Lakeview Drive, Weslaco, TX 78596, 956-565-3919, www.worldbirdingcenter.org.

Falcon State Park

The fact that visitors find exceptional fishing at Falcon State Park—especially for bass—is not a surprise when you realize the park's 573 acres hug the southern end of the 98,960-acre Falcon International Reservoir.

While boats constantly crisscross the clear blue waters of the lake, the park isn't just about the fish or towing water skiers. It's also great for bird watching, hiking, and observing wildlife.

The park's gently rolling hills are covered by cactus, ebony, hibiscus, huisache, mesquite, wild oregano, and wild olive. It has a one-mile, self-guided nature trail, and three miles of mutli-use trails that make a complete loop around the park.

The area is popular with bird watchers since it's the northwesternmost outpost for many tropical species, and is home to uncommon varieties such as the varied bunting and the small green kingfisher.

U.S. President Dwight D. Eisenhower and Mexican President Adolfo Ruiz Cortines dedicated Falcon Dam in 1953. The International Boundary and Water Commission (Mexico and the United States) built the dam for conservation, flood control, irrigation, power, and recreation, creating a beautiful sixty-mile-long lake.

The park was named for the dam that was named for the old town of Falcon after the original townsite was flooded when the dam was created. The town was moved several miles away. It is unclear from historical documents exactly who the city of Falcon is named for. Some sources cite one or two brothers who were early settlers in the area, another the wife of a city father. Most likely it was after the entire Falcón family.

In the mid 1700s, the king of Spain granted several thousand acres of land to José Clemente Gutiérrez who later sold the land to José Clemente Ramírez. In 1780, Ramírez married

Margarita de la Garza Falcón, uniting the area's two most distinguished families. The town was originally called Ramireño de Abajo but some people believe the name was changed to honor the wife of the founder because the area already had a city named Ramireño.

Blas Maria de la Garza Falcón and Miguel de la Garza Falcón were the two brothers. The brothers established ranches in the area in 1762, and those who settled the region looked to Captain Blas Falcón as their leader. He was instrumental in bringing in other settlers and was certainly the wealthiest, bringing with him a large stock of cattle, goats, and sheep.

Blas Falcón was born in 1712 in Nuevo León, Mexico, the son of a general and two-time governor of the state of Coahuila. In 1747, Blas Falcón led an exploration along the Rio Grande and two years later brought forty families to settle the area, founding the city of Camargo and establishing a mission and presidio there.

In 1766, Blas Falcón was given the task of settling land on

Remains of an old church break through the waters at Falcon Lake State Park

—Texas Department of Transportation

the Nueces River and succeeded there as well. In 1767, he returned to Camargo where he died later that year.

A statue of Blas Falcón may also be found on Shoreline Boulevard in Corpus Christi.

Miguel Falcón also held a captain's commission and explored the northern bank of the Rio Grande from Eagle Pass to the mouth of the river. He later explored the river through the Big Bend to La Junta de los Ríos (the confluence of the Rio Grande and Rio Conchos) at the present day city of Presidio. He was responsible for bringing many settlers into the area that is now Zapata County.

He was born in 1699 in Monterrey, Mexico, and died in 1753 of an unknown illness at the Presidio San Francisco Xavier de Gigedo on the San Gabriel River in Texas.

It should also be noted that a Texas Ranger captain named Cesario G. Falcón was stationed in the area in 1870 to 1871.

Location: The park is located fourteen miles northwest of Roma, off Farm Road 2098. Open daily.

Amenities: Biking, boating, camping, dump station, fishing, park store, picnicking, playground, restrooms, screened shelters, showers, swimming, water/electric/sewer sites, water skiing.

Contact: Falcon State Park, P.O. Box 2, Falcon Heights, TX 78545, 956-848-5327, www.tpwd.state.tx.us.

Goliad State Park and Historic Sites

Goliad State Park is one park that has it all, from biking and hiking its nature trails to paddling on the river to swimming to learning about more than 250 years of Spanish colonial and Texas history, including a massacre that rivals the Alamo.

Shaded campsites along the San Antonio River are popular, as is fishing. Then there's wandering the park's trails or going for a refreshing swim in the junior Olympic-sized pool.

Or maybe paddling a canoe or kayak is what you'd like to do. The park is a take-out point for the Goliad Paddling Trail that opened in 2007. It's a 6.6-mile river trail on the relatively quiet San Antonio River. The paddling trail showcases a variety of plant and animal life—cypress, oaks, pecans, deer, armadillos, hawks, herons, kingfishers, and turkeys.

Located on a bank of the San Antonio River, the 188-acre park features a reconstruction of Mission Nuestra Señora del Espiritu Santo that was built by the Civilization Conservation Corps in the 1930s.

The mission and Presidio La Bahia were originally established near Matagorda Bay and moved to their present site in 1749. "Mission Nuestra Señora del Espiritu Santo" means the mission of "Our Lady of the Holy Spirit" in Spanish, and refers to Mary, the mother of Jesus. "Presidio La Bahia" means the "Fort on the Bay" in Spanish, referring to the post's original location on the Gulf Coast.

The mission was also the first large cattle ranch in Texas.

The park also contains the birthplace of General Ignacio Zaragoza, the Presidio La Bahia, the ruins of Mission Nuestra Señora del Rosario, and is near Fannin Battleground State Historic Site.

Ignacio Seguín Zaragoza, considered the George Washington of Mexico, was born here in 1829. After Texas won its independence, his father moved the family to Matamoros, Mexico. In 1844, Zaragoza entered a seminary in Monterrey, but left in 1846. He ran a mercantile business for a while, then joined the militia of Nuevo León in 1853 with the rank of sergeant.

Zaragoza rose in rank quickly and fought in several battles to bring democracy to Mexico. In 1861, he was named minister of war and the navy under Benito Juárez, but later resigned to command the Army of the East, defending the city of Puebla in 1862 against the invading French army. His men won the day and his delay of the French forces at Puebla shortened French intervention in Mexico and rekindled the spirit of Mexicans to win their independence.

That daylong battle in Puebla took place on May 5, and Cinco de Mayo remains one the most celebrated holidays in Mexico and among those with Mexican heritage in the U.S.

Zaragoza died of typhoid fever in Mexico City later that year. Juárez named a city in his honor and declared the Fifth of May a national holiday. A statue in his honor was dedicated at Goliad State Park in 1980.

The Presidio La Bahia is about a quarter-mile south of the main portion of the park on U.S. Highway 183 and is operated by the Catholic Diocese of Victoria. It was built in 1749 to protect the mission and the frontier. It was in this presidio that Colonel Fannin and his men were held prior to their execution. Just east of the presidio is a memorial monument that marks the burial site of Fannin and his Texians.

Mission Nuestra Señora del Rosario was established in 1754. It is located just west of the city and the site is still being studied so it may be visited only by appointment. The mission's name means "Our Lady of the Rosary" in Spanish, again referring to Mary.

Fannin Battleground State Historic Site is nine miles east of the park. On this site, Colonel James Fannin and 284 of his men surrendered to Mexican General José Urrea after the Battle of Coleto. Urrea told them they would be treated as prisoners of war and moved them to Presidio La Bahia to be guarded. Seven days later, General Antonio López de Santa Anna ordered Fannin, all of Fannin's men, and other prisoners captured in the area executed on Palm Sunday, March 27, 1836. It is believed that 28 prisoners escaped, but 342 men were killed on grounds that are now in Goliad State Park.

Fannin, who had been wounded earlier, was left behind as his men were executed. He was told he, too, would be shot and he asked that he not be shot in the head and requested a decent burial. The officer in charge promised Fannin he would carry out his wishes and Fannin gave the man his watch as a token of his appreciation. Fannin was then shot in the face, his body stripped and thrown onto a pile with all the others who would be dumped in a common grave. Other wounded prisoners were also dragged out of the hospital area and shot.

The massacre led to repeated shouts of "Remember Goliad!" along with "Remember the Alamo!" during the Battle of San Jacinto that secured Texas independence (see details under San Jacinto Battleground in the Gulf Coast section).

James Walker Fannin, Jr., was born in 1804 in Georgia. He entered the U.S. Military Academy at West Point in 1819, but dropped out in 1821 and returned to Georgia. In 1834, he and his family moved to Texas and settled at Velasco where he owned a small plantation and was a slave trader.

He worked for Texas independence from Mexico, calling on the United States to help American settlers battle Mexican authority. When that help didn't materialize, he fought in the battles of Gonzales and Concepción in 1835. General Sam Houston commissioned Fannin a colonel in the Texas Army near the end of that year.

In 1836, he recruited volunteers for an expedition to take Matamoros from the Mexican army, but when he learned that city had been fortified, he withdrew his men to Goliad. At one point, James Bonham showed up with a message from Alamo commander William Travis asking for Fannin to reinforce his surrounded fortress, but Fannin had his own problems to deal with. He tried to retreat in the face of General Urrea's advance, but he and his men were captured and taken back to Goliad where he died with the remainder of those captured.

Fannin County and the city of Fannin were named for him.

There are two different versions of where the name Goliad comes from.

One version notes that the city was referred to as *Goliat*, Spanish for "Goliath" because the presidio there was such a large fortress.

Although that version may make more sense, it's the second version that is more accepted. The second version claims the name is an anagram of the name Hidalgo (the H being silent in Spanish so it is not used) to honor Padre Miguel Hidalgo the priest who began the Mexican independence movement in the early 19th century.

Miguel Hidalgo y Costilla was born in 1753 near Guanajuato, Mexico, and was ordained in 1779. As pastor of a church in Dolores, he tried to improve the well-being of his parishioners by starting a pottery factory and a leather-curing business, grew mulberry trees to support silkworms, cultivated olive groves and vineyards, and started workshops for blacksmithing, carpentry, harness making, and weaving wool.

After Napoleon conquered Spain, he set his brother on the Spanish throne, prompting many Mexicans to rebel against French dominance over their country. Hidalgo and others plotted a people's uprising against the established authority in 1810. On September 15, he gave a sermon calling for independence that became known as the *grito* or "shout."

A peasant army formed around Hidalgo and they sacked several cities, killing many innocent people. Although he was praised as a liberator, Hidalgo failed as a general and after his forces suffered several defeats, many of his followers deserted and Hidalgo lost heart for his cause. He was captured, defrocked as a priest, and shot in 1811.

Hidalgo was a father in three ways—he was a priest, he fathered two illegitimate children, and he is considered the father of Mexican independence even though his effort to achieve that goal failed.

It should be noted that he was nicknamed *Zorro*, Spanish for "fox." Whether his daring exploits inspired the writings of Johnston McCulley to create his own Zorro fighting against the Mexican government is uncertain.

In 1931, the city of Goliad donated the property to the state which transferred it to the State Parks Board in 1949.

Fannin Battleground was transferred to the Texas Historic Commission in 2008.

Location: The park is located just south of the town square in Goliad. Open daily; museum hours are 8 A.M. to noon and 1 P.M. to 5 P.M. Fannin Battleground is located about nine miles east of Goliad on U.S. Highway 59. It is open daily from 8 A.M. to 5 P.M.

Amenities: Boating, camping, dump station, fishing, hiking, museum, park store, picnicking, playground, pool, restrooms, screened shelters, showers, tours.

Contact: Goliad State Park, 108 Park Road 6, Goliad, TX 77963-3206, 361-645-3405, www.tpwd.state.tx.us. Fannin Battleground State Historic Site, FM 2506, Fannin, TX 77960, 512-463-6323, www.thc.state.tx.us.

Lake Casa Blanca International State Park

Lying on the border with Mexico, Lake Casa Blanca is a jewel for family recreation, offering a 1,650-acre lake for boating, swimming or water skiing; a couple of miles of trails for hiking and biking; five recreation halls or pavilions; and basketball, tennis, and volleyball courts. And it's adjacent to a public golf course.

The lake was constructed by Webb County in 1951 for recreational purposes. The state acquired the 370-acre property from the county and the City of Laredo in 1990 and the park was opened to the public in 1991.

Casa Blanca means "White House" in Spanish and likely refers to the houses built of white caliche blocks that were common in the area.

Location: The park is located just east of the Laredo Airport off U.S. Highway 59. Open daily 7 A.M. to 10 P.M.

Amenities: Biking, boating, camping, dump station, fishing, group recreation hall, hiking, park store, picnicking, playground, restrooms, showers, swimming, water skiing, wheelchair accessible.

Contact: Lake Casa Blanca International State Park, 5102 Bob Bullock Loop, Laredo, TX 78044, 956-725-3826, www.tpwd.state.tx.us.

Resaca de la Palma State Park

Resaca de la Palma is the newest Texas state park, opening in December of 2008. This 1,700-acre bird hideaway is the largest tract of native habitat in the World Birding Center. More than 500 bird species have been identified in this area, more than in most states.

A gorgeous piece of property, natural levees around shallow ponds are thickly wooded and full of marsh vegetation—inviting geography for the hundreds of bird species who make their home here or use it as a stopover during migration.

The park has no camping or boating, but plenty of areas to get into a natural wilderness or spy on birds like the American redstart, purple gallinule, summer tanager, or yellow-breasted chat.

Visitors at Resaca will have the option of riding a free tram on a three and one-half mile loop around a portion of the park with two stops. You can get off, hike, bird-watch and then catch the next tram. The park has six and one-half miles of hiking trails, many areas relatively remote and densely wooded. Two trails are open to biking, as is the tram road.

For more details on the World Birding Center, see Bentsen-Rio Grande Valley State Park above.

Sections of the old riverbed are known locally as *resacas*.

These ponds usually have water, but are no longer connected to the Rio Grande. *Palma* is Spanish for the palm trees common to this area.

Location: The park is located on New Carmen Road, off U.S. Highway 281 four miles west of Brownsville. Office hours are Monday through Friday 8 A.M. to 5 P.M.

Amenities: Biking, hiking, picnicking, restrooms, tours, wheelchair accessible.

Contact: Resaca de la Palma State Park, P.O. Box 714, Olmito, TX 78575, 956-350-2950, www.worldbirdingcenter.org.

Bibliography

Archives
Fairfield, Alabama, City Clerk
Texas Parks and Wildlife Department
Texas State Archives
Texas State Historical Association
U.S. Army Corps of Engineers, Fort Worth District

Books
American Antiquarian and Oriental Journal, Stephen D. Peet, editor, Leland Stanford University, Chicago, Illinois, 1891.
Built in Texas, Francis Edward Abernathy, University of North Texas Press, Denton, 2000.
Encyclopedia Britannica, Chicago, London, 1981.
The Encyclopedia of North American Indians, Frederick E. Hoxie, editor, Houghton Mifflin Company, Boston, 1996.
The Encyclopedia of Texas, Ellisa A. Davis and Edwin H. Crobe, editors, Texas Development Bureau, Dallas, 1922.
Fort Lancaster, Lawrence John Francell, the Texas State Historical Association, Austin, 1999.
Frontiersmen in Blue: The United States Army and the Indian, 1848-1865, Robert M. Utley; University of Nebraska Press, Lincoln and London, 1967.
Historical and Biographical Record of the Cattle Industry and the Cattlemen of Texas and Adjacent Territory, Antiquarian Press, Ltd., New York, 1959.
A History of Central and Western Texas, Captain B. B. Paddock, editor, Lewis Publishing Company, Chicago, 1911.
History of Henderson County Texas, J.J. Faulk, Athens Review Printing Company, Athens, 1929.
A History of Wood County, Thomas T. Ewell, Frank Gaston Publisher, Granbury, TX, 1895.
How Come It's Called That? Place Names in the Big Bend Country, Virginia, Duncan Madison and Hallie Crawford Stillwell, 1958, 1968, 1986.
In the Cattle Country: History of Potter County, Della Tyler Key, Tyler-Berkley Co., Amarillo, 1961.

The Indian Texans, James M. Smallwood, Texas A&M University Press, College Station, 2004.

The Indians of Texas, W. W. Newcomb, Jr., University of Texas Press, Austin, 1961.

Muleshoe and More, Bill Bradfield and Clare Bradfield, Gulf Publishing Co.; Houston, 1999.

The New American Bible, Oxford University Press, London, 1995.

The New Handbook of Texas, Ron Tyler, editor in chief, the Texas State Historical Association, Austin, 1996.

Off the Beaten Trail, William Edward Syers, Texian Press, Waco, 1971.

The Texas Almanac 2008-2009, Elizabeth Cruce Alvarez, ed., *Dallas Morning News*, Dallas, 2008.

The Texas Legal Directory, Bentley and Pilgrim, Democratic Statesman, Austin, 1877.

Texas Parks and Campgrounds, George Oxford Miller, Lone Star Books, Lanham, 2003.

1001 Texas Place Names, Fred Tarpley, the University of Texas Press, Austin and London, 1980.

A Treasury of Texas Trivia, Bill Cannon, Republic of Texas Press, Plano, 1997.

What If? 2, Robert Cowley, American Historical Publications, Inc., G. P. Putnam's Sons, New York, 2001.

Magazines, Newspapers and other Periodicals
Texas Highways, Austin, TX
Texas Parks & Wildlife, Austin, TX
Lufkin Daily News, Lufkin, TX
Southwestern Historical Quarterly, Texas State Historical Association, Austin

Manuscripts
Roy Banford Inks: He Lived Life in High Gear, Mildred Inks Dalrymple, Inks Lake State Park, Burnet, TX, November 1986.

Pamphlets
Along the Route, a Brief History of the Santa Fe

An Early History of Fayette County, Leonie Rummel Weyand and Houston Wade, *La Grange Journal*, 1936.

A History of the Texas Railroads, S. G. Reed, St. Clair Publishing Company, Houston, 1941.

Texas State Park Guide, Texas Parks and Wildlife Department

Web Sites
www.abileneks.com
www.ancestry.com
www.battleshiptexas.org
www.brazosbend.org
www.cctexas.com

www.en.wikipedia.org
www.fairfieldct.org
www.fairfieldtexaschamber.com
www.fortmckavett.org
www.friendsofpfalls.org
www.friendsofgc.org
ftp.rootsweb.ancestry.com
www.geocities.com/mckevitt_2000/people.html
www.georgeobservatory.org
www.honeycreekfriends.com
www.huntsville.about.com
www.jdbedwell.com/geneology
www.landmarkinntx.com
www.longhorncaverns.com
www.mexconnect.com
www.newadvent.org
www.nimitz-museum.org
www.palodurocanyon.com
www.patrickcleburne.com
www.portisabellighthouse.com
www.portisabelmuseums.com
www.sanjacinto-museum.org
www.supremecourthistory.org
www.tamu.edu
www.texascoa.org
www.texascapes.com
www.texasstaterailroad.com
www.texasstaterr.com
www.thc.state.tx.us
www.tpwd.state.tx.us
www.usstexasbb35.com
www.whitehouse.gov
www.worldbirdingcenter.org

About the Author

Allan C. Kimball is an award-winning writer and photographer with a long career at daily newspapers in Texas. Over the years he has interviewed several presidents, discovered clandestine government air strips, and covered stories as diverse as chili cook-offs to prison boot camps, disastrous tornadoes to sea turtle rehabilitation, gubernatorial races to beer-drinking goats. As a member of the Baseball Writers Association of America, he also covered Major League Baseball. And he has chased killer bees throughout Central and South America.

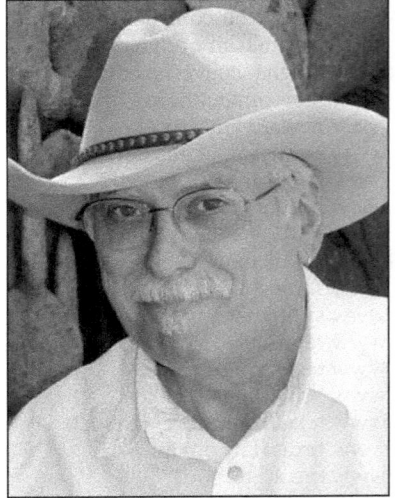

Allan is also the author of *The Big Bend Guide: Travel Tips and Suggested Itineraries*, the Western fiction trilogy *Rainbows Wait for Rain*, the historical novel *The Legend of Fort Leaton*, and the travel guide *Fun with the Family in Texas* among others.

He and his wife Madonna live in Wimberley, Texas.

www.ingramcontent.com/pod-product-compliance
Lightning Source LLC
Chambersburg PA
CBHW060255100426
42742CB00011B/1760